Natural and Artificial Parallel Computation

About the cover

The cover design is a composition built from images of two highly parallel computing devices, one artificial and the other natural, which illustrate recent research at Syracuse University.

One is an 'insertion' sorting chip which works by comparing, in parallel, a newly arriving item with each of those already stored in correct order in the chip's memory. All smaller items are immediately and simultaneously moved into the memory cell at the next-lower address, while those which are not smaller are left where they are. This action thus reclaims a memory cell into which the new item can be placed so as to maintain the correct ordering. The circuit was designed in the Electrical and Computer Engineering Department by S. Ramirez-Chavez, F. H. Schlereth and J. V. Oldfield.

The other is a lizard's retina—an array of light-sensitive cells ('photoreceptors') forming the input stage of the animal's vision system. How fine the optical resolution is in a particular region of the visual field depends on how close together the photoreceptors are in that region. The color coding shows how this density of photoreceptors varies over the surface of the retina. These data were obtained by G. A. Engbretson and P. J. Rousche of the Department of Bioengineering and Institute for Sensory Research, and then rendered as a computer graphics model by J. J. Ventrella.

Natural and Artificial Parallel Computation

edited by

M. A. ARBIB and J. A. ROBINSON

The MIT Press
Cambridge, Massachusetts
London, England

This book was printed and bound in the United States of America.

Library of Congress Cataloging-in-Publication Data

Natural and artificial parallel computation / edited by M.A. Arbib and
   J.A. Robinson.
      p.   cm.
   Includes index.
   ISBN 0-262-01120-4
   1. Parallel processing (Electronic computers) 2. Neural networks
(Computer science) I. Arbib, Michael A. II. Robinson, J.A. (John
Alan)
QA76.58.N37 1990
006.3--dc20
                                      90-6660
                                        CIP

To our distinguished Syracuse colleagues

ERICH M. HARTH
and
JOSEPH J. ZWISLOCKI

for their fundamental contributions to neuroscience

Contents

III
PARALLELISM IN THE BRAIN

IV
PARALLELISM IN ARTIFICIAL INTELLIGENCE

Foreword

This volume is the outcome of a Symposium held at Syracuse University on March 1 and 2, 1989, to mark the formal inauguration of its new Center for Science and Technology. The celebration of fresh scholarly opportunities by a Symposium focussing on the state of current knowledge and the future of the field is an old and familiar academic tradition. The occasions are more rare when bricks, mortar, glass and steel directly express the cross-disciplinary and integrative challenges created by a rapidly advancing technology: but the academy must also, by its very nature, build or remodel buildings to meet the changing demands of established disciplines and accommodate the new.

The Syracuse University Center for Science and Technology was made possible by the support of the State of New York, through its Urban Development Corporation, and was conceived and designed to foster synergism between Schools and Departments which depend on or work at the frontiers of computer science and electrical engineering, or which apply computer technology to problems in physical science, neuroscience, engineering and information management. In addition to the Schools of Computer and Information Science, the School of Information Studies, the Department of Chemistry and a large part of the Department of Electrical and Computer Engineering, the new Center houses two pivotal research organizations: the *New York State Center for Advanced Technology in Computer Applications and Software Engineering* and the *Northeast Parallel Architectures Center.*

On behalf of Syracuse University I would like to thank my colleagues Per Brinch Hansen and Alan Robinson, and our distinguished colleague from the University of Southern California, Michael Arbib, for the way they designed the Symposium. It was a fine opportunity not only for our own students and faculty, but also for those from many institutions throughout the Northeastern United States, to share in the work and savor the challenges presented by some of the greatest experts in an exciting and rapidly developing field. The university was greatly honored by the participation of the guest speakers and is grateful for their willingness to adapt their presentations for publication in this volume.

For thousands of years we humans have asked fundamental questions about ourselves and sought answers as best we may. *The proper study of mankind is man,* wrote Alexander Pope at the beginning of the modern age:

> *Sole judge of truth, in endless error hurled;*
> *The glory, jest and riddle of the world!*

More often than not, our study has been limited by the techniques available. Yet there have always some who managed to transcend the methodology of their times, even though their contribution may have been appreciated only decades or even centuries later. Others have recognised the potential of ideas from other disciplines and so opened up new directions in their own.

All of us who are curious about the nature of 'being' have to ponder the continuing riddle of consciousness, to pursue the long and arduous task of describing and modelling the elegant complexity of the nervous system, and to translate patterns at the molecular, cellular and system level into explanations of the way we see, hear, move, learn and develop our own individuality. No one approach will lead us to the truth or save us from error, but with each advance in knowledge, and each new methodology applied, there is always the possibility that yet another aspect of ourselves will be illuminated and that our expanded understanding will help to develop useful technology or to serve in other ways the needs of society.

Karen Hiiemae

Professor of Biology and Bioengineering
Syracuse University

Acknowledgements

It is a pleasure to acknowledge here those who helped to put together the symposium on which this book is based, as well as those who made the task of producing the book easier than it would otherwise have been.

Melvin A. Eggers, Chancellor and President of Syracuse University, and Gershon Vincow, Vice-Chancellor for Academic Affairs, generously and crucially supported the whole project from its inception.

Professor Karen M. Hiiemae originated the idea and championed it throughout with constructive enthusiasm and wise advice.

The symposium itself ran as smoothly as it did thanks to Wendy Harris, who managed all of the logistics with patience, skill, and tireless ingenuity.

Marcia Harrington expertly directed all artistic aspects of the entire book design and its graphics, and steered the project safely around all word-processing obstacles.

The material for the cover was provided by Dr. S. Ramirez-Chavez, Mr. J. J. Ventrella, and Professors J. V. Oldfield, F. H. Schlereth and G. A. Engbretson.

Our task was made lighter by the friendly cooperation and encouragement we enjoyed throughout from Teresa Ehling of M.I.T. Press.

I

INTRODUCTION

Chapter 1

INTRODUCTION: NATURAL AND ARTIFICIAL PARALLEL COMPUTATION

MICHAEL A. ARBIB AND J. ALAN ROBINSON

Natural science and the sciences of the artificial

Our brains are hugely complex natural parallel computers. Even though by comparison the most advanced of today's artificial parallel computers are mere toys, there are enough similarities to tempt us into supposing that ideas useful for understanding brains might also help us to understand actual and possible parallel machines, and conversely. The contributors to this book agree, and have willingly accepted our invitation to surrender to the temptation. Each contribution supports, indeed illuminates, this general theme in a specific setting.

Designers of parallel programming languages and architects of parallel computer hardware evidently see the structure and performance of the brain as both an encouraging precedent and a daunting challenge as they aspire to create ever more complex parallel computing systems.

Neuroscientists find parallel computers a source of ideas for modelling and understanding the structure and function of human and animal brains.

The language in which cognitive scientists think and talk about the natural functions of perception, memory, learning and reasoning is enriched by concepts and metaphors borrowed from the artificial world of communicating automata.

Artificial intelligence workers are well aware that the intelligent machines they aspire to build will have to be highly parallel ones, like the brain, and that although nature already knows how to build intelligent systems out of ordinary matter, she keeps the secret so well hidden that AI engineers may have to work out for themselves how to do it.

A parallel computer is an information-processing system made of components which mutually contribute to each other's changes of state through the exchange of messages over a network of communication links. So is a brain. We gain insights into both sides of the comparison by understanding the differences between the brain's biology and today's technology as much as by dwelling on the similarities. It will not be the first time this kind of mutually beneficial cross-fertilization has happened between parts of natural science and related areas of engineering.

Consider for example how the life sciences, physiology in particular, have assimilated the laws of thermodynamics; these were first empirically encountered by the inventors of artificial heat engines, and then more scientifically formulated following systematic study of the fundamental limitations on the efficiency with which these machines could transform energy into work. As with human-built energy-conversion devices, so with those contrived by nature.

A similar set of universal principles underlies the representation, communication, algorithmic computation, and control of information, whether the systems involved are natural or artificial. In fact, it was just such observations that led Norbert Wiener to subtitle his epochal book on cybernetics as *Control and Communication in the Animal and the Machine.*

So even if we ourselves discover some clever engineering trick by tinkering at the workbench, it is quite possible that evolution may already have hit on it or something like it. Possible, but not certain: nature seems to have little use for wheels, but certainly likes pipes, pumps and valves.

In casting about for new parallel hardware and parallel software designs, therefore, we might be able to copy (to the extent that we can discern them) some of the more successful schemes by which brains manage to do what they do.

Since it is an artifact, a parallel computer is in a straightforward but narrow sense much easier to understand than a brain. Its entire relevant structure is completely set forth in the drawings and specifications of its designers. Not that it is part of the concept of a computer that we should have this kind of complete knowledge of it: it is, so to speak, just a historical accident that we do. If today's parallel computers had been 'natural' objects first found on the Moon, it would have been a very difficult task to make those drawings and specifications (look how long it took to decipher the Rosetta Stone). We ourselves may be artifacts, or we may not—how could we tell?—but either way the neuroscientists still have the same puzzles to solve.

It is an often-noted irony that in artificial intelligence research the aura of intelligence seems to disappear from a performance once we know how it is done and how to program a computer to do it.

When the world chess champion Garry Kasparov recently played against the computer program Deep Thought, everyone knew (as he did) that its highly respectable 'expert' standard of play was produced by a relatively simple algorithm, albeit carried out on a monstrous scale at enormous speed. Mr. Kasparov's own performance, however, remains both for us *and for him* an awesomely inexplicable display of deep knowledge, fast, accurate, intuitive decision-making, and direct, holistic perception of significant patterns. (And he did beat the machine).

As matters stand at present no one can say how much longer Mr. Kasparov's supreme human chess skill will continue to withstand the inexorably larger scale and far higher speed which future versions of Deep Thought will bring to the contest. Not much longer, probably. But we are not likely to learn much from his defeat. Consider the analogous case of human and mechanical locomotion.

A century ago the fastest human runner might still outpace the fastest automobile; today such a contest would be an absurd mismatch. The artifact would always win the race. So what? Superiority of performance is a different dimension from explanatory simulation. Of course the Lamborghini goes much faster than Jesse Owens or Carl Lewis, but our knowing its engineering details is no help at all in explaining how humans run.

However, in this narrow sense, we really understand only rather simple algorithms which run on relatively simple serial architectures. We can get a complete overview of them, and pretend to be the computer carrying them out. This makes us feel that there is nothing hidden from us and that everything is clear.

It is a different matter when we have to cope with the behavior of the large-scale parallel computers which are just beginning to be widely available, such as the Connection Machine, and of those whose designs are still evolving, such as the various neural network machines. In these machines we are to various degrees dealing with deliberate imitations of the design of the brain itself.

Presumably a complete authentic replica of the brain would be just as hard to understand as the original—how could it not be? This paradox of simulation will be ruefully familiar to those who have in other contexts simulated a system so faithfully as to reproduce even its unpredictability and unintelligibility. We may never be able to understand parallel computers as well as we understand serial ones. It would seem that the only kind of computer we find it easy to pretend to be is an old-fashioned serial one of the von Neumann variety.   This is probably no accident.

Whereas the classic design of the von Neumann serial computer has remained virtually the same for almost half a century, there is no comparable fixed design scheme for parallel machines— though we may note the irony that one of the classical designs for 'non-von Neumann' parallel computers, the cellular automaton (a 'tilework' of locally connected identical finite-state machines), is also the work of von Neumann.   We are living at present in an experimental period in which all manner of parallel design possibilities are being tried, and there is as yet no fixed, clear view of what one can feasibly program parallel computers to do. For that matter, if our goal is to understand what computers can *feasibly* do then we still have some way to go even in the case of the serial computer.

It would seem, then, that the brain side of the comparison is the less well understood, with only a few rough sketches to go on, and only a glimpse here and there of the specifications and the drawings; but from another point of view we do understand more about the brain than about a computer.   We have the unfair advantage of the insider.   You have a peculiarly privileged access to (at least the conscious part of) what your own brain is doing, as I do of mine.   As yet you and I cannot swap these vantage points, and so each must rely on the other for reports of what can be observed to be going on.

Despite a modern disinclination to accept such 'private' evidence as a proper basis for science, it is a rich mine of clues which it is absurd to ignore.   Introspection may be private but what of that?   We need all the evidence we can get.

We do not know whether computers can ever (be programmed to) do certain things, but we already know that brains can do them.   They play chess, compose symphonies and write novels, recognize and enjoy friends, control the juggling of five tennis balls, and invent scientific theories.   Moreover they can, within limits, watch themselves doing so.

Experimental and theoretical computer science

In *The evolution of computing* Ralph Gomory reviews the remarkable advances which have been made over the past fifty years in the technology of information processing.   Both the size and the cost of computing machines have shrunk as dramatically as their storage capacity, speed and computing power have increased.   The physical limits are still a long way off, and although one day they will be encountered, the real limits on harnessing computing power are with us already.   They are limits imposed by our inability (as yet) to understand what we want

*✻ Maybe, but today Software exceeds Hardware.
certainty*

computers to do and our consequent ignorance of how to program them to do it. Software limits rather than hardware limits.

In a certain sense we do not know what the machines we already have can do. Today's, let alone tomorrow's, computers can do things which no one has yet figured out how to program them to do. Their existence mocks us and spurs us on.

It is the job of theoretical computer science to find out what computers can do and what they cannot do, and in the former case to say how, and in the latter case, to say why not. The task of practical computer science is to develop the principles of hardware and software design which underlie the engineering of applications such as those mentioned above.

Parallel programming methodology, parallel machine architecture, and applications of parallel supercomputers

One group of concerns clusters about parallel programming methodology and applications. In Part II, three of our authors deal with these matters from different standpoints.

It is one thing to be given access to a powerful parallel computer, and quite another to be able straightforwardly and systematically to program it to do something useful in a reasonably efficient way. Per Brinch Hansen discusses, in *The nature of parallel programming*, the issues which arise in the general problem of programming parallel computers and stresses the crucial role played by suitable notations and programming languages.

It is a characteristic feature of serial von Neumann computers that we use them according to the 'equation'

general-purpose hardware + software program = special-purpose hardware.

This 'hardware plasticity' goes back to Turing's mid-1930s conception of a 'universal' computing machine which when given the coded description of any particular computing machine will exactly simulate the behavior of that machine. The technological application of this (still) amazing theoretical fact is that all we need to do is to build one universal machine in hardware form; this in effect then gives us access to all the infinitely many different possible hardware machines, provided that we know how to code their descriptions (*i.e.*, write suitable programs for the universal machine to execute). This beautiful idea of 'general-purposeness' has been fully exploited for serial computers. David May in *Towards general-purpose parallel computers* airs the possibility of designing general-purpose parallel computers which can similarly be turned into special-purpose parallel computers by giving them a suitably encoded description, or program. Of course, what makes the design of parallel computers interesting, even vitally necessary, is that Turing's theorem says nothing about the speed with which the universal machine simulates another machine. In the practical worlds of computing and biological survival, the timeliness of a solution is at least as important as its correctness.

Geoffrey Fox then takes us, in *Applications of parallel supercomputers: scientific results and computer science lessons*, through an illuminating variety of actual scientific computations on parallel machines, their common theme being that they are real 'working' computations carried out by serious scientists in the course of their regular work. That is to say, the rationale of each computation is to be part of the solution of a 'user' problem rather than to be a contribution to computer science. His discussion brings out vividly the way in which the availability of parallel computing resources has changed the fundamental working outlook of such users in their various fields of science, and has brought into being a new discipline, 'computational science', which deals with the general issues that arise when computational power is deployed on so enormous a scale as is now possible in the new parallel supercomputers.

Parallelism in experimental and theoretical neuroscience

So how do brains actually work, then? It is the neuroscientists' job to find out and explain it to us. There are at least two ways they go about this: experimental and theoretical. The experimental approach probes, monitors and dissects real brains and observes real neurons in action. The theoretical approach elaborates and tests brain models. Each succeeds most in close interaction with the other.

The task of the experimental neuroscientist is similar to, although vastly more complicated than, what engineers call *retro-engineering*. Confronted by a 'black box' produced by company A, the goal of the retro-engineers working for company B is to unravel and reconstruct its design and purpose by painstakingly tracing out its structure and systematically testing its behavior: a splendid intellectual game, and in no way easy or boring. It may not be too fanciful to envisage, as the experts get better and better at this, the rise of the art of *anti-retro-engineering*, whose practitioners will seek to design as much inscrutability as possible into artifacts without adversely affecting their performance or cost. Our authors in Part III, and their colleagues, no doubt occasionally suspect that something of the sort lies behind the organization of the brain. Albert Einstein's gentle faith that the creator of the universe is subtle but not malicious was that of a physicist rather than a neuroscientist.

In Part III's four chapters we begin with Michael Arbib's Janus-like view of the natural and the artificial: *Cooperative computation in brains and computers*. He explores the tight reciprocity between computational neurobiology—whose goal is to understand the brain using the methodology of computer science to model the data—and neural engineering, in which what can be learned from study of the brain is repackaged as technological principles and turned to advantage in the design of distributed architectures for intelligent machines. He lays particular stress on the integration of perception and action—whether in the animal or the robot—and introduces a two-level methodology of schema theory and neural networks for the analysis of complex, intelligent systems. In the realm of biology, this relates the language of cognition to that of neuroscience, while in technology it provides the bridge between work in distributed artificial intelligence and the design of artificial neural networks.

Patricia Goldman-Rakic and Michael Merzenich then give us fascinating glimpses of what it is like to grapple with the challenge of retro-engineering the brain, and in so doing take us for a brief visit to a pair of forward observation posts on the frontier of contemporary experimental neuroscience.

Goldman-Rakic's *Parallel systems in the cerebral cortex: the topography of cognition* reveals how learning involves making parallel 'sideways' connections between neurons at the same level in the brain. It is not always possible to account for certain phenomena by simple sensor-to-motor linear throughput connections. Among these are experimentally observed features of 'working' (short-term, scratch pad) memory. In addition to the 'columnar' or 'vertical' connections of neurons which a number of neuroscientists have found in the cortical structure of the vision and other systems of the brain, there must also be 'row' or 'horizontal' connections linking these groups of neurons to each other in parallel. This means that the neural computations involved in short-term memory and decision-making are very much more complex than those which the relatively simple 'stimulus-response' paradigm suggests.

Merzenich describes and explains, in *How the brain functionally rewires itself*, beautifully clear experimental evidence he has obtained which shows how the brain responds to both correlated experience and disabling damage by reorganizing itself so as to encode new experience or restore some of the lost functions. In doing this the brain exhibits the phenomenon of 'synaptic plasticity'—in effect, the dramatic reshaping of connections between existing brain cells—the functional equivalent, if not the literal fact, of 'rewiring' parts of the brain. The same phenomenon underlies Edelman and Reeke's work which is described in the fourth chapter of Part III. That the brain can, and apparently routinely does, vary the topology of its network of communication links in this way is a fascinating discovery in its own terms, but should also inspire and challenge the computer architects as they ponder appropriate design ideas for the next generation of parallel computers. It is a prominent characteristic of almost all of today's parallel computers that their networks of communication links are fixed once for all as part of the structure of the machine. A notable exception is the Hillis Connection Machine (CM) produced by Thinking Machines Corporation. Although the wiring is (of course!) physically fixed—the machine is laid out as a conventional hypercube—it is designed deliberately to be capable of behaving as if it were in fact 'functionally rewiring itself' as its program is executed. David Waltz in Part IV discusses several CM applications and enlarges our view of this remarkable parallel computer.

The chapter *Neural Darwinism* by Gerald Edelman and George Reeke, describes a computer experiment, based on Edelman's theory of *neuronal group selection,* in which an artificial organism is exposed to an environment of sensory inputs which are processed by its nervous system according to selection principles abstractly the same as those at work in the biological evolution of species.

Theirs is a detailed attempt to reproduce phenomena found in real brains by running a brain model on a computer. Modelling is the basic technique of natural science. Indeed, one could say that scientific knowledge consists essentially of a repertoire of successful models—mostly in the form of equations or sets of equations whose mathematical properties reflect those of the systems they model—of various aspects of nature. The use of the computer in this methodology merely speeds up the process of comparing features of a model with corresponding features of its intended original. It is the mark of a good model that it can be used literally to imitate the behavior of a system, or simulate it. Thus with a good model of the brain one ought to be able to simulate actual brain behavior, at least to some degree. The Edelman-Reeke simulation is in effect part of a program of testing the theory of neuronal group selection, in which the central postulated mechanism is the selection of functional variants from populations of neurons that emerge as a result of the variation which occurs during the development of each individual brain.

Cognitive Science and Artificial Intelligence

The relationship between cognitive science and the science (if it can as yet be called that) of artificial intelligence is a special case of the natural-artificial theme which runs throughout the book. Neither of the two contributions in Part IV falls entirely under one or the other of these headings, but rather falls (to different degrees) under both, although probably David Waltz would admit to being more strongly motivated by the goals of cognitive science—to explain how the mind actually works and to simulate this working in suitably designed artifacts—than by the goals of artificial intelligence—to solve certain intellectual problems by any means possible, no matter how artificial they may be. Alan Robinson is driven by the ambition to develop machines which can prove theorems, whether or not they thereby shed any light on how mathematicians do so; but he is also drawn towards trying to see how humans understand and discover proofs, both for its own sake and for the sake of learning 'how nature does it' in order to imitate and perhaps surpass her.

Waltz explains, in *Memory-based reasoning*, how the novel highly parallel CM computer can be programmed to exhibit mindlike capabilities using mindlike principles of organization. The level of conceptual organization of his examples corresponds roughly to the subconscious parallel mental patterns of operation which seem to underlie both the associative retrieval of old concepts and the formation of new concepts by clustering and grouping of specific experiential traces in memory. This chapter is in its way a hymn to the CM as a powerful new tool for cognitive science, an interestingly different facet of its personality from that which attracts Geoffrey Fox in Part II—its ability to perform 'ordinary' scientific computations at supercomputer speeds.

Robinson's *Natural and artificial reasoning* examines ways in which 'natural' mathematical proofs—the characteristic products of human brains—differ from the 'artificial' proofs which have been produced by serial computers or will soon be produced by parallel computers. A number of algorithms for carrying out various artificial reasoning tasks are defined and shown at work on examples. Since at the highest cognitive levels, and in the conscious processing of information at all levels, human minds appear to operate in a serial rather than a parallel mode, certain kinds of reasoning will always remain strictly artificial because essentially parallel. Presumably it is some aspect of the brain's design which restricts the conscious mind to being a serial processor of information. As such it is no more than a contingent fact that thinking is serial: we can imagine parallel modes of thought, and simulate them on parallel computers. This reminds us that hitherto we have had to deal only with differences of *degree* between (serial) computers and ourselves—they do only the same sort of thing that we do except that they do it much faster and on a much larger scale. Henceforth we will have to deal also with differences of *kind*—it is not that we cannot think as quickly in parallel, we cannot think that way *at all*. Logics devised for *parallel* reasoning will thus be the special province of machines, and we will not always be able to follow directly what is going on. The best we will be able to do is to troop through arbitrary 'meanwhile-back-at-the-ranch' serial narrative records of their behavior, spreading out over time for separate perusal events which in fact occur simultaneously. For that matter, it is only in this artificial way that we shall ever be able actually to follow the workings of our own brains.

Minds, brains

This is not a philosophical book. Its authors more or less skirt around—we hope in a common sense sort of way—philosophical issues raised by our topic. This is not to be taken as being itself a particular philosophical position on such issues; rather it is our position that such issues deserve a whole book to themselves.[*] Meanwhile, much remains to be done to expand our understanding of the brain and its functioning, and so we must soldier on with experimental inquiry and theoretical modelling, whether or not we take time to wonder whether consciousness will occur in sufficiently accurate artificial brains, and so on. We don't even know with certainty that consciousness occurs in other human brains, let alone in the brains of the heroic experimental animals from whom so much has been and will be learned and to whom so much is owed.

It certainly looks like it, though, and the day may come when we are forced to say the same about an artifact.

---

[*]   Such as *The Construction of Reality* by Michael Arbib and Mary Hesse, Cambridge University Press, 1989.

Chapter 2

THE EVOLUTION OF COMPUTING

RALPH E. GOMORY

Progress in silicon technology

One of the great events of our time is the rapid and almost irresistible advance of computing, with all that it has already meant to everyone's life and what it will mean in the future. What is it that is driving this evolution which all of us have seen—changing and advancing computers in a most remarkable way—and will it continue?

Progress in this field certainly has something to do with the underlying silicon technology. Many of you have seen over and over again charts like Figure 1, which illustrate the seemingly relentless advance in the number of memory bits on a chip, or the number of logic circuits that can be placed on one square centimeter of silicon.

As the features in the silicon get smaller, more and more computing can be done on each chip, and the power that this is giving us is portrayed in Figure 2. What this shows is that the one-micron (one millionth of a meter) technology of today can give us, on a single chip or a very small number of them, nine to twelve MIPS (or millions of instructions per second) of computing power. And that power will grow as we move, in not many more years, to features only 0.7, 0.5, and 0.35 micron in size.

Will this progress continue? I think the answer is undoubtedly yes. It is very unusual for a technology to advance like this for twenty years, but I think it will keep on doing so.

Making the bits smaller

Why? There is one very simple, underlying fact: a small bit—a small one or a small zero—is as good as a big bit, and what we

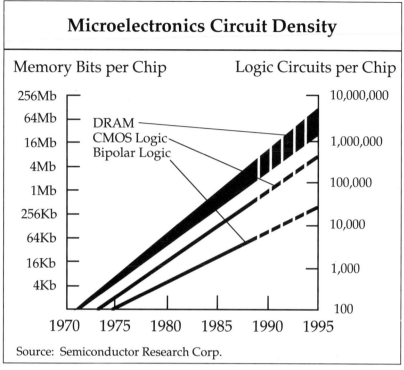

Figure 1

are doing in the computer industry is making the bits smaller every year. That is about it, and it's like pushing on an open door.

Our products are unlike those of any other industry, in this respect. Automobiles, for example, have to be big and strong enough to carry people up hills. They must do real physical work. But when we compute, we don't do any work in that sense. So the underlying thing that is transforming the world of computing is that the bits get smaller every year, and I will shortly give you some reason to believe that this will continue into the indefinite future. Smaller, of course, translates into cheaper. Faster is very important (and I will talk about speed later on), but cheaper is also very important. Let me illustrate that with a simple example.

When I joined IBM in 1959, twelve hundred of us shared one computer, a 704. We sent in our programs every day, and we got our results back the next day, and we thought we were the princes of the earth. Now, that 704 could probably have made a pretty good word processor. After all, it was only slightly inferior to an elementary personal computer of a few years ago. But believe me, the thought of linking those several rooms of machinery, worth a few million dollars, into a word processor, and thereby putting the twelve hundred of us out of business, never crossed our minds.

Microprocessor Capability

TECHNOLOGY FEATURE SIZE	MILLIONS OF INSTRUCTIONS/SECOND
1 micron	9 - 12
0.7 micron	13 - 17
0.5 micron	27 - 35
0.35 micron	37 - 48

Figure 2

The only real difference today is that you can buy a roughly equivalent machine for a thousand dollars. And because you can, the things you can do with it—simply as a result of its cheapness—are totally transformed, and it is used for totally different purposes. So what Figure 2 actually says is that computing is going to keep getting cheaper, as we learn to make things smaller and smaller. In practice, that can be enormously difficult to do, but it is doable.

Figure 3, for example, shows a small portion of an experimental chip with lines 0.7 micron across. That is smaller than was thought to be the limit of this technology only six or seven years ago. Limits, in this business, have a way of receding as we approach them. But the price one pays is increased complexity in the tools and facilities needed to build ever smaller circuits.

Electron beam lithography, for example, is much more complicated than today's optical lithography, which cannot go on forever drawing finer and finer features. X-ray lithography, which we may eventually need, is even more complicated and expensive.

A modern chip manufacturing facility costs on the order of a thousand dollars per usable square foot. That is partly because, even though it is three stories high, you only get to use the middle floor. The rest of the building houses equipment to clean the air, supply processing gases, and so on.

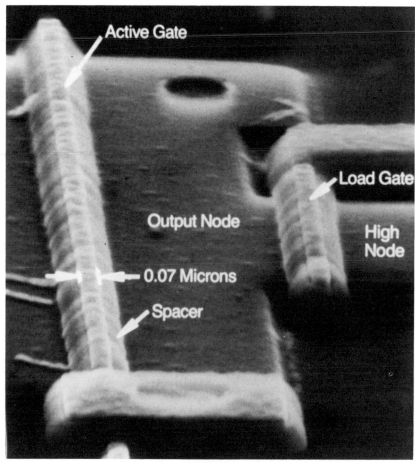

Figure 3

So yes, the bits will keep getting smaller every year. It will be done at great cost, in advanced facilities, with advanced tools, by thousands of skilled people constantly refining the processes involved. But it will happen.

The magnetic disk

Of course, silicon technology and its attendant packaging are only part of what goes into computing, and only a part of its rapid evolution. Storage—the magnetic disk file—is another major component. People often speak condescendingly of magnetic disks as mere mechanical objects, quite unlike the refined electronics that you find elsewhere inside a computer. That's a real mistake, because the sophistication of disk technology is, if anything, harder to imagine. And oddly enough, it too will continue to evolve. You must remember that the way disk technology works is that there is a head which senses magnetic marks on the surface of the disk. As the disk spins at engine speed—thirty-six hundred rpm—this little head flies above it.

How close to the disk? The head flies about a third of a micron—a third of a wavelength of light—above the surface. That is a distance smaller than present-day semiconductor dimensions, which is all the more remarkable when you realize that disks, when you examine them closely as in Figure 4, are not altogether flat.

Now, the only way that you can put more bits on a disk, basically, is by moving the head a little closer to the surface. Magnetism being what it is, you cannot sense small bits at a distance. There is no beaming of magnetism, as in optics. And yet, every projection which we make shows that disk storage will march forward in the same relentless way (Figure 5) that it has in the past. In storage, as in chips—even though storage is mechanical, and even though the heads are flying a third of a wavelength of light above a surface spinning at thirty-six hundred rpm—we have every reason to believe that progress will continue straight ahead. Here, too, the bits will get smaller. And keep in mind that almost everything I say here is probably over-conservative, because I haven't allowed for anything new— merely   for   the   evolution   of   what   we   already

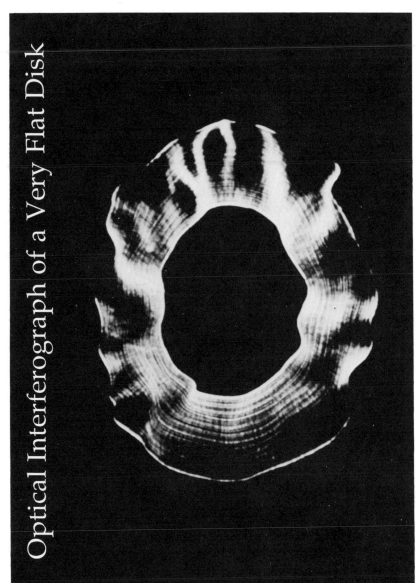

Optical Interferograph of a Very Flat Disk

Figure 4

Progress in Storage

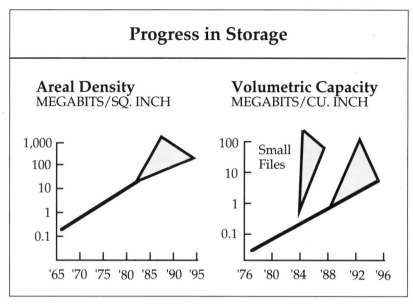

Areal Density
MEGABITS/SQ. INCH

Volumetric Capacity
MEGABITS/CU. INCH

Figure 5

Optical Storage Scenario

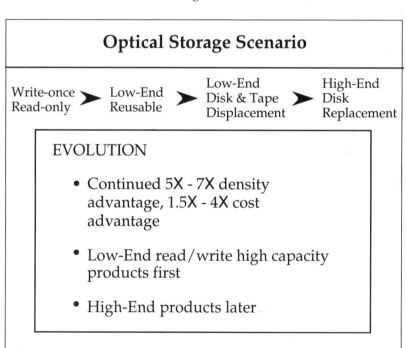

Write-once Read-only ➤ Low-End Reusable ➤ Low-End Disk & Tape Displacement ➤ High-End Disk Replacement

EVOLUTION

• Continued 5X - 7X density advantage, 1.5X - 4X cost advantage

• Low-End read/write high capacity products first

• High-End products later

Figure 6

understand.   On that basis alone, the historic pace will be maintained.

Of course, there are new elements to consider, too. For example, in addition to magnetic storage there is optical storage: (Figure 6). Optical storage has the advantage that you don't need to have the head as close to the bits because you can aim a beam of light at the disk, look at the reflections and see how the surface has been altered. Optical technology has a five-to-seven-times storage density advantage—that many more bits per square inch—over magnetic storage, although that doesn't translate in the early stages into a similar cost advantage, because the disks have to be spaced farther apart.   Still, it will be useful.   Optical storage will evolve from its present state, which is barely writable—just emerging from the write-once-then-read-only phase.   Rewritable optical disks will appear first in low-performance files.   Then, as their performance improves, they will probably become serious competitors to magnetic technology, and the contention between the two will mean that progress, from the point of view of those who use computers, will be even more rapid than was indicated earlier.

Storing information in molecules

Figure 7 may seem unrelated to data storage, but it does relate to the point I want to make: that the world of computing is based on making things small, and that this is an open door we are pushing on.   What this illustration shows are two surfaces— silicon and gallium arsenide—as seen by the scanning tunneling microscope, or STM, which is a relatively new form of microscopy.

I myself never thought to live to see pictures of individual atoms, but that's what these are.   They are not x-ray pictures of a crystal, where in fact you are looking simultaneously at millions of atoms combined into a single image.   These are individual atoms, and if there is a little flaw on the surface due to one particular atom being out of place, you will see it.   Today, then, we have a curious technology which enables us to see details at the atomic level.   Now what does that ultimately mean for computing?

I think Figure 8 suggests what it might mean.   Again, the little bumps scattered all over the surface are atoms.   The mountain in the middle is an organic molecule—or perhaps a couple of them— that have been pinned down on the graphite surface.   To understand this, you need to know that the scanning tunneling microscope is a mechanical beast—another reminder (like the disk file) that we should not sell mechanics short.   As I suggested earlier, people tend to think of mechanics as crude.   I

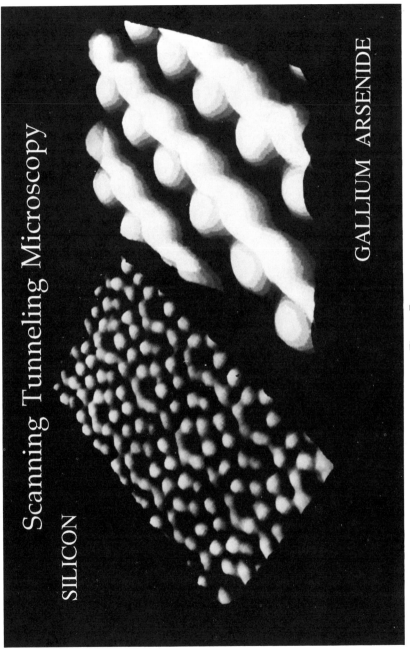

Scanning Tunneling Microscopy

SILICON

GALLIUM ARSENIDE

Figure 7

Storage at the Molecular Level

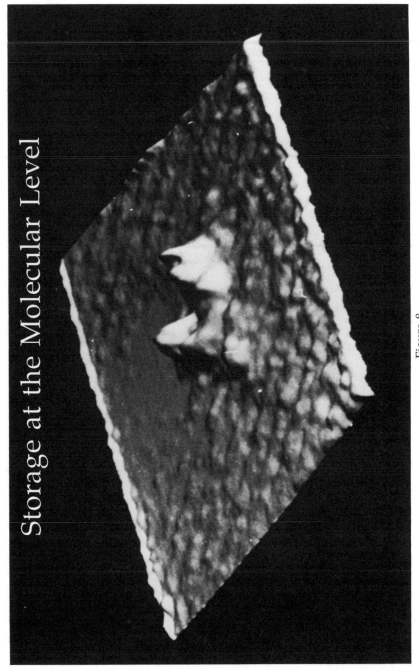

Figure 8

will take the opposite position: I say that a wavelength of light is crude; it's very big. With mechanics, you can be much more precise than a wavelength of light, and the STM is a good example of that.

The STM is a little tripod with a pin that comes down in the middle. You apply a voltage to the pin, and if you position its pointed end very close to the surface you want to examine, a small current will flow. The amount of that current measures how close the pin is to the surface. So far, I haven't described anything very remarkable. The amazing thing about the STM is that, by precise mechanical control, the pin can be kept only five angstroms (about one atomic diameter) above the surface, without banging into it. Not only that, but you can mechanically march the pin along, scanning the surface from a height of five angstroms, while observing, from the way the current varies, the profiles of the atoms below.

That is how these pictures were made. Furthermore, with the same instrument, you can march the pin up to a spot on the surface, apply a higher voltage to change that spot, walk the pin away, and then return later and see the change. In other words, you can make a mark and you can read a mark, and this has been done in the laboratory. Let's say that the little mountain in Figure 8 is fifteen or twenty angstroms across—maybe a little more. Today, at one micron or ten thousand angstroms, the smallest marks we make in practice are at least five hundred times larger. That is how far we have to go in making little marks before reaching the molecular level. And that, in turn, is another reason why I take the view that we have an almost open field ahead of us, with all the transforming power that implies.

More natural forms of input

Lots of inexpensive computing power, for example, will let people interact with computers in more natural ways. As Figure 9 indicates, it takes very little computing power to accept input from a keyboard. Using a mouse takes a little more power. Still more is needed for the machine to read your handwriting, and a lot more if you want to be able to talk to it. To a large extent, what is making these more convenient modes of interaction practical is the computing power now available, in a very inexpensive form, on a single chip.

Handwriting recognition at reasonable speed and with reasonable accuracy is basically here. Handmarking recognition which allows commands to take the form of easily drawn symbols is a promising extension.

The current state of speech recognition is harder to characterize, but one experimental system has a twenty-thousand-word vocabulary but only if you --- pause --- between --- the --- words.

Again, it is cheap MIPS that will eventually make all these things, and more, doable.

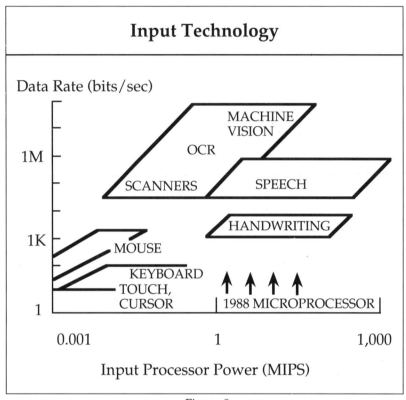

Figure 9

Parallel processing for speed

In view of the following chapters, I am not going to say a lot about parallelism. Clearly, it is real, and it is useful. I think that in every case the highest performance machine, for whatever purpose, will soon be a parallel machine. And it is quite possible that the machines with the best price-to-performance ratio will also be parallel machines. As you will read elsewhere in this book, parallelism has already been a winner in special-purpose applications. In IBM, for example, we have a number of highly-parallel machines of a type we call EVE, for Engineering Verification Engine. EVE simulates the gate-level logic of new computers not yet built, and does it much faster than the best software simulators. But that is all EVE does.

The question is, as David May asks in his chapter: what about general-purpose parallelism? In every case, I think, parallel machines will be the fastest. The question is how general-purpose they will be. May emphasizes the important role of communications between the processors. I totally agree with him, and it is my view that what I call, in Figure 10, the switch, will be the dominant question in determining how parallelism is used.

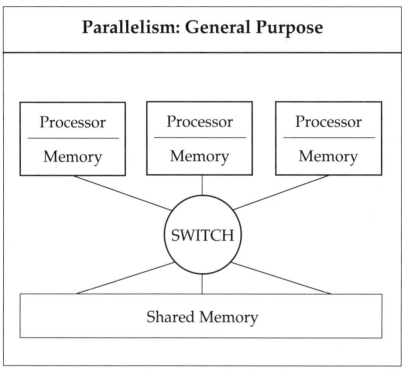

Figure 10

Figure 11 is a more specific representation of one of IBM Research's experimental parallel machines. And here you can get some sense, at the top of the diagram, of the effort we are making (which includes a combining switch) to get these processors to work together on a variety of problems.

The trouble with having a special-purpose machine is not that it isn't good at what it does, but that it doesn't do many things. If the machine's field of employment is too narrow, it may not be economically feasible. That is why general-purpose machines

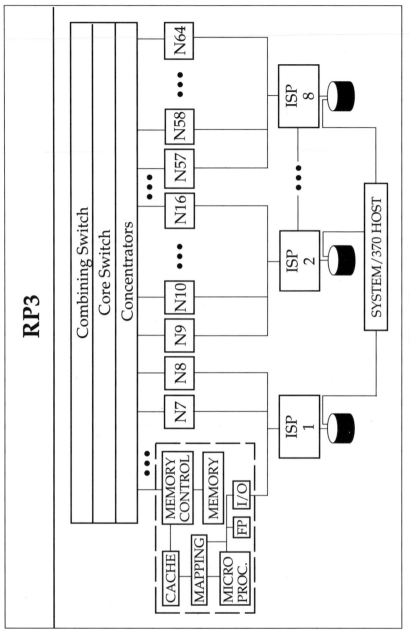

Figure 11

very often win out. One answer to this problem may lie in an intermediate realm of software which is neither general-purpose nor very special-purpose, but which has the characteristic that almost every application uses it. I refer here to the common software functions which, as I will explain shortly, are getting split off into separate subsystems. These functions would seem to be a natural field for parallelism.

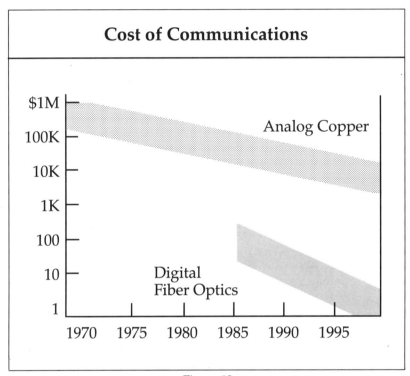

Figure 12

Low cost communications

While these and other evolutions are taking place in computing, let us not forget that the cost of communications (Figure 12) has also been dropping radically, through the introduction of optical fibers and appropriate light sources for them. Thus, not only is computing becoming incredibly cheap, and also rather fast, but the business of sending bits over long distances is simultaneously being transformed by the tremendous bandwidth available through digital fiber optics.

Hardware versus software

Meanwhile, there are so many differing views about hardware, software, and their changing roles that the result is a somewhat confusing picture. According to some people, hardware is becoming a commodity that no longer matters; the software is what's important. I think that they both continue to matter, in different ways. Other people denigrate software, because it hasn't made the progress that hardware has made. I don't even understand the point of that remark. I think that if software could be improved by making the lines of code smaller, as we do with the bits in hardware, it would be quite easy to make more progress. But that's not the case.

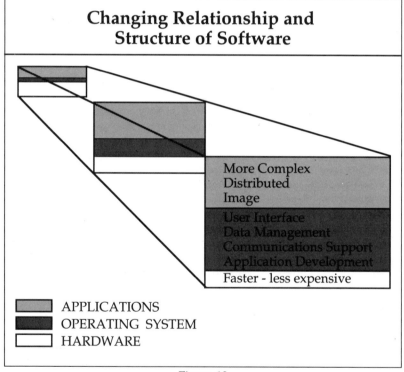

Changing Relationship and Structure of Software

More Complex
Distributed
Image

User Interface
Data Management
Communications Support
Application Development

Faster - less expensive

APPLICATIONS
OPERATING SYSTEM
HARDWARE

Figure 13

So what are the roles of hardware and software, and how is their relationship changing? Way back in time, as I have tried to illustrate in Figure 13, the total system bundle contained a lot of hardware (the bottom band) and relatively little software. What has happened since is this: every year the hardware gets cheaper, but—and this is the curious part—it still performs approximately the same function. It still does the same one hundred and twenty eight, or whatever, instructions. It moves data around, compares them, and puts them back. Today's hardware does this faster and cheaper, but it still does what it did before.

As these traditional hardware functions have become cheaper to perform, what the world wants to do with them, and what is economically doable, has become more and more complex. Today's computer users don't just add up columns of numbers any more. Today's users want to order, electronically, from other companies exactly what they need, based on sophisticated inventory rules. Besides sending out bills, they want to schedule their assembly lines. And yet all of these real world tasks, which are a lot more complex than adding up a column of figures, have to be translated into a sequence of the same old one hundred and twenty eight instructions.

In short, as hardware gets cheaper the applications get more complicated, and the software, whose burden it is to translate the applications into a fixed set of instructions, has more to do. So the pile of software sitting on top of the ever-cheaper hardware gets deeper and deeper over time. Furthermore, as the software pile gets deeper in its attempt to translate complexity into a fixed target, it gets too complicated to be one undifferentiated blob. It starts to split up into more manageable layers and subsystems. This is what has happened and what, I think, will continue to be the basis for a very definite structural evolution in software.

System software evolution

Back in 1950, as suggested in Figure 14, when you wrote an application, you wrote it all. If you were lucky, you had some run-time support. By 1960, operating systems were beginning to take over some of the tasks that all programs have to carry out, and there was data management at the file level; you didn't need to write your own file input-output routines. Since then, other common tasks have been split off, piece after piece. The user interface has become its own subsystem. Communications has become its own subsystem. The application writer simply invokes them, and they go to work.

As the pile of software continues to break up into subsystems, certain other things occur. The interfaces between the subsystems tend to become cleaner and better defined. This allows the subsystems to communicate across the interfaces at ever higher levels of abstraction. Also, the subsystems themselves (which, as I noted earlier, seem like natural candidates for parallelism) are

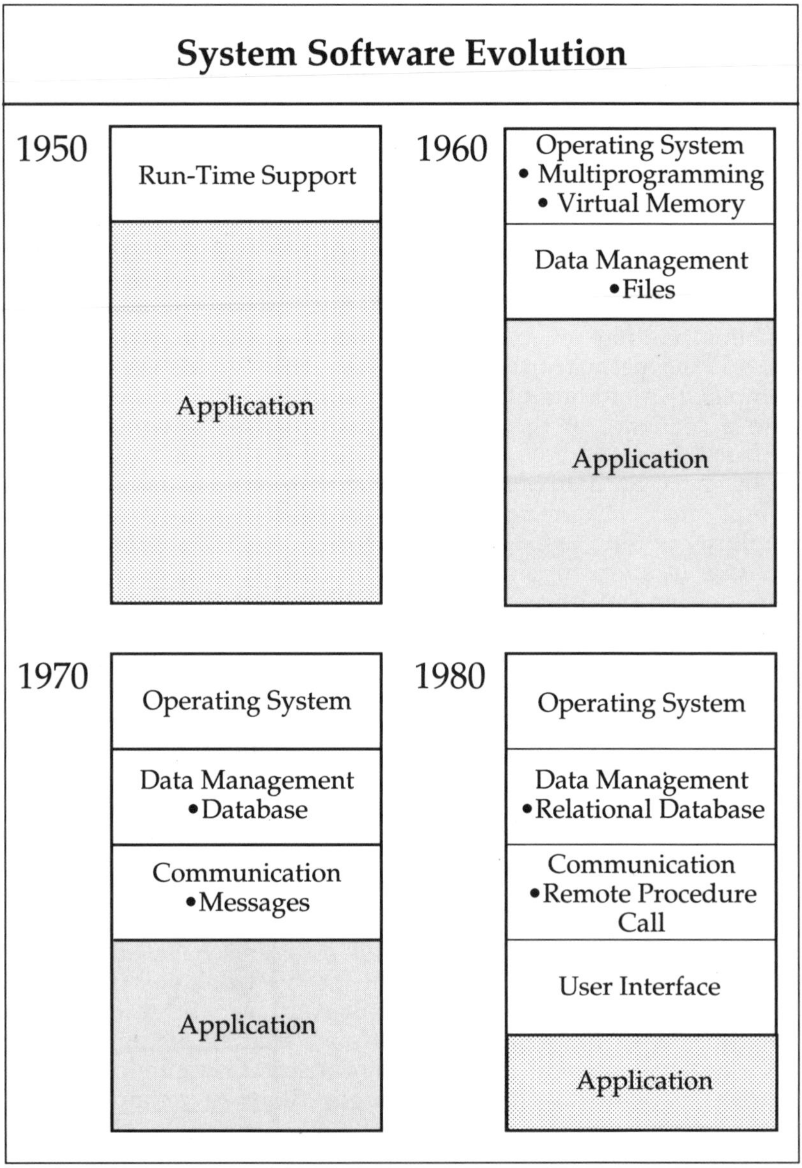

System Software Evolution

1950	Run-Time Support
	Application

1960	Operating System • Multiprogramming • Virtual Memory
	Data Management •Files
	Application

1970	Operating System
	Data Management •Database
	Communication •Messages
	Application

1980	Operating System
	Data Management •Relational Database
	Communication •Remote Procedure Call
	User Interface
	Application

Figure 14

providing more and more function. For example, the ability to deal not only with local data but with data distributed throughout a whole network might be built into the data-management subsystem.

Transparent access to network resources

Together, the semiconductors which are making computing cheap, and the optical fibers which are making communications cheap, are making networks with distributed data and applications technically and economically possible. The physical potential is there. To succeed, however, these networks must be made transparent to their users. You should not be aware of the fact that you are talking to programs and people at a distance, or of certain inevitable delays. This too is starting to happen, thanks to the standards for interconnection, transmission protocols, and so on, which are emerging.

What future applications will be like

Now, what will all these evolutions I have touched on—in the underlying technologies, in parallelism, in software and in networking—mean in terms of computer applications? For one thing, many applications of the future will be geographically widespread. In a few years, for example, you should be able to go into a retail clothing store and summon up, from your favorite manufacturer's computer, three-dimensional full-color images of suits that are not in the store. You might even, if things go well, be able to try on (hypothetically) one of these suits and see how it looks—wrinkles and all. Such widespread interconnection of applications, with more or less instantaneous response, will become increasingly common.

A second characteristic of future computer applications will be more accurate visualization and modelling of real world objects. We are just starting to see the potential of this, today. Already it is possible, for example, to see in a very realistic way a building that is not yet built, to work on its appearance, and to get it more correct than would otherwise be the case. Even more importantly, it is becoming possible, with tremendous amounts of numerical computation, to create models of reality that not only look real (like the unbuilt building) but act real. The simulated airflow over an airplane wing behaves exactly like real air flowing over a real wing. The ability to model, realistically, the behavior of alternative designs—their movement through the air and vibration—was of major assistance.

So the power that cheaper, faster computing gives us to create models that both look like, and act like reality is another important applications direction.

Finally, in addition to being widespread and acting more like real objects, it is safe to say that future applications will contain more intelligence. This intelligence may take many forms, from natural language processing to rule-based expert systems, neural networks, and other things which may be out ahead of us.

During this very brief overview, I have touched on certain fundamentals:

- Miniaturization as a wide open door, with plenty of opportunity remaining for further reduction in the cost of computing, and all that implies.

- The changing relationship of hardware and software, with the hardware becoming ever cheaper and the software ever more complex and modular.

- The tremendous possibilities of transparent networks.

- And finally, the future uses of computers, which I think will be enormous.

We have all seen great progress in computers, but it is my strong belief that we are still today very much only at the beginning.

II

PARALLEL COMPUTATION

Chapter 3

THE NATURE OF
PARALLEL PROGRAMMING

PER BRINCH HANSEN

Summary

This chapter discusses the nature of parallel programming without going into technical details. It uses a sorting problem to illustrate what it means to solve a problem in parallel, how we write parallel programs, how parallel computers execute them, and how fast they run. I expect that scientific users of parallel computers may find ease of programming more important than maximum performance. I suggest ways to make this possible.

Asking the right questions

Parallel programming is the art of writing programs for computers that perform many operations simultaneously. Parallel computers with tens and hundreds of processors are already commercially available. Researchers are now working on computers with thousands of processors. Programming these machines sounds like an exciting idea until you try it. It is often too complicated, but for the wrong reason: most of our programming languages and computer architectures do not really support parallelism as well as they could.

It seems natural to begin by asking some fundamental questions:

- What does it mean to solve problems in parallel?
- How do we write parallel programs?
- How do parallel computers execute such programs?
- How fast can parallel programs run?
- Can we make parallel programming easier?

I will try to answer these questions by stripping away the inessentials and penetrating to the core of the problem.

One step at a time

A well-chosen example is often an important source of insight. I will use a sorting problem to illustrate the ideas of parallel programming. Once you understand these ideas, the example becomes merely a detail in the great scheme of things.

Bridge players often sort their hands by picking up one card at a time and inserting it where it belongs. This is the simplest way to sort a small number of cards. But, if you are sorting thousands of cards, there are much faster methods. One of them is called *merge sorting*. As early as 1945 John von Neumann wrote computer programs for merge sorting. Let me describe how you would use this method to sort eight numbers manually.

- Write each number on a separate card and place the cards in front of you in any order

- Pick up two cards at a time and put them down as an ordered pair of cards. You now have four ordered pairs

- Take the first two pairs

- and merge them into a single, ordered sequence of four cards

$$\boxed{1}\ \boxed{2}\ \boxed{4}\ \boxed{6}$$

- Then combine the last two pairs into an ordered sequence

$$\boxed{3}\ \boxed{5}\ \boxed{7}\ \boxed{8}$$

- Finally, merge the two ordered sequences of four cards each into a single, ordered sequence of eight cards

This completes the sorting.

Let me explain the merging more carefully. The first card in the merged sequence is the smallest of the eight cards. Since the two original sequences are ordered, the smallest card is the first card of one of these sequences. Take this card and place it below the two sequences as the first card of the merged sequence

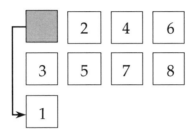

- Continue to remove the smallest remaining card and add it to the merged sequence until one of the original sequences is empty

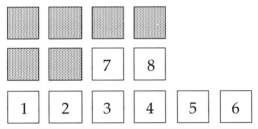

- Then add the rest of the other sequence to the merged one.

The mergesort works by repeatedly merging shorter, ordered sequences into longer ones. Eight sequences of length 1 are merged into four sequences of length 2, which, in turn, are combined into two sequences of length 4, and, finally, into one sequence of length

8. You can picture the sorting process as a tree of merging steps

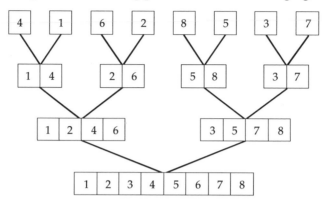

I have described merge sorting as a *sequential process* performed one step at a time. This is indeed how it would be done on a traditional computer. Merge sorting can, however, be speeded up by performing the merging steps simultaneously on a parallel computer.

Running in parallel

The mergesort solves a problem by dividing it into smaller instances of the same problem. The subproblems can be solved independently of one another. This property makes the algorithm well-suited for parallel execution.

We can build a parallel computer that sorts eight numbers. This machine is organized as a *tree*. It consists of 15 processors connected by 16 communication channels. The processors and channels are drawn as circles and arrows

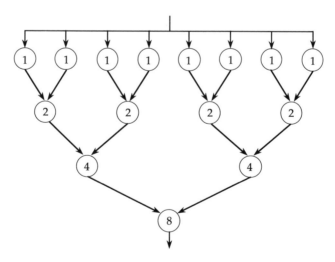

The eight processors at the top are the *leaves* of the tree. The single processor at the bottom is the *root* of the whole tree. Each processor in the middle is the root of a smaller tree within the larger one.

The eight numbers move from top to bottom in the tree. Each leaf receives a single number from a shared channel and sends it to its successor in the tree. Each root receives two sequences of numbers from its predecessors and sends them as a merged sequence to its successor. The main root sends the eight numbers through a channel in ascending order. Each processor merges either 1, 2, 4 or 8 numbers as shown in the circles.

The processors operate in parallel. Processors which are at the same horizontal *level* in the tree communicate simultaneously with their neighbors. Each root holds only two numbers at a time. When a root has sent a number below, it immediately receives another one from above. Meanwhile its successors can process the previous number.

In general when a tree machine sorts N numbers, we will simplify the discussion by assuming that N is a power of two. In other words N is a number in the series

$$1, 2, 4, 8, ..., 1024, ...$$

Since the number of processors doubles from one level to the next, the total number of processors in the tree machine is

$$1 + 2 + 4 + ... + N.$$

This adds up to $2N - 1$. So the machine needs 2047 processors to sort 1024 numbers. If N is large the number of processors is almost 2N.

In practice we do not always have two separate processors and channels for each of the sorted numbers. We often have a parallel computer with a much smaller number of processors and channels. We use these processors and channels to *simulate* a large number of slower processors and channels. This simulation is a crucial part of the implementation of a programming language for parallel programming.

Getting down to fundamentals

A parallel computation may involve millions of small steps. The mind obviously cannot comprehend such a multitude of simultaneous events in detail. We must impose order on the complexity by describing it in terms of a small number of general concepts. The most important *abstractions* in parallel programming are processes and communication.

A *process* is an abstract model of a computation. A sequential process is a sequence of steps which take place one at a time. A parallel process is a set of processes performed simultaneously. And a *communication* is a transfer of data from one process to another. These concepts are the essence of parallel programming. The rest is detail.

From now on we will view the parallel mergesort as a tree of processes. Whether these processes run on real or simulated processors is a technical detail.

When you have discovered powerful thinking tools, it becomes essential to express them in a *concise notation*. For parallel computations we need a programming language which can describe individual processes and combinations of processes precisely. I will not discuss the merits of particular programming languages. Instead I have invented a simple notation which will give you the flavor of a parallel language.

The simplest processes in a parallel merge tree are the sequential leaves. A leaf is connected to two channels.

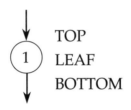

TOP

LEAF

BOTTOM

All leaves behave in the same way. We can therefore write a single procedure that describes the behavior of these identical processes. In a programming language this procedure might look as follows:

```
LEAF (top, bottom) =
    1.   receive (x, top);
    2.   send (x, bottom).
```

The notational details are unimportant. The procedure consists of two numbered steps. Each step describes an action performed by a leaf:

1. Receive a number x through the top channel.

2. Send the same number through the bottom channel.

When a leaf has done this, it terminates and ceases to exist.

From a user's point of view a sorting tree is a single process that receives N numbers through one channel and sends them in ascending order through another channel.

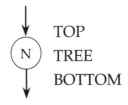

TOP
TREE
BOTTOM

A closer look reveals that a sorting process takes one of two forms. A tree that "sorts" one number only is just a single leaf. A tree that sorts more than one number consists of a root process and two smaller trees connected by a left and a right channel.

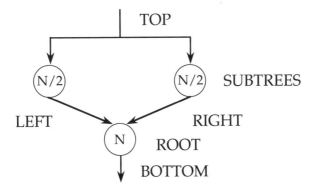

TOP

SUBTREES

LEFT   RIGHT

ROOT

BOTTOM

In this picture each subtree is viewed as a single process. Internally it may be composed of other processes, but right now we choose to ignore these details.

The following procedure defines the behavior of a tree that sorts N numbers

TREE (N, top, bottom) =
  if   N = 1 **run**   LEAF (top, bottom)
  if   N > 1 **run**
            TREE (N/2, top, left),
            TREE (N/2, top, right),
            ROOT(N, left, right, bottom)
        in parallel.

Again the programming symbols are not important. Here is what they mean:
1. If N = 1 a tree is just a single leaf. The effect of the command

run LEAF (top, bottom)

is to activate a leaf process with access to the top and bottom channels of the tree. When the leaf terminates, the tree ceases to exist.

2. If N > 1 a tree splits into two subtrees and a root process running in parallel. When all three processes have terminated, the whole tree disappears.

The above procedure defines a tree in terms of smaller trees. A parallel process which is defined in terms of other processes of the same kind is called a *recursive process*.

A root is a sequential process that receives two ordered sequences from a left and a right channel and sends a merged sequence through a bottom channel. I will omit the programming details of this process and describe it in English.

ROOT   (N, left, right, bottom) =
1. Receive the first left and right numbers;
2. Send the smaller of the two through the bottom channel and replace it by the next number (if any) from the same left or right sequence;
3. Repeat step 2 until the left or right sequence is empty;
4. Copy the rest (if any) of the other left or right sequence.

Parallelism is a mechanism for splitting larger computations into smaller ones which can be performed simultaneously. A notation for recursive processes is essential in a parallel programming language. The reason is simple. In a highly parallel program it is impractical to formulate thousands of processes with different behaviors. We must instead rely on repeated use of a small number of behaviors. The simplest problems that satisfy this requirement are those that can be reduced to smaller problems of the same kind and solved by combining the partial results. Recursion is the natural programming tool for expressing these *divide and conquer* algorithms.

A good programming language has an air of economy and an element of surprise. The economy comes from using a small number of concepts: processes, channels and communication. The surprise is the elegance and utility of recursive, parallel processes. This wonderful concept can be used not only for sorting, but also for fast Fourier transforms, n-body simulation, computational geometry and matrix multiplication on parallel computers.

Hidden complexity

A programming language should hide irrelevant details of computer hardware and support more abstract models of computation efficiently. You will immediately appreciate the significance of this requirement if you catch a glimpse of what really happens when a parallel computer executes a program.

In a parallel computation the number of processes often exceeds the number of physical processors. This is only too obvious when you run thousands of processes on a parallel computer with ten processors only. Programs that are more parallel than the computer itself are executed by switching the processors rapidly between processes to give the illusion that they are executed simultaneously on a slower, parallel computer.

The simplest kind of parallel computer is a *multiprocessor* which consists of tens of processors connected to a common memory. A language implementer views a multiprocessor as a *queueing system* with a finite population of customers (the processes) and multiple servers (the processors).

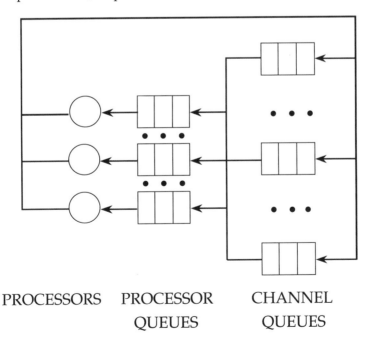

PROCESSORS   PROCESSOR   CHANNEL
QUEUES   QUEUES

In the common memory each process is represented by a small block of memory called a *process record*. This record holds the parameters and local variables of the process. Each processor has a separate queue of processes that are ready to run. The queue is a list of process records chained together.

An idle processor removes a process from its queue and executes it until the process, for example, is ready to send a message through a channel. The processor then puts the process in a queue associated with the channel. Immediately afterwards the processor resumes the execution of another process from its own queue.

When a process is ready to receive from the same channel, a message is copied from the record of the sending process to the record of the receiving process. The delayed process is then moved from the channel queue to one of the processor queues. Sooner or later the corresponding processor resumes the execution of the process.

To achieve the highest performance of a parallel computer it is important to divide a computation evenly among the processors, so that all of them can work at full speed whenever possible. This is called *load balancing*.

On a multiprocessor it is easy to balance the load, if the processors share a table defining the lengths of all processor queues. When a processor removes a process from a channel queue, it scans the table and puts that process in the shortest processor queue. Load balancing is in effect achieved by letting communicating processes *migrate* from processor to processor.

If several processors simultaneously attempt to manipulate the same queue, they must be forced to do it one at a time in unpredictable order. So parallelism introduces an element of chance in computation. The study of machines with *nondeterministic* behavior is a fertile area of research in computer science.

A well-designed parallel language enables the programmer to ignore these implementation details of processes and communications. However, the programmer cannot ignore the efficiency of the language implementation.

Limits to parallelism

The parallel mergesort is not particularly efficient. To understand why, we need a theoretical model of its performance.

The most critical performance figures for a highly parallel program are the execution times of process activation, communication and termination. We will assume that each of these steps takes exactly one unit of time. This is a reasonable approximation for the parallel mergesort written in the programming language Joyce and executed on a multiprocessor (the Encore Multimax).

It is customary to compare the running time T_1 of a parallel program on a single processor with its running time T_p on p processors.

For large N the *serial running time* is approximately

$$T_1 = N (L + 5) \text{ units}$$

where L is the number of process *levels* in the tree. T_1 includes the activation and termination of 2N processes and the communication of N numbers through all levels in the tree. I cannot go into further details here. You will find them in Brinch Hansen (1989b). For mathematically inclined readers: it turns out that

$$L = \log N + 1$$

where logN is the binary logarithm of N. A tree that sorts 1024 numbers has 11 process levels. It takes 16384 time units to run the sorting on a single processor.

The *parallel running time* is approximately

$$T_p = N (3 + (L + 2)/p) \text{ units.}$$

Most of the steps are now executed p times faster. But there are 3N steps which cannot be speeded up by the use of multiple processors. These serial steps can be attributed to the initial creation of the process tree and the sequential communications of the root. (See the paper cited above). The following curve shows the predicted running times (in time units) for sorting 1024 numbers on 1 to 10 processors. The plotted points were measured on the Multimax.

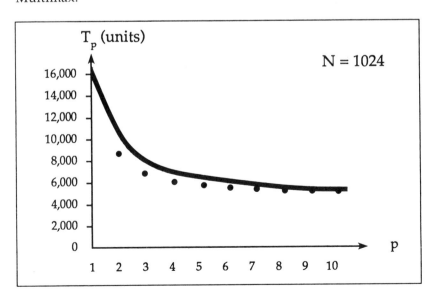

The *speed-up* $S_p = T_1/T_p$ defines how much faster a program runs on p processors compared to a single processor. Ideally p processors should make a parallel program run p times faster. If the speed-up is less than p, it means that some processors are idle part of the time.

The next figure shows the predicted and measured speed-up of the parallel sorting of 1024 numbers. The approximate model is fairly accurate.

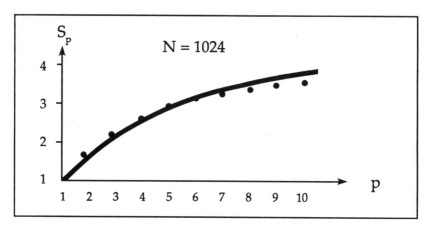

No matter how many processors you use, parallel merge sorting cannot be speeded up by more than

$$S_{max} = (L + 5)/3$$

For N = 1024 the maximum speed-up is five only. The limiting factor is the number of serial steps in the parallel algorithm. This is known as *Amdahl's law*. Many other parallel algorithms have similar limitations.

As you add more processors, the algorithm runs slightly faster, but wastes more and more processor time. In practice one should probably stop adding more processors when

$$S_p = p/2$$

since more than half of the processing capacity will be wasted beyond this point. Consequently the speed-up of the parallel mergesort is limited to

$$S_p = (L + 8)/6 \qquad \text{for } p = (L + 8)/3$$

For $N = 1024$ the sorting program runs only three times faster on six processors. And it does not pay to use more processors. This modest speed-up is acceptable for parallel computers with tens of processors, but not for thousands of processors.

After this brief discussion of the nature of parallel programming it is time to draw conclusions.

Looking ahead

As we move from tens to thousands of processors, our parallel algorithms will often be unable to run that much faster. There is only one way out of this problem: we must perform numerous experiments with new algorithms until we know how to use highly parallel computers well.

Scientific computer users, who are primarily interested in getting numerical results fast, will constantly have to reprogram new parallel architectures and may become increasingly frustrated at the difficulty of doing this.

Parallel programs are often written in the conventional languages Fortran and C extended with subroutines for parallelism. To my taste these programs are difficult to read and lack the beauty which scientists expect of their own research. This state of affairs puts a scientist in an unreasonable dilemma: should you study the unnecessary complexity of existing programs or reinvent similar ones?

I am convinced that the *most important task in computational science is to make the programming of parallel computers easier*. This is even more important than increasing computational power, and we should be prepared to sacrifice some performance to solve the programming problem. With this important goal in mind, I propose three requirements for the next generation of parallel hardware and software.

REQUIREMENT 1: Parallel programs must be written in abstract notations that hide irrelevant hardware detail and express parallelism concisely.

The essence of parallel computing is process creation and communication. These basic operations are implemented in software on most parallel computers. Consequently they are an order of magnitude slower than subroutine calls in Fortran. Due to the lack of hardware support for the process concept, the parallel mergesort is only slightly faster than the best sequential method for sorting (quicksort)!

REQUIREMENT 2: Process creation and communication must be hardware operations which are only an order of magnitude slower than memory references.

In the future we can expect to see highly parallel programs which use a mixture of process structures simultaneously. Sorting trees and image meshes may, for example, coexist. A computation may also change its process structures from one phase to another. When a parallel program spawns numerous processes with changing topologies it is not meaningful to ask the programmer to specify on which processor each process should run. This leads me to the last requirement.

REQUIREMENT 3: Most parallel computers must be able to distribute the computational load automatically with reasonable efficiency.

The driving force

I will end on a personal note. Parallel programming is not just about computation. It is about beautiful ideas that happen to be useful. The study of parallelism is driven by the same powerful ideas as the rest of science and mathematics. They are the concepts of *number, form, arrangement, movement* and *chance*. In mathematics, these notions led to arithmetic, geometry, combinatorics, calculus and probability. In parallel programming, they reappear as data, processes, networks, communication and nondeterminism.

The most enjoyable thing about computer programming is the insight it provides into the deep similarities of all creative endeavors.

Acknowledgements

This essay has been improved by valuable advice from Gideon Frieder, Milena Brinch Hansen, Carlos Hartmann, Erik Hemmingsen, Anand Rangachari and Ernest Sibert.

The work was conducted using the computational resources of the Northeast Parallel Architectures Center (NPAC) at Syracuse University, which is funded by DARPA, under contract to Rome Air Development Center (RADC), Griffiss AFB, NY.

Suggested Further Reading

Athas, W.C. and Seitz, C.L. Multicomputers: message-passing concurrent computers. *Computer*, Vol. 21, pp. 9-24 Aug. 1988.
A status report on a research project.

Barnes, J., and Hut, P. A hierarchical O(NlogN) force-calculation algorithm. *Nature*, Vol. 324, pp. 446-449, Dec. 1986.
A parallel divide and conquer algorithm for the n-body problem.

Bitton, D., DeWitt, D.J., Hsiao, D.K., and Menon, J. A taxonomy of parallel sorting. *Computing Surveys*, Vol. 16, pp. 287-318, Sept. 1984.
Includes sorting algorithms that are much faster than the parallel mergesort.

Brinch Hansen, P. Joyce - a programming language for distributed systems. *Software - Practice and Experience*, Vol. 17, pp. 29-50, 1987.
Explains Joyce by examples.

Brinch Hansen, P. A multiprocessor implementation of Joyce. *Software Practice and Experience*, Vol. 19, pp. 553 - 578, 1989a.
A detailed explanation of how parallel processes and communication channels are implemented.

Brinch Hansen, P. Analysis of a parallel mergesort. School of Computer and Information Science, Syracuse University, Syracuse, NY, 1989b.
An exact performance model of the parallel mergesort.

Dally, W.J. *A VLSI Architecture for Concurrent Data Structures*. Kluwer Academic Publishers, Norwell, MA. 1987.
Proposes a programming language and a parallel computer based on message-passing.

Fox, G.C., Johnson, M.A., Lyzenga, G.A., Otto, S.W., Salmon, J.K., and Walker, D.W. *Solving Problems on Concurrent Processors*. Vol. 1. Prentice Hall, Englewood Cliffs, NJ, 1988.
Explains how many scientific problems can be solved on hypercube architectures. Chapter 11 outlines a parallel divide and conquer algorithm for the fast Fourier transform.

Gehani, N., and McGettrick, A.D. *Concurrent Programming*. Addison Wesley, Reading, MA, 1988.
A collection of classical papers on parallel programming languages.

Gustafson, J.L.   The scaled-size model: a revision of Amdahl's law. *Supercomputing 88*, pp. 130-133.   International Supercomputing Institute, St. Petersburg, FL. 1988.
Reports impressive performance of parallel computations by redefining the meaning of speed-up. The problem size is scaled up in proportion to the number of processors to finesse the limitations of Amdahl's law.

Hillis, W.D.   *The Connection Machine*.   MIT Press, Cambridge, MA, 1985.
A clear description of a revolutionary idea: a parallel architecture with 64,000 synchronous processors executing identical processes in lock step.

Hoare, C.A.R.   *Communicating Sequential Processes*. Prentice Hall, Englewood Cliffs, NJ, 1985.
A mathematical theory of communicating processes.

Jenkins, R.A.   New approaches in parallel computing. *Computers in Physics*, Vol. 3, pp. 24-32, Jan.-Feb. 1989.
A recent survey of parallel architectures.

Kahn, G.   and MacQueen, D.B.   Coroutines and networks for parallel processes.   In B. Gilchrist (editor), *Information Processing 77*, pp. 993-998.   North Holland Publishing, Amsterdam, The Netherlands, 1977.
Presents an elegant parallel language with recursive processes.

May, D.   The influence of VLSI technology on computer architecture. *Supercomputing 88*, pp. 247-256, International Supercomputing Institute, St. Petersburg, FL, 1988.
Includes a short overview of the nonrecursive language occam and the transputer processor which has machine instructions for process creation, communication and termination.

Preparata, F.P., and Shamos, M.I.   *Computational Geometry: An Introduction*.   Springer Verlag, New York, NY, 1985.
Chapter 3 describes a parallel divide and conquer algorithm for finding the convex hull of a finite set of points in the plane.

Quinn, M.J.   *Designing Efficient Algorithms for Parallel Computers*. McGraw Hill, New York, NY, 1987.
A short introduction to parallel sorting and searching, matrix multiplication, and graph algorithms.

Whiddett, D.   *Concurrent Programming for Software Engineers*. Halstead Press, New York, NY, 1987.
Explains the three major paradigms for parallel programming: monitors, message-passing and remote procedures.

Chapter 4

APPLICATIONS OF PARALLEL SUPERCOMPUTERS: SCIENTIFIC RESULTS AND COMPUTER SCIENCE LESSONS

GEOFFREY C. FOX

Introduction

Parallel computing has come of age. Both commercial and university-built parallel computers with supercomputer performance are now available.

In this chapter we describe a number of major computations which were carried out in 1988-1990 at Caltech on a variety of parallel machines: hypercubes, transputer arrays, the Connection Machine, and the AMT DAP. We compare their performance with that of several advanced-architecture serial machines, including the conventional CRAY and ETA-10 supercomputers, on the same problems. From our varied use of parallel machines we derived a number of lessons concerning hardware, software, and performance, including the idea of an appropriate match between problem category and type of parallel architecture. It is our hope that these lessons will both encourage scientific users to use parallel machines properly and help computer scientists to design better hardware and software.

We also discuss the emergence of a new academic discipline—*computational science*—motivated by the larger and more important role played in science by computation in general, but especially by parallel computation. We can expect computation, and especially parallel computation, not only to revolutionize many existing scientific fields but also to open up new ones for which traditional approaches have failed. We can thus expect *computation* to join *theory* and *experiment* as a third fundamental part of the scientific method. It has been clear for some time that parallel computers are crucial to this revolution. Our own research has wandered between science, computational science, computer science and applied mathematics. We have concluded that existing academic disciplines will need to be changed to take proper advantage of the revolution offered by unbelievably powerful computers. We discuss this issue and describe two new graduate programs at Caltech: the well-established Computation and Neural Systems and the fledgling Physical Computation and Complex Systems.

It is the enormous advances in computer technology, reviewed by Ralph Gomory in Chapter 2, which allow the implementation of practical parallel machines and which therefore have led to the increasing importance of the computational approach in science and engineering. During the 1980's these advances have fueled the explosive growth of the personal computer and workstation industry and have shrunk an entire mainframe onto a chip. By the year 2000, even a microprocessor will be a parallel computer containing from ten to a hundred processors of varying sophistication, each with up to half a million transistors. These parallel computer chips will then be cascaded, first into boards and then into racks, to build massively parallel systems. In this way, the gigaflops peak computing speed of today will have become a teraflops before the year 2000 arrives. Progress thereafter will continue far beyond the teraflops level: by the year 2000 we can expect a supercomputer capable of ten teraflops— an awesome machine with perhaps ten thousand individual processors and a hundred billion words of memory.

Parallelism will thus soon be a feature of all computers, but supercomputers especially will be dominated and revolutionized by it. By a supercomputer, at any particular time, we mean the best computer one can build at that time for between $20 and $30 million, which happens to be the cost in 1976 of the CRAY 1, a very fast sequential computer. Today a typical supercomputer is a machine built by Cray Research, whose most modern system (the CRAY Y-MP) is a parallel machine with eight extremely powerful nodes.

Before 1988 the parallel computations which were already being done were both intriguing and encouraging, but could not then compete with the major calculations possible in the (conventional) supercomputer centers of the National Science Foundation and the Department of Energy. These centers were instrumental in the birth of computational science in universities. They made possible, for example, such serious calculations as those in lattice gauge theory, which require the equivalent of between 1,000 and 10,000 hours on a CRAY XMP.

However, starting in the middle of 1988, there was a major transition: several parallel computers became available in configurations capable of supercomputer-level performance and robust enough to support large scale computations. These machines are detailed in Table 1. In chapter 10 of this book David Waltz discusses the Connection Machine and David May describes transputer arrays in chapter 5.

TABLE 1. PARALLEL SUPER-COMPUTERS USED IN SECTIONS 4-17		
Machine	**Configuration**	**Key Characteristics**
NCUBE - 1 hypercube	1024 nodes SANDIA 576 nodes Caltech	Scalar nodes, with about 0.1 megaflop per node
Transputer Array (MEIKO)	32 nodes Caltech Large system coming into use at Edinburgh University in 1989-90	Scalar nodes, each with about 4 times the speed of NCUBE - 1 node
Mark IIIfp hypercube (Designed and built at the Jet Propulsion Laboratory)	128 nodes Caltech (mainly used in 32 nodes so far)	Each node is a (short vector) pipeline FPU. 1-2 megaflops with a rather disappointing compiler. 5-8 mega-flops per node in assembly language (easier than microcode used in previous WEITEK chip sets)
Thinking Machines Connection Machine CM-2	64K nodes Los Alamos 16 K nodes ANL/Caltech 64K 1-bit nodes is really 2048 32-bit nodes for floating point work	64 K single bit node system peaks out at about 2 gigaflops
AMT DAP 510	1024 nodes ANL	Mesh of 1-bit processors. Each is faster than those of CM-2, but there are fewer of them.

The many different new computer architectures have made performance evaluation critical. We will use the work of Messina's group to compare performance of our applications on parallel machines with other interesting architectures. Table 2 lists the broader range of parallel machines covered in that work, including some not yet available in supercomputer configurations (Messina 1990).

The Caltech Concurrent Computation Program

In my own research group, we have concentrated on applications. Our simple idea is that a good way to develop and understand parallel machines is to use them, and that furthermore the only users guaranteed to develop real applications are scientists who use parallel machines to address major scientific and engineering problems. This idea led us in 1983 to start the Caltech Concurrent Computation Program in order to investigate the hypothesis that *the hypercube is a suitable concurrent computer for general purpose scientific and engineering calculations.*

TABLE 2. ADVANCED ARCHITECTURES STUDIED IN THE CALTECH PERFORMANCE EVALUATION PROJECT

Machine	Description
NCUBE 1	Hypercube with custom scalar processors
Mark III	Hypercube with MC68020/68882 processors
Mark IIIfp	Mark III hypercube with XL Weitek chip set
INTEL iPSC/1	Intel 80286/80287-based hypercube
BBN Butterfly	MIMD network of MC68020/68881-based processors
Alliant FX/8	Shared memory vector multiprocessor
Sequent Balance	NS 32032/32081-based shared memory multiprocessor
Sequent Symmetry	Intel 80386-based shared memory multiprocessor; Weitek chips
Encore Multimax	NS32332-based shared memory multiprocessor
Cydrome Cydra 5	Very Long Instruction Word machine
CRAY X-MP/48	4-node vector super-computer
CRAY-2	4-node vector super-computer with large memory
SCS-40	Vector mini-super-computer, CRAY X-MP compatible
ETA-10 E	4 vector processors with shared memory
Connection Machine 2	Massively parallel SIMD machine with 64k nodes; Weitek chips

Our approach is captured by the slogan: *use real hardware to solve real problems with real software.* Accordingly we have built and used a series of in-house hypercubes and developed the necessary systems software and user support to allow the use of these machines for the solution of interesting computational problems. We have set up multidisciplinary teams of computationally-oriented Caltech faculty and Jet Propulsion Laboratory scientists in a variety of fields. These applications groups obtained from the Caltech Concurrent Computation Program not only parallel computer resources but also funding for students and postdoctoral research fellows. We felt that proper development of parallel processing would be helped by involving first-class users and challenging new parallel systems to solve real problems. These user teams were provided access to real parallel computers, initially at modest but interesting performance levels, and now at supercomputer performance levels. We also set up a central research team to investigate basic algorithms, systems software (strongly motivated by applications), benchmarking, and architectural analysis.

Our accomplishments in the past seven years include the development of a very successful series of in-house hypercubes culminating in the Mark IIIfp hypercube which achieves supercomputer performance. Our results have helped to inspire four commercial companies to produce concurrent computers with the hypercube architecture, and indirectly helped the transputer systems through collaboration with the University of Southampton. We have used in-house and commercial machines to demonstrate that distributed-memory concurrent computers can indeed be used with high efficiency for the majority of science and engineering applications that typify Caltech's computationally intensive research. Our faith in parallel computing was quantified by the formulation of a theory and models for the performance of the first hypercubes and then for more general parallel machines.

These successes inspired many Caltech faculty to become active in large scale computations using advanced architecture computers. A committee chaired by Aron Kuppermann recommended that Caltech institutionally sponsor a supercomputer center using state-of-the-art parallel machines. Following this, we split off, in early 1988, the hardware and software support (*i.e.*, the 'Computer Center') component of the Caltech Concurrent Computation Program to form the nucleus of Caltech Concurrent Supercomputer Facilities. This is Caltech's major in-house facility for numerical computing, and is directed by Paul Messina. At the Jet Propulsion Laboratory concurrent computer design and use has become a major new thrust which can be attributed to interactions with the Caltech Concurrent Computation Program.

It has been shown that many parallel computer systems, including the hypercube, shared-memory, and SIMD architectures, work well in a wide range of scientific problems. We must now ask new questions concerning, for example, the cost, technology, and software tradeoffs that will drive the design of future parallel supercomputers and (a crucial and harder question) what is the appropriate software environment for parallel machines and how should one develop it.

Present concurrent software systems are functional but do not provide a productive software environment. Better software tools are essential if parallel machines are to become widely used, especially in commercial environments.

These new questions have changed our strategy in several ways. We do not intend to develop further in-house hardware such as the Mark IIIfp hypercube, but will center our work on commercial hardware. We will no longer concentrate on the hypercube architecture, but will study and use a broad range of machines. This is illustrated by Caltech's recent acquisition of transputer arrays and of a 50% share in a Connection Machine. We expect to concentrate on distributed-memory machines in the immediate future, as these not only exhibit good cost performance but also exploit our experience base. We also expect commercial software to be insufficient, and we hope to expand our effort in software tools significantly.

We intend to increase our collaborations, especially in the area of applied mathematics and computer science. These will center on our plan (described later) to establish Computational Science as an academic discipline and on the development of the software tools. We will use collaborations to extend our experience base in this area.

A classification of problems

During the course of our research, we developed a classification of problems which allows us to describe succinctly which problems are suitable for which machines.

DOMAIN DECOMPOSITION

All the applications considered here, and essentially all other successful uses of highly parallel machines have obtained their parallelism from *data parallelism* (Hillis 1986) or equivalently from *domain decomposition* (Fox 1988a). This notion implies that a computation can be considered as an algorithm applied to a data set. Concurrency is obtained by acting simultaneously on different parts of the data set. This data set can be a collection of grid points, galaxies, possible chess moves, neurons, database records, and so on. Whatever the architecture of the computer, parallelism comes from evolving these entities simultaneously. The three major commercial architectures obtain their parallelism from this source, but implement it differently.

Radical architectures such as dataflow may exploit other forms of parallelism, but this has yet to be proved practical.

We should say that some *functional parallelism* has also been exploited, as in the battle management simulation discussed later. However, this does not lead to the essentially unlimited parallelism typically coming from the decomposition of large data sets. Functional decomposition is a useful way of augmenting, but not replacing, data parallelism.

How easily, and under what circumstances, can one simultaneously evolve different parts of the data set and so use domain decomposition to achieve parallelism? We can extend the idea of a data domain into the physical, or space-time aspect of applications. This allows a classification of the *architecture of problems* and a quantification of the matching of problems with computer architectures.

SPACE-TIME STRUCTURE

We will call the underlying data set, discussed above, the *space* associated with the problem. Any implementation (simulation) of the problem on a computer involves work or computation performed on the elements of its space. The computation can be indexed by a variable which we call *time*. Let us consider some examples.

In the simulation of a three-dimensional physical system, the space is a discretized version of conventional physical space. Time is again just discretized physical time. Our general nomenclature thus reduces to the conventional one for such physical simulations.

In the calculation of the distribution of electromagnetic waves in a radar antenna problem, we would step through time solving Maxwell's wave equation. This can be contrasted with iterative solutions to elliptic equations which could involve a similar spatial operator, say, ∇^2. In the latter case, we can consider successive over-relaxation or Gauss-Seidel iterative methods for solving the sparse matrix problems. For such an algorithm, the space is again a conventional three dimensional space, but now iteration count, rather than physical time, plays the role of time.

Finally, consider full matrix problems—inversion, multiplication, eigenvalues, etc. Now the space is more abstract, being the two-dimensional array of matrix elements. A typical algorithm is LU decomposition, where one successively eliminates rows and columns from the matrix; time is then naturally defined as the index of the eliminated variable.

TEMPORAL CLASSIFICATION OF PROBLEMS

We divide problems into the following three increasingly general classes according to how they behave with respect to time.

Synchronous problems are those which change in a spatially homogeneous fashion, even on a microscopic time scale. This case arises when nature is viewed microscopically in terms of a set of similar fundamental quantities transformed by identical algorithms. The QCD simulations which are described later provide a good example of this.

Loosely synchronous problems are again those which change spatially in a homogeneous manner, but possibly only when this is averaged over a macroscopic time interval. In between macroscopic synchronization points, the different parts of the space may evolve independently, with no microscopic synchronization. This is seen clearly in spatially irregular physical simulations where we step in time from t_0 to $t_0+\delta$ to $t_0+2\delta$, ... These time points provide the macroscopic synchronization, but if the problem is spatially irregular, quite different computations could be involved for each data point in the time evolution. This temporal behavior is natural when one models nature macroscopically in terms of nonfundamental (and correspondingly different in space and time) objects. Examples would be a heterogeneous circuit simulation, or the clustering algorithm mentioned later in the chapter.

Asynchronous problems are those which show no regularity in time; each spatial element evolves in time with no natural mutual synchronization. An event-driven simulation, such as the computer chess example discussed later, is an example of this kind of problem.

Properly asynchronous are those asynchronous problems that are not loosely synchronous, and *properly loosely synchronous* problems are those which are loosely synchronous but not synchronous.

We should emphasize that these are properties of problems and not of the software implementation. For instance, most hypercubes standardly have asynchronous communication systems, even though these machines are typically used for loosely synchronous problems. On the other hand, occam on the transputer and CrOS III on the Caltech hypercubes (Fox 1988a) are synchronous operating systems. Their success can be traced to the loose synchronization property, which typically involves interprocessor communication only at the synchronization points. Synchronous communication is sufficient even for properly loosely synchronous problems. However, an asynchronous communication system not only supports the simple time behavior of loosely synchronous problems, but its greater generality naturally supports debugging and other user environment features that lead to the whole implementation being asynchronous.

Embarrassingly parallel or *spatially disconnected* problems are those in which the basic entities given by domain decomposition are computationally independent. Spatially-disconnected applications give excellent parallel performance for asynchronous problems which when nontrivially spatially connected provide major challenges. The relevance of this classification is illustrated in Table 3 which summarizes 84 parallel applications or algorithms surveyed in (Fox 1988b). Ninety per cent of these applications were either synchronous, properly loosely synchronous, or embarrassingly parallel. Such applications afford parallelism that scales to many nodes.

TABLE 3. SUMMARY OF 84 SEPARATE APPLICATIONS ON PARALLEL COMPUTERS

Number of Applications	Application Field
9	Biology
4	Chemistry and Chemical Engineering
14	Engineering
10	Geology and Earth/Space Science
13	Physics
5	Astronomy and Astrophysics
11	Computer Science
18	Numerical Algorithm

Number of Applications		Application Classification	Running Total	
34	(40%)	Synchronous	34	(40%)
30	(36%)	Properly loosely synchronous	64	(76%)
6	(7%)	Embarrassingly parallel - runs on SIMD	70	(83%)
6	(7%)	Embarrassingly parallel - needs MIMD	76	(90%)
8	(10%)	Truly Asynchronous	84	(100%)

Lattice Monte Carlo simulations

GENERAL REMARKS

Lattice theories give rise to one of the most computationally intense classes of problem. These problems arise from numerical approaches to statistical physics, or from quantum field theories. Even in today's modest problems, one has to evaluate an integral which can have over one million dimensions (degrees of freedom).

In computing an integral for a problem of this class by the Monte Carlo method, one averages over a very large sample of configurations. These configurations are generated successively by making a series of small changes—usually for single sites to ensure that one keeps the configurations distributed correctly. The calculations which are currently hardest —dynamical QCD with a 16^4 lattice—take from 50 to 100 hours of time on a full-size CM-2 running at two gigaflops to produce each statistically distinct (uncorrelated) configuration. The slow evolution produced by the successive application of a single-site update has encouraged development of cluster update methods, but these are known at the present only for the simpler theories. This is a critical issue; clustering could not only speed up the computation but also alter the necessary architecture, as we will illustrate later.

In general, parallelism is straightforward for these problems— one uses domain decomposition of the underlying regular space. There have been several algorithmic improvements recently— which can usually be viewed as better sampling in the Monte

Carlo computation of the integral. The continual need to improve algorithms favors relatively general-purpose machines with flexible high-level software. This suggests that in the long run commercial parallel machines will be more successful than the many special-purpose computers constructed within the high-energy physics community.

DISCRETE SPIN ISING AND POTTS MODELS

Here one studies a regular array of simple spins. These problems are ideal for bit-serial machines like the AMT DAP or the CM-2, although one cannot use the WEITEK floating-point units on the latter for these bit-oriented problems.

We are currently using the AMT DAP 510 to investigate a 256^3 three-dimensional Ising model. It is conventional to rate machines by the speed at which they generate new configurations—measured in spin-updates per second. The DAP 510 compares well with the fastest supercomputers, performing at 0.6 x 10^9 spin-updates per second compared with the Hitachi S-820/80, which is only 40% faster. However, this performance rating is misleading, since the update is only a small part of the overall calculation. In fact, we have only crudely coded the update stage on the DAP 510 so that it runs a factor of 100 slower than the value quoted above. Even this slow update consumes only 1% of the total time.

CONTINUOUS SPIN TWO DIMENSIONAL $O(2)$ AND $O(3)$ MODELS

These systems involve spins that are NxN matrices of the group $O(N)$ and can model materials important in high-T_c Superconductivity (Ding 1989). Last summer we finished a major $O(2)$ calculation using the novel 'over-relaxation' single site update algorithm. This used the 128-node FPS T Series hypercube at Los Alamos and realized two megaflops per node. These calculations are being continued for the $O(3)$ group by my graduate student John Apostolakis.

The T Series hypercube is a poorly designed machine and is suitable only for a small class of regular calculations; its scalar performance is poor compared to its vector performance, and it has slow communication. We used a 256 x 256 lattice, allowing one dimension to be decomposed over nodes, and the other dimension to be viewed as a large vector (multiples of 128). This achieved good performance from the node based on the inflexible WEITEK chip. Some of our calculations have been marred by hardware glitches, requiring, for instance, that one avoid the hardware vector divide and long vector (> 256) instructions.

Niedermayer and Wolff (Baillie 1990b) have introduced effective clustering methods which currently we believe are unsuitable for the FPS architecture. We expect to use the MEIKO transputer array to continue these calculations. The CM-2 would perform well on the algorithm we used for the T Series, but we currently believe that a true MIMD architecture may be needed for the clustering calculation. The regular vectors needed by the T Series make this old hypercube essentially SIMD in character; more precisely, it requires synchronous problems for good performance. The currently-known clustering algorithms are properly loosely synchronous. We are currently experimenting with SIMD implementations which, although inefficient, may still have sufficiently good performance (Coddington 1990).

PURE GAUGE QCD

QCD or Quantum Chromodynamics is the theory of quarks and gluons that is believed to describe the strong or nuclear interactions of the fundamental particles.

This calculation can be both vectorized and parallelized. It can achieve good performance on essentially all architectures with MIMD, SIMD, or vector characteristics (Baillie 1990a). The large number of floating point calculations dwarfs overheads such as communication.

Even a modest calculation on a 16^4 lattice requires 262,144 degrees of freedom, 19 megabytes of memory and of the order of 10^{15} floating point operations. This problem was originally tackled (Otto 1984) on the first 64-node Cosmic Cube Hypercube with a $12^3 \times 16$ lattice, and was repeated in 1985-86 on the 128 node Mark II hypercube with a larger 20^4 lattice. These machines had peak performance below 5 megaflops. We have implemented this application on several more powerful machines with the following approximate performance:

CRAY XMP (1 processor)	60 megaflops
NCUBE (1024 nodes)	80 megaflops
JPL Mark IIIfp hypercube (128 nodes)	500 megaflops
Connection Machine CM-2 (64K nodes)	900 megaflops

Table 4 gives more details of the performance of the Mark IIIfp hypercube on this application. The good results in this table needed the consolidation of communication into single calls wherever possible. This was done by grouping communication associated with 8 or 16 separate time values into 2 communication calls. The performance was reduced by almost a factor of two without this blocking. The three spatial dimensions can be decomposed, and the table compares one-, two-, or three-dimensional decompositions. At fixed lattice size, one finds improved performance for decompositions that minimize surface area of the block in each node. Currently, interesting problems involve around a 16^4 lattice, which shows a speed-up of 84 on the 128-node Mark IIIfp hypercube.

TABLE 4. TIMES (IN SECONDS) OF FOUR SWEEPS OF UPDATES ON
MARK IIIFP HYPERCUBE

Total Lattice		8^3 x 16	16 x 8 x 8 x 16	16^3 x 8	16^4	32 x 16^3	32^2 x 16^2	32^2 x 16^2
NODES	DIM.							
1	0	123	246	492	984	1968	3936	7872
2	1	69.75	133.0					
4	1	39.25	69.16	135.3				
	2	39.67	73.76	142.8				
8	1		39.6	76.0	152.0			
	2	21.32	39.4	74.0	148.1			
	3	11.82	22.05	42.0	79.1	152.3		
32	2		11.5	21.3	42.5	78.6	148.3	
	3	6.31	11.74	21.9	41.65	77.96	151.7	
64	2							
	3	3.37						
128	2					23.07	42.94	85.87
	3		3.38	6.29	11.7	21.8	41.68	78.8
128 node speedup	3		72.8	78.2	84.1	90.3	94.4	99.9

The column labelled Dim. indicates the dimensionality of the decomposition.

These physics results involved 8,000 lines of C and WEITEK XL assembly code—the commercial compiler for this pipelined chip set is poor. The CM-2 results correspond to 3,000 lines of *LISP. One needs eight virtual processors (corresponding to eight separate calculations) to get good performance.

Curiously, this version of the code vectorizes poorly even though we know that with an optimized implementation, this application performs well on vector supercomputers. The flexibility of parallel machines is illustrated by Chiu's calculations. These use a random block lattice where, in the largest simulation, a different 40^4 lattice is calculated on each node of the 1024 node NCUBE hypercube at SANDIA; an embarrassingly parallel application.

DYNAMICAL FERMION QCD

This ultimate QCD calculation is dominated by inverting the 65536 x 65536 (on a 16^4 lattice) sparse matrix. This is currently done with a conjugate gradient or minimal residue method. The CRAY 2 uniprocessor code runs at 10^8 floating point operations per second and the full-size Connection Machine CM-2 can perform about 2 x 10^9 floating point operations per second. We anticipate this problem will need 10^{16} floating point operations—about 3,000 CM-2 hours—for even initial studies.

Currently, no effective clustering algorithms are known for either the pure gauge or fermion QCD problem. The regular 'dumb' algorithm used so far does not require a sophisticated architecture. This could change when an effective clustering method is introduced.

The Department of Energy has awarded large blocks of time (about 6,000 hours) in 1989-90 to two collaborations for 'Grand Challenge' QCD calculations on the CRAY 2 and ETA-10. The National Science Foundation has certainly already devoted much more time than this at the supercomputer centers on this problem.

Conventional and parallel supercomputers are compared in Table 5.

TABLE 5. APPROXIMATE DYNAMICAL FERMION QCD PERFORMANCE FOR THE "GRAND CHALLENGE"		
Machine	**Performance (megaflops)**	**Time Allocated in 1989 and comments**
ETA-10 (1 processor)	350	1 year
CRAY-2 (1 processor	100	1 year
Mark IIIfp (128 nodes)	750	
NCUBE (1024 nodes)	100	Not competitive
CM-2 (64K nodes)	> 1,000	
Several SIMD Coarse Grain special purpose computers	1,000 - 10,000	limited by software

With several months running on the CM-2 or Mark IIIfp, parallel supercomputers are very competitive with the ETA-10 and CRAY 2. The scalar node MIMD architecture of the NCUBE is not well optimized for this highly regular, vectorizable problem (which is a synchronous algorithm).

Computational fluid dynamics (CFD)

Caltech has so far not solved any large CFD applications on parallel machines. However, the parallelization methodology is clear. At one time, we thought that decomposition of irregular problems would be a stumbling block, but it is now clear that it is straightforward. Powerful methods based on neural networks and other heuristic optimization methods apply very generally.

An irregular adaptive mesh, illustrated in Figure 1, is naturally implemented as a linked-list data structure (Williams 1989). This is hard to vectorize on conventional supercomputers, but parallelizes well at least in MIMD machines such as the NCUBE. It would be interesting to study the SIMD implementation. Seemingly, SIMD machines could cope with data access irregularity, but the irregularities in the computational graph (varying multiplication of nodal points) cause inefficiencies in the SIMD case which are absent for MIMD machines.

Figure 1

Subatomic string dynamics

The flexibility of MIMD machines is illustrated by the numerical investigation of the dynamics of strings. Strings are at the heart of modern research on unified theories. The dynamics of a one-dimensional string naturally involves the two-dimensional world sheet swept out by the string's motion in the overall embedding space of dimension d. The current computations take the simplest case $d = 3$, but this theory is notorious for having an important—and perhaps the only viable—formulation in the seemingly unphysical choice of $d = 26$ dimensions.

The world-sheet is flexibly parameterized by means of techniques borrowed from finite element theory, with nodal points generated by dynamical random triangulation. The string theory specifies an integration over the two-dimensional metric on the world-sheet. This is implemented by integrating over random choices of the mesh.

The computation is *embarrassingly parallel* since the largest system (288 points on the world-sheet) can easily fit into a single node of our machines. Parallelism is obtained by decomposing the space of Monte Carlo configurations. Note that this problem is geometrically irregular and vectorizes with difficulty; furthermore, it does not appear to run well on SIMD parallel machines. We initially ran our simulations on a network of SUN workstations, putting into practice the slogan *the network is the computer*. Our major calculations have used the 512-node NCUBE, the 64-node SYMULT 2010, and the 32-node MEIKO transputer array. These have node performances in ratio 1 : 2 : 4 respectively, and given the perfect speed-up and size of parallel systems, total performance in ratio 1 : 0.25 : 0.25 respectively. These are major supercomputer-level calculations with a 144 nodal point simulation taking 400 hours on the 512-node NCUBE. Comparing our code with a similar CRAY implementation, we estimate our NCUBE outperforms the CRAY XMP by a factor of about four.

High temperature superconductivity

A Toronto group has been using the Caltech NCUBE to study the Quantum Anistropic Heisenberg Model. This problem is related to the Ising and Potts systems discussed earlier, with the difference that one is studying the dynamical rather than the statistical properties of a spin system.

Typically, an 8 x 8 lattice is evolved separately on each node by the NCUBE, with approximately 10^6 independent evolutions needed. This algorithm is reminiscent of the (far more complex) neutron transport calculations studied at Department of Energy laboratories. An *embarrassingly parallel* algorithm, it was easily implemented in C on the NCUBE. The 256-node NCUBE achieved three times the performance of the original FORTRAN implementation for the CRAY XMP, which clearly vectorized poorly. Current calculations correspond to several hundred hours of CRAY XMP time.

Exchange energies in solid helium 3

In his Caltech Ph.D. dealing with condensed matter, Callahan calculated exchange energies in solid He^3 by means of a Monte Carlo method. Rather modest systems were used, with 54 to 128 particles arranged in a three-dimensional spatial mesh which were further extended in time. The 512-node NCUBE required parallelism in several aspects of the problem. The forces are not nearest-neighbor, and decomposition of their calculations over space leads to a factor of four in parallelism. Decomposing time (direction of path) leads to another factor of 16. This 64-fold data-parallelism is combined with from 2 to 8 independent runs.

In an unfair comparison, the 64-node NCUBE has an efficiency of only 64%, but outperforms the CRAY XMP by over a factor of two. However, the CRAY computation used an early implementation of the C language for the CRAY which achieved only a few megaflops on this problem. Our implementation used Salmon's CUBIX environment (Fox 1988a), allowing the identical code of about 2500 lines of C to run on either the NCUBE hypercube or CRAY.

Callahan's thesis involved a total of about 250 hours computation on the 512-node NCUBE—another supercomputer-level calculation.

Astrophysical particle dynamics

N-body calculations have been revolutionized by a clustering technique whose basic idea is simple. Consider a cluster of M stars for which we need to calculate the interaction with a single star (far) outside the cluster. This straightforwardly requires about M steps, but we can gain a factor of M by ignoring the details of the cluster and just computing with its center of mass. One can apply this idea by recursively generating a tree (a quad tree in two dimensions) with, at most, one particle in the cluster at the lowest level of the tree.

The naive calculation takes $O(N_p^2)$ time for each simulation (time) step for a system of N_p particles, while explicit implementation shows that the clustering method takes time $O(N_p log_2 N_p)$.

The cluster method has superior performance for $N_p \geq 1000$ particles. The current limit of $O(10,000)$ particles for the $O(N_p^2)$

algorithm is increased by an order of magnitude for the cluster method. The possibility of large N_p of $O(10^{16})$ particles opens up several important astrophysical calculations including:

(1) the study of the growth of fluctuations in the early universe;

(2) the dynamics of globular clusters where one finds in nature $O(10^{5-6})$ stars, which is a difficult calculation since very short range interactions (binary stars) are critical;

(3) galactic structure and the collision of galaxies.

We have just finished several calculations of the last type, each of which used about 200 hours on the 512-node NCUBE.

This computation has several interesting features. The cluster tree is rebuilt at each time step. This stage is negligible in the sequential version, but takes about 30% of the concurrent execution time in the $N_p = 180,000$ particle simulation. Initially, we found load-imbalance, but this was solved by dynamically redistributing particles at each time step. The information for this was found from the 'workload' at the previously-calculated time step. Orthogonal recursive bisection is used to distribute the particles. Communication is required to fetch those parts of the tree that are stored outside the node and will be needed for updating particles within the node. This ensures maximum re-use of the communicated data and low communication-overhead—at most 10%. This approach, however, uses 75% of the available NCUBE memory and limits the simulation-size. In spite of this, we are able to consider, on the current NCUBE, large problems that are difficult to implement on the limited-memory CRAY XMP. Future such hypercubes with several megabytes of memory per node will allow much larger values of N_p

The program was implemented with 3,400 lines of C code for the NCUBE. Some timing information compared with FORTRAN CRAY code is given in Table 6 for a single time step. We see that the 256-node NCUBE outperforms the CRAY XMP implementation for 10^5 particles, even though the hypercube efficiency is quite low. The CRAY efficiency is even lower.

We can compare this with the results on the $O(N_p^2)$ particle dynamics algorithm for a vortex approach to fluid dynamics. This vectorizes well on CRAY and runs with > 95% efficiency on the NCUBE. In this case, the CRAY XMP is four times as fast as the 256-node NCUBE.

Considering SIMD architectures, we are not certain how to implement the clustering algorithm so as to get good performance on machines like the CM-2. This is related to the previously-discussed difficulties with Monte Carlo clustering and adaptive grids on SIMD machines. Note that the 'regular' clustering and multiscale algorithms such as multigrid or the FFT run quite well on SIMD machines. The implementation difficulties for synchronous machines occur with geometrically irregular cluster algorithms. This application is properly loosely synchronous.

TABLE 6. PERFORMANCE ON ASTRONOMICAL PARTICLE DYNAMICS

	10^4 particles	10^5 particles
CRAY - XMP some optimization	10 seconds	130 seconds
256 node NCUBE — time — efficiency	21 seconds 24%	118 seconds 56%

Astronomical data analysis

This group (S. Anderson, P. Gorham, S. Kulkarni and T. Prince) has pioneered the use of the NCUBE for astronomical data analysis (Anderson 1990). Our Caltech NCUBE system has a small (4 disks) parallel disk farm connected to the main hypercube. The disks are controlled by a SUN-4 which also has additional peripherals, including the necessary tape drives.

RADIO ASTRONOMY

In the most exciting work, radio data from the Arecibo radio telescope were taken on December 26, 1988 in particularly advantageous circumstances, namely that the holiday spirit reduced the ambient interference—especially from a nearby naval base. Data are taken with a 0.5 millisecond time interval and Fourier-transformed (a large 2^{24} one-dimensional FFT) to look for peaks corresponding to radio pulses from a rapidly-rotating neutron star. A total of five pulsars were discovered using the NCUBE in 1989. Two of these are located in the globular cluster M15, making a total of three known pulsars in this globular cluster. The discovery of these pulsars has prompted a re-analysis of current ideas concerning the origin of neutron stars in globular clusters. The computation involves both the FFT (which is efficiently implemented on the hypercube) and an I/O intensive stage which takes a total time comparable to the FFT. This first I/O dominated stage is overlapped with a calculation which corrects for frequency dispersion in the interstellar medium. The measured I/O performance of the system is a modest 40 Kbytes per second per drive, including all overheads. Our ESMD disk drives on the

NCUBE are rated at a factor of 25 higher performance than this, which suggests the need for better I/O software on the NCUBE.
The second of the two pulsars is part of a binary system. It therefore required a further computation-intensive acceleration correction to remove the orbital effects of the binary system. This additional computation has negligible disk I/O but substantial internode communication. Processing 90 minutes of data taken at Arecibo takes about two hours for the dispersion correction and FFT stages (which was enough to discover the first pulsar in M15). About 40 hours of 512-node NCUBE time were needed for the second pulsar. The major I/O and large memory requirements of this calculation make it hard to compare the NCUBE with a CRAY or IBM 3090 performance.

OPTICAL ASTRONOMY

Traditionally the resolution of ground-based optical telescopes is limited by atmospheric turbulence to about one second of arc (1/3600th of a degree). However, it is possible to eliminate the effects of turbulence using interferometry techniques familiar from radio astronomy, and achieve resolution of 30 milliarcseconds. Using the 200-inch Mount Palomar telescope, one divides the total aperture into approximately one thousand 15 cm disks. The correlations between these disks are summarized in 10^6 Fourier coefficients. These are averaged over many samples or frames lasting from 10 to 100 milliseconds over which the turbulence is essentially constant. This technique has been implemented on the NCUBE where a 20-minute Palomar exposure on an asteroid was analyzed for 10 hours on a 256-node subcube. The best image resolution ever seen for an asteroid was obtained. The results show that a similar analysis can resolve a binary star. In each case, one finds a factor of 30 improvement in resolution for each linear dimension.

This novel method is still in its infancy. It illustrates graphically how powerful computers can open up new approaches to scientific problems.

QUANTUM CHEMISTRY REACTION DYNAMICS

Kuppermann's group (M. Wu, P. Hipes, A. Kuppermann, and S. Cuccaro) has been developing a fundamental approach to the understanding of chemical reactions. A goal is the description of reactions such as those which are the basis of chemical lasers. This is a difficult computation (Wu 1990).

Operationally, this problem involves solving Schrödinger's equation in the novel hyperspherical basis set, a computation which breaks down into two phases.

In Phase 1 there is a series of 5 steps which is repeated 51 times. Steps 1, 2, and 4 are embarrassingly parallel. Step 3 needs significant parallel algorithms adapted from work by Patterson at

JPL. Step 5 is I/O. This phase has been fully implemented for a particular reaction on the 32-node Mark IIIfp hypercube with 3,000 lines of coding. The total runtime was 9.8 hours, of which 2.2 hours were I/O (step 5). This will be improved soon with the high performance CIO (Concurrent I/O hardware on the Mark IIIfp). The same calculation on the SCS-40 (which typically has about 25% the performance of the CRAY XMP) took 71 hours.

TABLE 7. IDEALIZED PERFORMANCE OF HIGH PERFORMANCE COMPUTERS

	CM-2 64K "huge" vector	CRAY XMP 1 Processor "long" vector	Mark IIIfp Hypercube 128 nodes "short" vector	NCUBE Hypercube 1024 nodes scalar
Super Regular (e.g., large full matrix)	≥ 3000	200	750	100
Typical Regular (e.g., QCD)	≥ 1000	75	500	100
Irregular (e.g., chess, clustering)	fails	10	100	50

The listed numbers are approximate megaflops

Phase 2 involves the integration of coupled linear systems of ordinary differential equations and uses a fourth-order special-purpose integration algorithm for chemistry simulations. The algorithm is dominated by matrix inversion (and not by LU decomposition!) with some matrix multiplication. I/O is also needed to initialize Phase 2 with the results of Phase 1 which determined the matrix elements. This involved 2,000 lines of code and 74 coupled ordinary differential equations integrated for 250 steps. Thirty-one energies were calculated simultaneously to reduce I/O overheads and the resultant calculation took two hours on the Mark IIIfp with an additional I/O overhead of 10%. The vector machines do well on this calculation, and these systematics are abstracted in Table 7.

Table 8 has an interesting comparison between two hypercubes (NCUBE, Mark III) and two algorithms (Gauss-Jordan, LU decomposition) for solving linear equations.

TABLE 8. EXECUTION TIMES ON NCUBE AND MARK IIIfp HYPERCUBES OF GAUSS-JORDAN (GJ) AND LU DECOMPOSITION FOR SOLUTION OF LINEAR EQUATIONS $M\underline{x} = \underline{b}$.

LU times in seconds on 256 Processor NCUBE

DIMENSION	LU DECOMPOSITION	16 RHS	64 RHS	256 RHS	1024 RHS
16	0.49	0.35			
64	2.08	1.49	1.60		
256	9.73	6.74	7.48	10.4	
1024	96.1	39.0	47.0	79.2	208.5
2048	515	111			

GJ times in seconds on 256 Processor NCUBE

DIMENSION	GJ DECOMPOSITION	16 RHS	64 RHS	256 RHS	1024 RHS
16	0.50	0.066			
64	2.09	0.238	0.266		
256	10.3	1.18	1.59	3.35	
1024	123	9.71	16.5	43.8	154.2

LU times in seconds on 32 Processor Mark IIIfp

DIMENSION	LU DECOMPOSITION	16 RHS	64 RHS	256 RHS	1024 RHS
16	0.027	0.025			
64	0.138	0.116	0.150		
256	1.42	0.720	1.12	2.77	
1024	40.9	6.97	12.9	36.4	131

GJ times in seconds on 32 Processor Mark IIIfp

DIMENSION	GJ DECOMPOSITION	16 RHS	64 RHS	256 RHS	1024 RHS
16	0.029	0.012			
64	0.167	0.064	0.096		
256	2.07	0.510	0.910	2.51	
1024	63.0	6.11	12.0	35.3	12

We list the dimension of Matrix M and the number of right hand sides (rhs) $\underline{b}$.

LU decomposition is always superior on sequential machines, but it is more sensitive to communication (especially latency) on parallel machines. The NCUBE looks good, compared to CRAYs, on problems which are irregular and vectorize poorly. Matrix algebra and, to a lesser extent, synchronous algorithms like QCD, show the vector machines at their best. This is not surprising—CRAYs were designed for this problem class! Table 7 attempts to show a progression from SIMD to long vector supercomputers to hypercubes with short vector nodes to scalar node MIMD machines. This corresponds to increasingly general-purpose machines. As we have already commented, machines like the NCUBE are not competitive in peak performance on regular problems, but they do offer good performance on a range of problems and their speed degrades slowly as one increases the irregularity of the problem.

Plasma physics

Plasma physics computations represent interesting challenges for distributed-memory machines because the use of 'particle in the cell' algorithms involves two distinct decompositions. Our example problem involves calculation of the orbits of plasma electrons, in their own electromagnetic field. In the first stage of the calculation, one finds the field using an FFT. This involves a decomposition with an equal number of mesh points on each node of the hypercube. Then, one transforms to a separate decomposition with an equal number of particles in each node; this latter is the particle update or 'push' part of the computation where the particle positions are evolved in the field. Each stage can be efficiently implemented on the hypercube, but transforming between the two distinct decompositions must be done at each time step (Liewer 1989). A general strategy for this uses the *crystal-accumulator* algorithm. This does not attempt to localize the calculations done 'on the fly' as information is routed through the hypercube.

This method was originally developed for neural network simulations. It can be implemented well only on machines like the NCUBE and transputer arrays. The Mark IIIfp and Ametek S2010, where calculation and communication subsystems are separated, do not support the crystal-accumulator well. This algorithm requires communication subsystems that support the combination of messages in a similar fashion to the way combining networks in shared-memory parallel computers can combine fetch and add operations.

Currently, we have measurements only for the more straightforward strategy where information is routed to the destination node and then combined, rather than being combined *en route*. This is almost certainly the best algorithm for the Mark III hypercube, which has separate communication and calculation subsystems. The combining overhead would be severe on this and similar machines, where the interface between communication and calculation on the node introduces a significant latency.

Grain dynamics by lattice gas

A very interesting use of the NCUBE was recently reported in Gary Gutt's Ph.D. thesis at Caltech. Earlier research by Werner had studied grain dynamics using the first hypercubes, employing detailed Newtonian dynamics to study the motion of sand and other granular material. This is an interesting alternative to conventional continuum approximations to material dynamics. Gutt proposes an intermediate model for such systems using cellular automata or lattice-gas techniques that have already been applied to fluids. Gutt's automata are quite dense (about one for every two lattice sites) and one must store the relative displacement of each automaton from the lattice site positions. Thus, this cellular automaton method does not use binary arithmetic, but rather 32-bit arithmetic. To improve performance, integer rather than floating-point arithmetic is used. The computation consumed about 200 hours of NCUBE 512-node time with the largest simulation involving 0.5×10^6 grains on a 8064 x 128 lattice. This involves Poiseuille flow down a pipe driven by gravity. We do not have a CRAY implementation of this code, but it is possible that irregularities in lattice-site-occupancy would make vectorization difficult. The parallelization on the NCUBE is straightforward and efficient.

Computer chess

Computer chess involves constructing a tree of possible moves and dynamically pruning it using the alpha-beta technique. On a parallel machine, the game tree ('data domain') is distributed over the nodes. We found that a real-time graphics display (using the NCUBE parallel graphics subsystem) was crucial in achieving a factor of five better performance. This allowed us to change the algorithm for processor assignment and improve the load-balance. A speed-up of 101 (170) was found on 256 (512) nodes for trees of a depth appropriate for the middle game. The speed-up increases as the problem gets bigger, *i.e.*, as one spends a longer time on each move. This illustrates the fact that for problems with real-time constraints, improving processor-performance raises parallelization-efficiency by increasing the size of the problem that can be solved in a given fixed time.

This was a very difficult code to design and develop, as the algorithm is asynchronous. Probably, the technical implementation and in particular the debugging were harder than the algorithmic issues. The result is 8,000 lines of C code using the commercial NCUBE operating system VERTEX with a special shared-memory enhancement to allow concurrent access and update of a distributed database—the so-called transposition table of currently-evaluated positions. In contrast, the earlier Caltech hypercube scientific calculations in this review use our internal loosely synchronous communications system CrOS which is faster than VERTEX on the NCUBE.

It is interesting to consider the future of computer chess. We estimate that the above program for the 256-node NCUBE has a U.S. chess rating of 2,100 at present. In a more familiar unit of megamoves searched per second, we have the results in table 9(A).

TABLE 9. (A) CHESS POSITIONS SEARCHED PER SECOND

Machine	Performance (10^6 moves/sec)
SPECIAL PURPOSE	
BELLE (1980)	0.075
HITECH (1985)	0.25
Deep Thought (1988)	2.5
GENERAL-PURPOSE	
256 node NCUBE	0.025
4 processor CRAY XMP	0.15

TABLE 9. (B) RATINGS OF THE BEST CHESS PLAYERS

Player	Rating
HITECH	2450
Deep Thought	2600
Kasparov	2850
1000 x Deep Thought	2850?

The NCUBE does quite well compared to a CRAY (a 512-node NCUBE is approximately one head of a CRAY XMP), but neither of them is competitive with special-purpose machines. However, we can consider using the same parallelization technique developed for the NCUBE, but for an array of special-purpose chess chips rather than for the general-purpose microprocessor used on the NCUBE. We conjecture that a system of some 8,000 special-purpose chips, like those in Deep Thought, would achieve a speed-up of 1,000 and be very competitive with Kasparov as shown in table 9 (B).

Each node processor of our computer world chess champion would have for chess about 100 times the power of a NCUBE node. The communication overhead for the NCUBE case is about 10%; the Deep Thought chips would need an internode bandwidth about ten times that of NCUBE to keep a manageable (50%) communication overhead. Such a system seems quite practical, but outside my group's resources. Rather, we are concentrating on a different approach: to improve chess programs by the use of position evaluators based on neural networks.

Further, we now realize that our parallel chess program can be improved by changing the sequential algorithm used at each node. This change could increase the effective performance of our parallel system by a factor of about one hundred.

Ray-tracing in computer graphics

The 512-processor NCUBE was used to render a one-minute-long animation entitled 'Self-Portrait', which shows a hypercube growing from zero through four dimensions and then rotating in four dimensions. The sequence consists of approximately 600 frames, each of which was rendered at 2048 x 1944 pixel resolution and filtered to 512 x 486 for transfer to videotape. The most complex scenes contain 169 polygons, 16 spheres, 32 cylinders and three light sources. Over the course of the sequence, approximately 8 billion rays were shaded and approximately 200 billion ray-intersection tests were performed. The entire calculation required about 300 hours on the 512-processor NCUBE system.

Ray-tracing is generally implemented as an embarrassingly parallel algorithm. In order to render an image which consists of a large number of pixels, each pixel is considered separately and independently. The calculation for each pixel is itself quite complex, involving anywhere from tens to thousands of floating-point operations, depending on the complexity of the scene. Since computer graphics images generally have 512 x 512 or more pixels, a decomposition in which individual pixels are assigned to processors can make efficient use of hardware with up to $O(10^5)$ processors. A minor subtlety arises because even within a single image, the complexity of individual pixels can vary by several orders of magnitude. Pixels at the edge of the scene, whose rays may miss the model entirely, are very easy to compute, while those near the interesting part of the image may involve hundreds of intersection and shading calculations.

If pixels were allocated to processors according to a 'tiled' decomposition like the following decomposition of 16 x 8 image for an 8-node machine:

```
1 1 1 1 2 2 2 2 3 3 3 3 4 4 4 4
1 1 1 1 2 2 2 2 3 3 3 3 4 4 4 4
1 1 1 1 2 2 2 2 3 3 3 3 4 4 4 4
1 1 1 1 2 2 2 2 3 3 3 3 4 4 4 4
5 6 7 8 5 6 7 8 5 6 7 8 5 6 7 8
5 6 7 8 5 6 7 8 5 6 7 8 5 6 7 8
5 6 7 8 5 6 7 8 5 6 7 8 5 6 7 8
5 6 7 8 5 6 7 8 5 6 7 8 5 6 7 8
```

the large fluctuations in the time to compute different pixels would translate into severe load-imbalance. The solution to this dilemma is to use a 'scattered' decomposition like:

```
1 2 3 4 1 2 3 4 1 2 3 4 1 2 3 4
5 6 7 8 5 6 7 8 5 6 7 8 5 6 7 8
1 2 3 4 1 2 3 4 1 2 3 4 1 2 3 4
5 6 7 8 5 6 7 8 5 6 7 8 5 6 7 8
1 2 3 4 1 2 3 4 1 2 3 4 1 2 3 4
5 6 7 8 5 6 7 8 5 6 7 8 5 6 7 8
1 2 3 4 1 2 3 4 1 2 3 4 1 2 3 4
5 6 7 8 5 6 7 8 5 6 7 8 5 6 7 8
```

instead of the 'tiled' one. Now each processor computes representative pixels from all over the image, and severe load imbalance is extremely unlikely. In fact, we can estimate that the load imbalance is proportional to

$$n^{-1/2}(\sigma_{pix} / \mu_{pix})$$

where μ_{pix} and σ_{pix} are the mean and standard deviation of the distribution of pixel computation times, and n is the number of pixels per processor.

A much more significant difficulty with the embarrassingly parallel approach to ray-tracing is that it requires that the entire database be available to each and every processor. This is no problem, in principle, for shared-memory machines in which the database is stored once in shared memory, but it is a major restriction for distributed-memory machines, as it requires that a separate copy of the database reside in each processor's local memory. Even for shared-memory architectures, the multiple access of nodes to a single database may introduce contention and performance-degradation. Thus embarrassingly parallel distributed-memory ray-tracers are capable of rendering only models which fit, in their entirety, within the memory of a single processor.

To address this problem, we are forced to distribute the database as well as the computation. It is necessary at this point to have some understanding of how the ray-tracing algorithm proceeds. For each pixel, a *ray* is generated which passes from the *view-point* through the pixel on the screen, and into the model space. Once this is known, a shading calculation is performed, which usually involves projecting a number of additional rays from the point of intersection toward the light-sources in the model and in the directions given by Snell's and Hero's Laws.

By far the most time-consuming part of the computation is determining which primitive object is struck by a ray. A complex scene can have up to a million primitive objects, so a naive linear search is clearly out of the question. Several related techniques are common for reducing the complexity of the intersection to $O(logN)$ where N is the number of objects. As described in Salmon's Ph.D. thesis, the Caltech group elected to construct a tree of *bounding boxes*, in which the leaves are primitive objects, and each internal node is a rectangular box large enough to contain all of its descendants. The intersection calculation begins by testing the ray with the root bounding box. If the root bounding box intersects the ray, then each of its children is tested recursively. Whenever a bounding box fails to intersect the tree, all its children may immediately be pruned as candidates for intersection as well.

The tree of bounding boxes is a natural data-structure to distribute to the processors. A copy of nodes near the root of the tree is duplicated in each processor. Thus, each processor can begin an intersection-calculation with data available locally. We call this common data-structure the *forest* because its terminal elements are pointers to sub-trees which are stored only once, in one of the processors of the parallel ensemble. When a processor needs to know the results of an intersection-calculation between a ray and a sub-tree, a remote procedure-call is made, and the remote processor which maintains the appropriate part of the database performs the calculation and sends back the result in a message. This approach has similarities with the parallel clustering algorithm used in the astrophysical-particle-dynamics application.

The communication-traffic in this program is highly asynchronous and unpredictable. This is one of the few algorithms we have studied which would not perform well under a loosely synchronous message-passing operating system. In fact, it is not just the communication but also the computation as a whole that is asynchronous. A processor must divide its time between its own work (traversing the forest for pixels which it is responsible for computing) and that requested by others. In order to manage the highly asynchronous computation, the MOOSE operating system was developed to allow numerous lightweight processes to run on each processor. Each sub-tree that is assigned to a processor is represented by a separate lightweight process, with its own queue of requests. A process is active when its input-queue is non-empty. Otherwise, the process is idle, and does not consume CPU resources. Note that computer chess was also asynchronous, but involved larger grain chunks which were irregular but essentially static. This application did not need MOOSE but rather the conventional asynchronous message-passing system VERTEX which is supplied with the NCUBE.

Battle-management

A JPL team headed by D. Curkendall has developed a sophisticated battle-management simulation. This includes threat-generation (launch missiles), tracking, engagement-planning (launch anti-missiles), and graphics. The total of 200,000 lines of code is one of the largest single parallel computer projects we have studied. Its size is much larger than the sum of all the lines of code described so far in the previous eleven subsections! The so-called SIM 88 project completely simulates up to 250 objects launched from 6 sites. There is an interesting hybrid approach to the simulation with each component (tracking satellite, planning platform) functionally decomposed with a very coarse-grained object-oriented model. Traditional data-parallelism is used with individual functions (objects) assigned to a subcube of the hypercube. Correspondingly, a hybrid software model CENTAUR for the Mark IIIfp hypercube supported general but slow inter-object communication and fast loosely synchronous CrOS communication within objects. Formally, the simulation is an asynchronous event-driven simulation at the object level, but the predictable and coarse-grain nature of the object-to-object communication allowed efficient loosely synchronous implementation within a simple conservative framework.

Let us focus on the tracking component, which used a parallel implementation of a traditional multi-target Kalman filter-tracker. Much of the calculation can be done independently in each node when one distributes the tracks. There are some significant overheads when tracks share measurements, and load-balance is an issue addressed by dynamically redistributing the data at each measurement-cycle. This is a loosely synchronous algorithm implemented as 4,000 (20,000) lines of C in the SIM 87 (88) versions.

The SIM 87 code shows good performance on a variety of shared-memory machines. These avoid the data-shuffling overhead for overlapping tracks. This algorithm was designed for the so-called boost-phase, when there is modest parallelism coming from the decomposition of a total of a few hundred objects. Even the 480-target problem does not perform well on the larger NCUBE systems due to the limited parallelism. The 85-target problem is even harder to parallelize.

We note that the communication-overhead is perhaps overestimated in the benchmarks, as it depends critically on the sophistication of the track-model. The newer SIM 88 implementation has a fully parallel tracking component that takes three times longer than SIM 87. The communication-overhead is reduced by this factor for SIM 88.

We expect the situation to change in the harder midcourse-phase where up to 10^5 real or decoy objects can be anticipated.

This will need new algorithms—perhaps neural networks—and the parallelism issues will be different, but we expect it to be easier rather then harder to exploit massively parallel machines. It appears that existing parallel machines with a few megaflops of performance will allow real-time tracking in the boost-phase; mid-course will require true supercomputers.

Ocean general circulation model

This is a salutary lesson in parallelizing dusty decks. Our original plan was that this 20,000-line FORTRAN CRAY code would typify issues involved in converting similar but larger and more sophisticated meteorological and climate-modelling codes.

TABLE 10. STEPS IN PARALLELIZING OGCM	
Step	**Time in days**
Get original FORTRAN running on CRAY and understand use of program	10
Generate working sequential code for SUN	10
Construct test dataset	10
Find that our FORTRAN environment on NCUBE hypercube needed upgrade as up to now we had used C language	10
Parallelize code	3
TOTAL	43

The program solves a three-dimensional ocean-model with the Navier-Stokes equations and driving terms from wind, temperature and salinity. It uses a time-stepped evolution with successive over-relaxation to solve Poisson's equation for the fluid. We kept a careful record of the time spent on this project, as shown in Table 10.

Parallelization involved a simple domain-decomposition implemented by changing DO loop indices in the original code and adding communication-calls. There was a frustrating difficulty with decomposing in the north-south dimension, which we now believe was an unphysical approximation introduced in the original sequential code to improve an original small-memory CYBER 205 version. As it stands, the code could be parallelized (decomposed) only in the other two directions (east-west, depth). The parallel code used all 256 megabytes of memory on the 512 node NCUBE and did not need the memory-management necessary in the CRAY version. The 512-node hypercube performance was comparable to that of CRAY.

A success, you might think, but there is a tragic end: the NCUBE version does not currently agree with that for the CRAY. This may be due to a bug introduced by the parallelization, but we doubt it. We have studied the CRAY code and believe it is technically incorrect; vectorization was implemented by allowing references outside the array's assigned memory. We do not know how to parallelize such practices! We tried to obtain help from the originators of the code, but to no avail.

We deduce from this experience that parallelizing existing code can be quite simple and quick. As Table 10 shows, the parallelization step took only three days. However, such endeavors should be undertaken only with the help of someone who really knows and is responsible for the sequential code.

Neural networks

Neural networks have been important in our research from three very different points of view. Most straightforwardly, one can use digital parallel computers, both SIMD and MIMD, to simulate neural networks. Here, one is mapping nature's parallel computer onto mankind's. One can view this as a sparse-matrix problem, and we were able to develop general mapping techniques which are applicable to other network simulations, such as electric-power-grid optimization and VLSI-chip-simulation. Some or all of such simulations will eventually be implemented on the special-purpose neural hardware being developed by many groups. This will give higher performance, but it is likely that general parallel computers will still be useful for networks whose structure does not easily map onto special-purpose architectures.

As was mentioned, we have used artificial neural networks of the type pioneered by Hopfield and Tank to address optimization-problems associated with parallel computing. Indeed, one can view parallel-algorithm-and-architecture research as 'just' an optimization problem—namely, to minimize the execution-time of a problem with varying algorithms on a varying parallel computer. Similarly, software-engineering can be viewed as 'just' minimization of the time that a user takes to write and maintain programs. A key characteristic of such optimization-problems is that one needs 'reasonable' but not exact minima. For instance, a typical communication-overhead obtained by careful user-decomposition is around 20%. It is normally sufficient that an automatic method would obtain a value of this overhead of, say, 30%; a factor of 1.5 off the true minimum. It has been shown that decomposition is NP-complete, *i.e.*, exponentially hard. However, this categorization refers to the difficulty in finding exact solutions. Methods such as simulated annealing and neural networks are able to find approximate minima in times that are linear (up to logarithms) in problem size. Further, these approaches to decomposition can be parallelized. Hence, one can construct dynamic decomposition and load-balancing tools that are implemented with neural networks running on the same parallel computer that is simulating the application being decomposed (see Figure 1). We have also shown how to apply similar neural network optimizers to message-routing.

Nelson and Bower have interpreted some of the observed structure of the cortex in terms of decomposition methodologies used in parallel computing. As shown in Figure 2, one can identify both the 'tiled' distribution in (A) and extreme 'scattered' distribution in (C). (B) shows an intermediate 'patchy' distribution; each of these three techniques is a basic parallel computing methodology. I expect that there are further fruitful analogies between the architectures of neural and digital computers. In particular, I am interested in studying the architecture of large artificial VLSI neural networks. This issue has received very little attention, but seems important; how should one hook up a large number of special-purpose neural network chips to build a neural supercomputer?

Lessons

Now we collect together some of the lessons we have learned from 'using real parallel computers to solve real problems with real software'.

APPLICATION LESSONS

One can achieve high performance on essentially all scientific computations which are either loosely synchronous MIMD or synchronous SIMD, provided that they are large.

We can view the above synchronicity conditions as requiring that the architectures of problem and computer match. Above, we refer only to the temporal aspects of the architecture. Earlier, we have discussed the matching of the spatial properties of problem and computer. This is expressed as the inequality

$$d_{computer} \geq d_{problem}$$

in terms of the underlying system-dimension d of the complex systems. This is natural for geometric systems, but we have also shown how to define dimension generally in terms of the local information flow in a system. In this approach, a hypercube is a good architecture because it has a high system-dimension $d = \log N$.

More research is needed to clarify Table 3 and see how far one can violate synchronization and still get good results for irregular problems on SIMD machines, *i.e.*, to what extent problem and computer architecture can be mismatched. Even for loosely

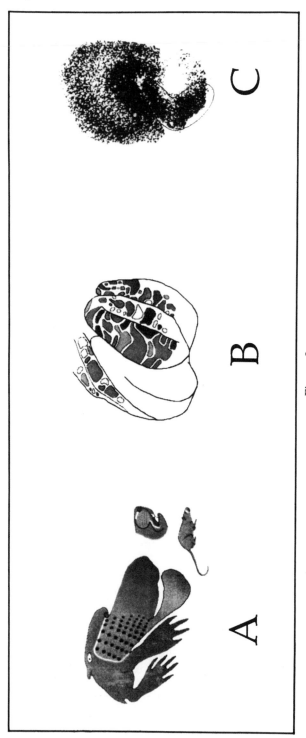

Figure 2

synchronous problems, synchronous communication is usually sufficient; communication is typically necessary only at the macroscopic synchronization points of the algorithm.

Domain-decomposition or data-parallelism is a universal source of parallelism that scales to large numbers of nodes.

These results are true on a broad range of computer architectures (SIMD, MIMD, shared-memory, distributed-memory, hypercubes, transputer-meshes).

University successes on parallel computers have come with 1,000-10,000 line codes written from scratch for a particular machine.

It is not clear how to extrapolate these successes to up-to-a-million-line commercial codes where one perhaps has less knowledge as to the inner workings of the program. This is illustrated graphically by the difficulties experienced in the oceanography project described earlier. Certainly, one must establish and use standard methods in parallel software to justify the expense of a new parallel implementation. These standards must apply across a range of architectures.

In many cases, it is easier to decompose for a parallel machine than to vectorize for a conventional supercomputer. This is especially true for small (university) codes. We can superficially extract from this the principle that universities should purchase parallel computers and industry should purchase vector-supercomputers!

The importance of parallel machines for artificial intelligence (AI) is unclear to me. If the AI application is implemented with neural networks, or as a memory-based-reasoning system as in Chapter 10, then the relevance and use of parallel computers is clear. More traditional AI systems parallelize less easily, although chess is a good example which *both* parallelizes *and* needs high performance. How many other such AI applications are there?

PERFORMANCE LESSONS

One can get high performance on essentially all scientific computations. Performance scales linearly in the number of nodes at a constant grain-size (problem-size proportional to machine-size). Fixed problem-size does not scale; this can be viewed as Amdahl's Law.

Some initial disappointments can be traced to imbalance in early commercial machines, such as the iPSC/1 and FPS T Series hypercubes.

We saw that machines like an NCUBE or a transputer-array, with many simple nodes, look particularly attractive compared to the CRAY-XMP-class machines on irregular problems where one finds that it is more natural and easier to decompose than to vectorize, that the NCUBE efficiency is low (maybe 50%) but the CRAY efficiency even lower (maybe 5%). Note that the average CRAY XMP performance in computer-center operation is about 25 megaflops with a 12% efficiency. The NCAR CRAY realizes a sustained 50 megaflops, which is perhaps the peak average performance. We have too high a standard for the efficiency of parallel machines!

Scalar-node MIMD machines are natural general-purpose machines with reasonable performance over a range of problems. As seen in Table 6, hypercubes have high efficiency on regular (*e.g.*, full-matrix and QCD) problems, but so does the CRAY-XMP-class machine. Hypercubes with vector nodes or SIMD machines are attractive for regular problems.

Different programming methodologies and lack of standards handicap performance-studies. As FORTRAN-8X is yet to be implemented uniformly, it is hard even to port between CRAY XMP and the ETA-10. This, for instance, is handicapping the 'Grand Challenge'. Of course, porting between parallel and sequential machines is hard, and our Caltech performance-evaluation team essentially re-implemented many algorithms from scratch. The different software-methodologies for shared- and distributed-memory machines cannot be avoided, as in some sense it is the more convenient environment that motivates shared-memory machines. It would be unreasonable to require shared-memory machines always to use message-passing, even though it leads to excellent machine-performance. Message-passing currently does minimize user-productivity.

DECOMPOSITION LESSONS

Here we refer to issues concerning the dividing-up of problems to minimize communication and equalize load on processors.

Three years ago, I thought decomposition or load-balancing was a hard problem, but, as we saw, it is surprisingly easy! Usually, the application-scientist can specify it from the natural geometric structure of the problem. Several heuristic methods provide automatic decomposition. These include recursive bisection, simulated annealing and neural networks.

Current hardware-trends have emphasized transparent message-routing where the user need not be aware of machine-topology. This is clearly convenient, but it is not strictly necessary for a broad class of problems. We note that most problems can be mapped with software to any reasonable-band-width topology with modest routing-overheads. In particular, for current Caltech codes there is an average overhead of less than 5% due to routing. This should be compared to overheads of perhaps 50% due to poor compilers (*e.g.*, for NCUBE and WEITEK), 50% due to the overall flakiness of the system, and 25% due to communication from node to neighboring hypercube-node. We must emphasize that these software-solutions have yet to be packaged nicely for general use. Not every programmer is comfortable with simulated annealing. Thus, automatic routing hardware is certainly convenient in the real world.

In current systems, message-start-up time, which includes hardware- and software-effects, is a much more serious overhead than either node-to-node through-routing, or channel-transmission between neighboring nodes.

HARDWARE LESSONS

So far, high-performance computation on moderately or massively parallel machines ($\geq$ 8 nodes) has been confined to distributed-memory machines. The comparison between distributed- and shared-memory architecture is hard because of the lack of comparable machines and experience.

Five years ago, there were many university-projects building novel machines, but in the future commercial systems will dominate the parallel field as they now do with conventional supercomputers.

The U.S. entrepreneurial environment will guarantee a wide range of architectures even without new university-projects. Portable software will be necessary to exploit these machines.

Many or perhaps all the current commercial parallel systems are disappointing in some ways. For instance, our NCUBE is now in full use as a production-supercomputer, but this took two years and at least $150,000 in software-development costs at Caltech. According to Bill Joy's law that sequential computers improve by a factor of two each year in cost-effectiveness, a two-year delay translates into a factor-of-four loss in cost-effectiveness compared to the conventional competition. Novel computers are bound to need more time to develop viable software than their sequential competition; this certainly handicaps their ability to compete.

As this implies, systems-integration is not yet well-addressed in the parallel machines. This includes issues such as general multiuser operating systems especially for distributed-memory machines; debugging; adherence to standards; input/output for disks and graphics (the architecture of the I/O system gets surprisingly little attention in the literature); high-performance appropriate hosts (not PC's or workstations) for a parallel supercomputer.

For MIMD machines, we have already mentioned some issues. Currently, machines like the NCUBE or transputer with scalar (floating-point) nodes seem more successful than machines with vector nodes. The user finds it hard to vectorize and decompose problems. One such optimization is enough. Given that such scalar-node systems are particularly attractive for irregular problems, maybe one should consider adding specialized support for the data-structures like linked lists needed for irregular problems. A several-megabyte (but not arbitrarily large) memory per node is needed to hold program, decomposed data, databases and re-used communication data. One can expect the differences between shared- and distributed-memory architectures to lessen as both are based on low-latency networks. Either local memory (for machines like the hypercube) or caches on shared-memory machines will require data-locality for good performance.

SIMD machines can support at least 50% of university scientific applications, as shown in Table 3. They currently give the peak performance for regular problems (see Tables 5, 7). Perhaps commercial applications are more irregular and will show a lower fraction appropriate for the SIMD architecture.

The above discussion suggests a possible structure of an integrated high-performance novel-architecture computer environment. Simple scalar-node MIMD machines support general problems with either vector or SIMD architectures as an accelerator for regular problems.

SOFTWARE LESSONS

Whereas the role of universities in developing hardware-systems may be limited in the future, we expect universities to have a critical role in the software for parallel machines where we cannot hope for the commercial systems to be adequate.

A key question is: what is the appropriate productive standard programming-environment for parallel machines? This could be based on four aspects: new languages and approaches (*e.g.* graphical techniques); compiler-generated parallelism; application-specific high-level environments; and explicit user-decomposition.

Note that essentially all successful applications of parallel machines have involved explicit user-decomposition which is low-level and machine-dependent. We expect that we must find more attractive and portable methods if parallel computers are to take over from the conventional architectures.

Asynchronous applications need more sophisticated operating-environments than do the loosely synchronous or embarrassingly parallel applications of the earlier sections. Each of the last three applications required different software systems (shared-memory VERTEX, MOOSE and CENTAUR respectively) for good performance. The simple but high-performance synchronous CrOS communication-system is adequate for the earlier applications.

Approaches like LINDA (shared message-space) or the new language occam appear not to address enough of the issues to be the appropriate productive standard programming-environment for parallel machines.

When we started work on hypercubes in 1981, I had great confidence that they would be successful because I could make a simple performance-model and prove that, for dedicated users, hypercubes would work. I don't have any way of making a similar prediction for the software-environment. I do expect parallelized FORTRAN to be important in the future for both SIMD and MIMD machines. I estimate that about 75% of Caltech 'hand-parallelized' codes could be written so that a compiler could find the parallelization semi-automatically with advice on decomposition from the user .

The challenge to universities: Caltech experience and Syracuse promise

The results we have described have come from interdisciplinary research teams whose participants have needed skills in software, numerical analysis, and the underlying application-areas. This approach was proposed in several national studies and has been an underlying principle behind the Caltech Concurrent Computation Program since its inception.

Our experience has suggested another key idea: *the training of individuals whose skills span those of a range of traditional disciplines.* Most of the students and postdoctoral fellows in our group have moved away from a concentration in a particular application-area and towards this interdisciplinary mold. The value of such an education is recognized by industry and the national laboratories; graduates of our program are typically highly-sought-after by these employers.

However, they are ignored by universities. For instance, my own students, although they played a leading role in pioneering the use of the hypercube and are highly talented even by Caltech's standards, have not received any job-offers from U.S. universities. This is not surprising; universities are conservative organizations built around traditional and often narrow disciplines. There is a rigid system designed for, and successful in, ensuring the continuation of high standards within established areas. This has the unfortunate side-effect of stifling new areas, and making it hard for interdisciplinary research.

The situation is not a direct difficulty for tenured faculty. For instance, I myself have been encouraged to perform interdisciplinary research, and I find it easy to establish collaborations between departments. However, I certainly am aware of the phenomenon. My computer-scientist friends know me as a physicist, whereas my colleagues in the physics department are not sure how to classify me, but are certain that I am no longer a physicist! More importantly, I have found it hard in the last three years to train graduate students. Originally, my students obtained Physics Ph.D.s with theses describing their physics research, with computational developments in appendices. As the sophistication and interdisciplinary nature of our research increased, this pattern became unnatural. My students benefited from a physics motivation, but wished, in many cases, to have their research judged primarily on its contribution to computation.

Several people have identified this interdisciplinary area and labeled it variously as *scientific computing, computational science,* or some similar term. We use the long-winded but descriptive *fundamentals of computational science and engineering* (FCSE).

There are several choices for creating an academic program around FCSE. One could view it as Applied Computer Science and implement FCSE as an area of specialization within Computer Science. My impression is that this choice would be considered natural by most of our faculty. However, this is probably not appropriate, for we do not need the underlying specialist training provided for researchers in Computer Science. Their research is typically based on electrical engineering or pure (discrete) mathematics, and usually there is little emphasis on (scientific) problem solving. I am therefore sceptical that this field is a natural home for FCSE.

Or one could view FCSE as Applied Mathematics, a field which is based on applications, often those in fluid-flow, combustion and similar fields. In this field an analyst would typically be interested in analytic properties of differential equations and numerical solution-techniques. Optimization and linear algebra are other major Applied Mathematics specializations. However, FCSE is founded on computation, not on mathematics as such, and has a broader range of applications. I believe nevertheless that FCSE has the greatest overlap with Applied Mathematics among existing fields; an expansion of this traditional field would be a natural implementation of FCSE.

At Caltech, a proposal for a new Ph.D. program in Applied Mathematics and Computational Science did not succeed. A proposed new Institute-wide option covering FCSE was pursued. In preparing this proposal, we realized that the new field of Complex Systems was synergistic with FCSE. Computers are naturally studied as complex systems, and further it is the possibility of computer-experiments that has opened up the field of complex systems. A proposed new interdisciplinary option, Computation and Complex Systems, was endorsed strongly by several Caltech faculty from many fields, but generated confusion when considered by the full faculty. Comments included, *Isn't this already part of Computer Science? Doesn't every one do computing? Surely Complex Systems includes everything?*

We tried to distinguish this Ph.D. program from existing disciplines by calling it *plectics*, a neologism coined by Murray Gell-Mann. (The name of our various proposed programs always created great debate; different choices for the name trod on different toes.   More substantive was the criticism that the proposed field did not have a well-defined core-knowledge).

We had proposed that students could base their computational work in essentially any scientific or engineering area.   How then could we maintain academic quality with such flexible requirements? We should mention here a well-established Ph.D. program founded at Caltech in 1986: Computation and Neural Systems.   This field studies biologically-motivated computation, including applied neural networks, optical and silicon implementations and cortex-models.   The base-knowledge is neurobiology, computer science, electrical engineering, and modelling.

We had come to realize that a key feature of our approach was an emphasis on a physical background rather than the electrical engineering , mathematical, or biological orientation of Caltech's existing programs.   This is seen in our exploitation of physical structure in parallel decomposition—here we use 'physical' in its general definition as 'natural'.   We also can view the theory of complex systems as a mapping of general systems into physical systems.   Simulated annealing and neural networks are *physical* optimization techniques.

Thus, we formulated, and obtained approval on June 12, 1989 for, a new Ph.D. program: Physical Computation and Complex Systems.   This program is described in the catalog as follows

> The objective of Physical Computation and Complex Systems is a unified approach to abstraction, modelling, and computation applied to the natural world.   This approach is based on a systematic use of physical analogies and methods.   The program involves fundamental education in mathematical physics, simple classical and quantum physical systems, fundamental properties of complex systems, physical optimization methods, and the appropriate computational techniques needed for large-scale problem-solving on advanced-architecture computers.

The requirements are focussed—students must have a strong physics training at the level of Caltech's senior-undergraduate or first-year-graduate physics-courses.   However, these physics-tools may be used in a broad range of research-topics, including computation (as in FCSE) and complex systems.   A list of possible research-areas is described as follows:

> Specific subjects of attention in Physical Computation and Complex Systems include: the relation of information, complexity, and computation; the role of classical and quantum information in the history of the Universe; performance-modelling with computers considered as complex systems; nonadaptive but nonlinear dynamical systems; fundamental general properties of adaptive complex systems, with examples

of such systems being chemical, biological and cultural evolution, learning and thinking; computational techniques for use of high-performance, advanced-architecture computers in modelling, simulation, and data-analysis; mathematical, algorithmic, and programming issues underlying such applications; impact on problem-solving of new approaches such as genetic algorithms, symbolic methods, cellular automata, neural networks, and multiscale methods; visualization and interpretation of massive data-sets generated by high-performance computers. This broad range of topics is unified by the use of analogies, methods, and approaches suggested by physical systems.

The program has strong faculty-support inside and outside physics at Caltech.

We should distinguish *Physical Computation*—the study of computational methods relevant for or based on physical systems, with *Computational Physics*—the study of physics using computer-simulation. Physical Computation and Complex Systems will have strong involvement from computational physicists, but will greatly extend the range of research of our students. It is not the complete answer to FCSE, but it is an exciting, focused beginning. It could grow into an Institute-wide program either directly or as a consortium containing Physical Computation and Complex Systems, Computation and Neural Systems, Applied Mathematics, Chemical Computation, and possibly other programs.

Our efforts were handicapped by the lack of a national movement in this area. It is crucial for FCSE to be discussed nationally. There are a few computational science efforts starting in universities, but with no common theme and little national recognition. This should be changed. Without major new educational initiatives, the U.S. will not be able to exploit the possibilities opened up by advances in computer-performance.

D. Sorensen of Rice University organized an important session on this question at the 1989 Supercomputing Conference at Reno. We saw two distinct approaches to computational science. Some universities viewed it as an expansion of computer science; others, similarly to the Caltech proposal, as an expansion of a scientific application-field.

I will be moving to Syracuse University in Summer 1990, and intend to start there a broad Computational Science program including both of these ideas: the use of computers in science and the science of using computers. We will include not only traditional computer science approaches but also the biological and physical analogies emphasized in the Caltech Physical Computation and Complex Systems program. We intend to have undergraduate, masters and Ph.D. programs in Computational Science at Syracuse.

Acknowledgement

I would like to thank Paul Messina and the many others whose research is discussed in this paper.

Suggestions for further reading

Anderson, S.B., Gorham, P., Kulkarni, S., Prince, T.A., and Wolszczan, A. Discovery of two radio pulsars in M15. Forthcoming in *Nature*, 1990.
Analyses of some of the new pulsars discovered on the NCUBE at Caltech.

Angus, I.G., Fox, G.C., Kim, J.S., and Walker, D.W. *Solving Problems on Concurrent Processors: Software for Concurrent Processors*, volume 2. Prentice-Hall, Inc., Englewood Cliffs, NJ 07632, 1989.

Baillie, C.F., Johnston, D.A., and Kilcup, G.W. Status and prospects of the computational approach to high energy physics. Forthcoming in *The Journal of Supercomputing*, 1990 (a).
Reviews the status of the QCD and string computations described in the chapter.

Baillie, C.F. Lattice spin models and new algorithms—a review of Monte Carlo computer simulations. Forthcoming in *International Journal of Modern Physics C*, 1990 (b)
Reviews conventional and clustering computational approaches for a range of spin systems.

Coddington, P.D., and Baillie, C.F. Cluster algorithms for spin models and MIMD parallel computers. Forthcoming in the *Proceedings of the Fifth Distributed-memory Computing Conference*, 1990.
Describes the parallelization of the clustering methods for Monte Carlo problems.

Ding, H.-Q., and Makivic, M. Quantum spin calculation on the hypercube. Forthcoming in the *Proceedings of the Fifth Distributed-memory Computing Conference*, 1990.
One of a set of large-scale two-dimensional condensed-matter calculations on the Mark IIIfp hypercube.

Felten, E.W., and Otto, S.W. A highly parallel chess program. In *Proceedings of International Conference on Fifth Generation Computer Systems 1988*, 1001-1009, ICOT 1988.
Presents the approach and performance of the parallel chess program.

Fox, G.C.   Questions and unexpected answers in concurrent computation.   In J. J. Dongarra, (editor), *Experimental Parallel Computing Architectures*, 97-121. Elsevier North-Holland, 1987.
Describes the Caltech Concurrent Computation Program.

Fox, G.C., Johnson, M.A., Lyzenga, G.A., Otto, S.W., Salmon, J.K., and Walker, D.W. *Solving Problems on Concurrent Processors*, volume 1. Prentice-Hall 1988 (a).
Describes the algorithms and software developed by the Caltech Concurrent Computation Program. See also Angus 1989.

Fox, G.C.   What have we learnt from using real parallel machines to solve real problems? 1988 (b).
Develops the temporal classification of problems given in the chapter. In Fox 1988 (c).

Fox, G.C., editor. *The Third Conference on Hypercube Concurrent Computers and Applications*. Jet Propulsion Laboratory of the California Institute of Technology, ACM Press 1988 (c).
The proceedings of the annual hypercube conferences contain a wealth of experience, especially from the Caltech groups in this third conference (see Heath 1986, 1987).

Fox, G.C., and Furmanski, W.   Hypercube algorithms for neural network simulation the Crystal-Accumulator and the Crystal-Router.
Describes the issues and one example in the use of hypercubes to simulate neural networks. In Fox 1988 (c).

Fox, G.C.   The hypercube and the Caltech Concurrent Computation Program: A microcosm of parallel computing, in B. J. Alder, editor, Special-purpose Computers, 1-40. Academic Press, 1988.
More on the Caltech Concurrent Computation Program.

Fox, G.C., and Furmanski, W.   The physical structure of concurrent problems and concurrent computers. Philosophical Transactions of the Royal Society of London.   A 326, 411-444, 1988.
Presents the concept of the 'problem architecture'.

Fox, G.C., Furmanski, W., Ho, A., Koller, J., Simic, P., and Wong, Y.F.   Neural networks and dynamic complex systems. Proceedings of the 1989 SCS Eastern Conference, 1989.
Presents optimization algorithms based on neural networks for real world and computer routing and decomposition problems.

Fox, G.C.   Parallel computing comes of age: Supercomputer level parallel computations at Caltech.   Concurrency: Practice and Experience, 1(1), 63-103, September 1989.
Gives more details, especially references, on some of the material presented here.

Furmanski, W., Bower, J.M., Nelson, M.E., Wilson, M.A., and Fox, G. Piriform (Olfactory) cortex model on the hypercube, 1987.
In Fox 1988 (c).

Gustafson, J.L., Montry, G.R., and Benner, R.E.   Development of parallel methods for a 1024-processor hypercube, *SIAM J. Sci. Stat. Comput.*, 9 (4) 609-638, 1988.
An impressive demonstration of parallelism on the 1024-node NCUBE-1 at Sandia.

Heath, M.T., editor.   Proceedings of the First Hypercube Conference, Hypercube Multiprocessors 1986, SIAM 1986.

Heath, M.T., editor.   Proceedings of the Second Hypercube Conference, Hypercube Multiprocessors 1987, SIAM 1987.

Hillis, W.D., and Steele, G.L.   Data parallel algorithms, *Communications of the.Association for Computing Machinery.* 29, 1170 -1183, 1986.
Describes how parallelism is naturally obtained for synchronous problems by specifying identical operations on individual elements of a data-set.

Liewer, P.C., and Decyk, V.K.   A general concurrent algorithm for plasma particle-in-cell simulation codes, *Journal of Computational Physics*, 85 (2) 302-322, 1989.
Describes one of the general methods of load-balancing particle-in-the-cell codes.

Fox, G.C ., and Messina, P.   Advanced computer architectures, Scientific American, 255 (10), October 1987.
An elementary presentation of parallel computing.

Messina, P., Baillie, C.F., Felten, E.W., Hipes, P.G., Walker, D.W., Williams, R.D., Pfeiffer, W., Alagar, A., Kamrath, A., Leary, R.H., and Rogers, J.   Benchmarking advanced architecture computers. Concurrency: Practice and Experience, 1990.
A detailed performance-evaluation of the machines in Table 2 using some of the applications presented here.

Nelson, M.E., and Bower, J.M.   Computational efficiency: a common organizing principle for parallel computer maps and brain maps?, in *Advances in Neural Network Information Processing*

Systems 2 (Touretsky, D.L., editor), Morgan Kaufmann, 1990 (in press).
Speculates on the relation between decomposition methods developed for parallel computers and the structure observed in the cortex.

Otto, S.W., and Stack, J.D. SU(3) heavy-quark potential with high statistics, *Physical Review Letters.*, 52:2328, 1984.
The first large-scale computation on the Caltech hypercube.

Williams, R.D. Supersonic flow in parallel with an unstructured mesh. *Concurrency: Practice and Experience*, 1(1):51-62, 1989.
Describes the generation and load-balancing of adaptive two-dimensional finite-element meshes on the hypercube.

Wu, Y.-S.M., Cuccaro, S.A., Hipes, P.G., and Kuppermann, A. Quantum mechanical reactive scattering using a high-performance distributed-memory parallel computer. Forthcoming in Chemical Physics Letters, 1990.
A detailed account of the chemistry and computer issues in the parallel reaction-dynamics computation of $H + H_2$ scattering.

Chapter 5

TOWARDS GENERAL-PURPOSE PARALLEL COMPUTERS

DAVID MAY

Summary

One of the major successes of computer science has been the development of an efficient *general-purpose* architecture for sequential computers. This has allowed the construction of standard languages and portable software which have been a primary factor in increasing the pervasiveness of the sequential computer. One of the major questions of current computer science research is whether a similar success can be achieved for general-purpose *parallel* computers.

A wide range of specialized parallel architectures can already be found in applications such as real-time control, image-processing, graphics and supercomputing. Several promising approaches to the architecture of scalable general-purpose parallel computers are suggested by our experience with these machines and by theoretical considerations. How efficiently such architectures can be implemented in current and future technology remains an open question.

Introduction

It is generally believed that the future of computing depends on the exploitation of large-scale parallel processing. However, although specialized parallel computers have been successfully used in many different application areas, there remain significant obstacles to the widespread use of general-purpose parallel computers. It is easy to understand these problems from the viewpoint of an intending purchaser of a computer.

A purchaser of a general-purpose sequential computer will have many expectations of his new machine. He will expect both a variety of standard programming languages and an extensive set of subroutine libraries to be available, and he will also expect to be able to execute his own libraries and programs written in standard languages such as FORTRAN, C, and LISP. If he wants to know how fast the new machine will run his programs, he will check the memory-size and the speed of the machine—in MIPS (millions of instructions per second) or MFLOPS (millions of floating-point operations per second)—and the combination will give him a good idea of the capabilities of the new machine.

A purchaser of a general-purpose parallel computer will have similar expectations, and will find several manufacturers able to offer him a 'general-purpose parallel computer'. He will discover that each of these machines is indeed 'general-purpose'—it has been used in a number of different applications. Here the similarity with the sequential computer ends. The parallel machine must be programmed in the manufacturer's proprietary language—or proprietary extension of an existing language. There are no subroutine libraries of any size—and certainly none which effectively exploit the capabilities of the machine. In trying to estimate the capabilities of the machine, the intending purchaser will look at the number of processors, their speed, the memory attached to each of them, the speed of communication between processors, and finally the intricate details of the machine organization. He will find it impossible to compare the machine's capabilities with those of other parallel machines—or even with those of sequential machines!

There are two closely-related problems. The first is discussed in the chapter by Per Brinch Hansen, namely, the need for effective programming languages implementable across a range of parallel computers. The second is the need for a common architecture for general-purpose parallel computers. In the absence of both of these, there is no basis for the creation of standard languages, operating systems, subroutine libraries and applications software. Parallel computers are simply not 'general-purpose' in the same sense as sequential computers.

VLSI parallel processors

Most current computers are built in VLSI technology. This technology has been used successfully for many different purposes. It can be used to construct—on a single silicon chip—general-purpose sequential computers. Here the problems have been those of using a new technology to implement an architecture which has been understood for many years. VLSI technology has also been used to construct general-purpose components for special-purpose parallel machines. There are also several programmable parallel computers which are certainly not general-purpose, and there are also many special-purpose parallel machines such as image- and signal-processing arrays.

It is therefore reasonable to ask whether it is possible to design *general-purpose* parallel computers at all, and whether VLSI technology is capable of implementing them.

Transputers—components for parallel machines

VLSI technology enables a complete sequential computer to be constructed on a single silicon chip. One example is the Inmos transputer (Homewood 1987), which integrates a central processor, a floating-point unit, four kilobytes of static random-access memory and a communications system onto a chip about one square centimeter in area.

Transputer

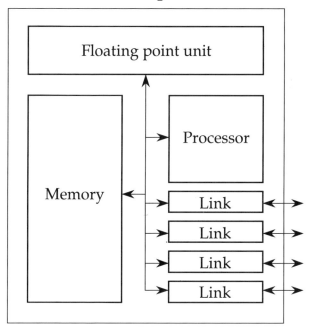

As a microcomputer, the transputer is unusual in that it has the ability to communicate with other transputers via its communication links. This enables transputers to be connected together to construct multiprocessor systems to tackle specific problems. The transputer is also unusual in that it has the ability to execute many software processes at the same time, to create new processes rapidly, and to perform communication between processes within a transputer and between processes in different transputers. All of these capabilities are integrated into the hardware of the transputer, and are very efficient. As a sequential processor, the performance of the transputer is about ten million instructions per second—and about two million floating-point operations per second.

The transputer is a general-purpose component for special-purpose machines, as can easily be seen from its major application areas. Transputers are used in a wide range of office equipment: they are used as controllers in laser printers and inkjet printers, to perform data-compression in facsimile machines and video-phones, to perform data-encryption and protocol-conversion in communications devices. Transputers are used in industrial applications: they implement real-time control systems, monitoring systems and robotics. They are used in avionics applications such as signal-processing and radar. In computers, the major transputer applications are in peripherals: they implement graphics, visualization, animation and database systems. All of these are 'embedded' applications and the end user does not actually program the transputers. Most of them are implemented as a specialized network of anything from one to a thousand transputers. The programs for the transputers are loaded when the product is switched on, and continue to be executed until it is switched off again.

The use of transputers has been greatly simplified by the development of the occam programming language (INMOS 1988b). Although designed in conjunction with the transputer, occam could be implemented on almost any parallel machine. It is based on the theory of concurrent processes and synchronized message-passing developed during the 1970s. These ideas gave rise to several experimental concurrent programming languages of which the best known is CSP (Hoare 1978). Occam combines an efficiently implementable subset of the CSP language with a simple sequential programming language. Subsequent developments in the theory of CSP have allowed the construction of a mathematical theory both for the sequential and the concurrent aspects of occam programs.

The occam language allows an application to be expressed as a collection of concurrent processes which communicate via channels. Each channel is a point-to-point connection between two processes; one process always inputs from the channel and the other always outputs to it. Communication is synchronized; when both processes are ready the data is copied from the outputting process to the inputting process and both processes continue.

Each transputer has a process-scheduler which allows it to share its time between a number of processes. Communication between processes on the same transputer is performed using the local memory; communication between processes on different transputers is performed using a link between the two transputers. Consequently, an occam program can be executed either by a single transputer or by a collection of transputers connected in a network. Three different ways of using transputers to execute the component processes of a typical occam program are shown below.

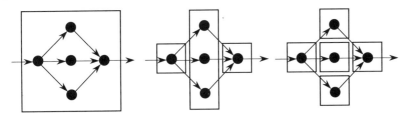

Most of the embedded-systems products incorporating the transputer are programmed in occam, sometimes with segments of program in standard languages such as C or FORTRAN where they are more appropriate—or where existing programs could be used.

Transputers have been used to construct a number of more general-purpose machines. These all consist of an array of transputers connected together in some kind of network. Experience with these machines—and with similar multiprocessors—has given rise to much debate about the most appropriate architectures for general-purpose parallel computers. However, it is clear that the exploitation of parallel processing in embedded systems has been much more successful than its exploitation in general-purpose computing.

Before returning to consider the further developments in computer architecture needed to provide general-purpose parallel computing, it is worthwhile to examine some of the features of the technology used to implement existing multiprocessor systems.

VLSI technology

Electronic systems are constructed as a hierarchy of modules. Integrated-circuit chips are mounted on modules, with each module containing one or more chips. The modules are then mounted on boards, and a collection of boards is held in a box—which also contains power-supplies and cooling. Switching devices—transistors — occur only on the chips.

One of the most obvious features of this technology is that interconnections consume nearly all of the volume—modules and boards contain only wires. Switching devices—transistors—occur only on silicon and themselves consume a tiny fraction of the available silicon area. Even a semiconductor manufacturer is effectively selling wire, not transistors!

Some significant improvements will come from semiconductor-manufacturing processes with more interconnect-levels—and from modules and boards allowing more interconnect-levels. However, it is likely that wire-density—the number of wires crossing a unit area—will continue to be the limiting factor in system construction. It is not the case, as is often supposed, that the number of connection-points on a chip is a limiting factor. The number of connection-points on a chip can easily be increased to the point where the density of wires needed to route connections away from the chip exceeds the capabilities of the module technology. Scaling down the size of the devices on a chip has continued steadily for many years and is expected to continue for many more. Present technology achieves transistor-gate-lengths of about one micron. As the device-size scales down, it is possible to reduce the size of the chips. Provided that the chip is not so large as to have a low manufacturing-yield, it is much more attractive to use the reduction in device-size to put more devices on a chip. In fact, there has also been a steady increase in chip-size over the years as manufacturing processes have improved.

Reducing the size of devices on a chip has several effects. A reduction in the size of the transistors gives rise to a linear increase in switching-speed. Moreover, the number of devices increases quadratically. These two factors provide a good justification for the use of parallelism: the speed of a sequential machine can be scaled linearly but the number of components of a parallel machine can be scaled quadratically.

Although reducing the size of transistors has the effect of increasing their speed, the opposite is the case with interconnections. Signal-propagation through a metal track (a 'wire') on silicon is limited in speed by its resistivity and by capacitance effects. Reducing the width of the track increases resistivity and reducing the distance between tracks increases capacitance. The result is that signal-propagation delays are increasing relative to switching-speeds.

The cost in silicon area in communication between chips is high—about 20% of the area of a transputer is occupied by connection-points onto which wires are connected, and there are further costs in area and power consumed by devices to transmit and receive data. Communication between chips over significant distances can be fast—a good transmission line can achieve near light speed (3×10^8 cm/sec). On chip, the resistance and capacitance effects limit speeds to much less than that of light— about 5×10^6 cm/sec in current VLSI technology.

In the technology used to manufacture transputers, a transistor can switch in about the same time as a signal will travel along one millimeter of a metal track. In designing a processor, it is therefore essential to ensure that the registers, arithmetic units and control logic are physically close together in order to ensure a high rate of data-transfer, rapid transmission of control-signals, and rapid distribution of clock-signals.

VLSI computer architecture

VLSI technology has significant implications for computer architecture. As processing is relatively inexpensive, it should be used to reduce the need for storing data, and to reduce the need for communications. To optimize performance, local operation is essential. Each processor should be equipped with a local memory to hold frequently-accessed programs and data. Communications should be supported via point-to-point connections rather than by connections shared between many processing elements. The transputers directly follow these architectural principles, allowing networks of simple sequential computers to be constructed. The transputers all operate independently of each other and pairs of transputers periodically synchronize with each other and communicate data as determined by their programs.

Most system designers are surprised at the suggestion that a processor should be used to save a few kilobytes of memory, that multiple copies of data and programs should be held to minimize communication, or that values should be recomputed to avoid the need to store them. However, all of these techniques have proved important in the design of effective parallel-processing systems. It does not seem likely that existing programming-languages and algorithms can be easily adapted to such systems. To exploit parallel processing effectively, new languages and algorithms are needed. Although this has not proved to be a major problem for embedded applications of parallel processing, it is likely to impede the widespread introduction of general-purpose parallel computers.

Algorithm development will continue to be just as important in parallel processing as it has been in sequential processing. Technology development provides a gradual improvement in performance—often at a considerable cost.

But reducing the number of operations required to execute an algorithm on n data items from n^2 to, say, $nlog(n)$ can have a dramatic effect. To return to the problem of sorting discussed by Per Brinch Hansen: sorting a thousand elements with an n^2 algorithm requires a million comparisons whereas with an $nlog(n)$ it requires only ten thousand comparisons. Replacing a widely-used algorithm with a much more efficient one can provide an immediate—and spectacular—performance improvement across a broad range of applications.

Most of the existing parallel machines have—like the transputers—been technology-driven. Indeed, there have been significant difficulties in constructing such machines even when closely following the constraints imposed by the technology. There is now a major opportunity to exploit the increasing capabilities of the technology to construct much more usable machines—not just faster ones. By designing general-purpose parallel architectures it will be possible to address the major obstacle to the use of parallel machines—the lack of software.

Parallel computers

One of the potential benefits of parallel computers is the ability to scale up *performance* by adding more processing-power. There are several different measures of performance. One of these—the only one which seems to be widely understood—is the speed of processing. Another is *responsiveness* - this is important because many computers are now used in environments requiring rapid responses. And finally there is *throughput* - the rate at which data can be input and output.

It is useful to distinguish two ways of applying parallelism to a problem. We can use parallel processing to solve a bigger problem in the same time (this is sometimes called *scale-up*) or we can use parallel processing to solve the same problem in less time (this is sometimes called *speed-up*). Scale-up tends to be easier than speed-up. For example, it is often necessary to scale-up a simulation, perhaps to increase the accuracy. This requires a corresponding increase in processing-power. However, this can often be achieved by executing several copies of an existing program in parallel. Speed-up is more difficult because the program must be decomposed into many parallel components which can be executed by separate processors.

Both scale-up and speed-up are commercially important—in some cases they create new applications of computers. Simulation is often used to understand physical phenomena; for this purpose speed is not always important. However, if simulation is fast enough—faster than real-time—it can be used for forecasting. Obvious examples are forecasting the weather—or the behavior of the financial markets.

Parallel computer architectures

Over the years a large number of parallel architectures have been developed. One example is the SIMD (single-instruction multiple-data) architecture used by the Connection Machine (Hillis 1985) and the (much earlier) Distributed Array Processor (Reddaway 1973). In a SIMD machine a single sequential instruction-stream controls a large number of operation-units each with its own local memory. Such machines are synchronous and at any time every operation-unit performs the same operation on its local data. SIMD machines can be very effective when performing the regular computations which arise in some numerical and image-processing applications.

Another important example is the MIMD (multiple-instruction multiple-data) architecture. MIMD machines have a number of processors each of which executes its own program. In some machines the processors all share a common memory, in others each processor has its own local memory and the processors are connected together in a fixed network. Recently there have been a number of reconfigurable machines (Nicole 1987) which allow the interconnection-network to be programmed—a step towards general-purpose MIMD machines. I shall discuss the applications of these machines later.

The best known—and most widely-exploited commercially— parallel machines are the vector supercomputers. Like the SIMD machines, vector machines are applicable to regular computations; their performance falls dramatically on programs which have few vector operations! One of the major reasons for the success of the vector supercomputers is that they can support standard sequential programming languages—although for high efficiency, proprietary extensions are often needed.

The various parallel architectures differ in terms of their implementability. For example, maintaining synchronous instruction-execution in a large SIMD machine requires the distribution of instructions to all of the operation units. In VLSI technology, the time taken for an instruction to travel throughout the machine is longer than the time taken for each operation unit to execute the instruction it receives. Either the speed of operation must be restricted to the rate at which instructions can be broadcast, or a faster (and more expensive) technology must be used to broadcast instructions. Consequently, it is not straightforward to construct high-speed SIMD machines in VLSI technology.

Each of the architectures has an associated programming-style. For general-purpose computing, what we need is a single architecture which will support *all* of the different programming-styles—effectively simulating each of the specialized machines efficiently. I am going to concentrate on MIMD machines because they seem to be able to do this more effectively than their rivals. For example, it is normally possible to use a MIMD machine to perform the kind of regular algorithms designed for SIMD machines. The converse is not true: it is not normally possible to use algorithms designed for MIMD machines on a SIMD machine.

Unfortunately, I know of no detailed study of the efficiency with which MIMD machines can emulate other parallel machines.

Another important property of the MIMD architecture is the ability to scale *all* of the performance characteristics: responsiveness, speed and throughout. Responsiveness is the most difficult characteristic to scale. Anyone with two telephones has experienced the problem of answering a call on one telephone in the midst of a call on the other. On the other hand, two people can easily deliver rapid response on two telephones. This is exactly analogous to the approach taken by a MIMD multiprocessor; it is almost impossible to emulate with a fast sequential processor—or with a SIMD array processor!

A final advantage of MIMD machines is that they are well-adapted to current VLSI technology—and to the technology we are likely to see over the next few years.

MIMD multiprocessors

There are two kinds of MIMD multiprocessor. In a common-memory multiprocessor, a number of processors access a number of memory-modules via an interconnection network. If there are few processors, the network may be a single shared bus. If many processors are used a more complex network is needed.

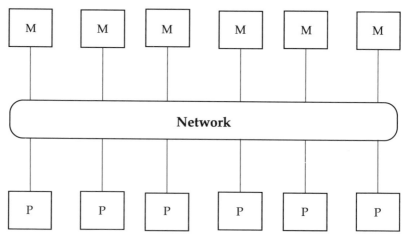

In a distributed-memory multiprocessor, a number of computers are connected via a network. Each computer consists of a processor with its own local memory.

Distributed memory MIMD machine

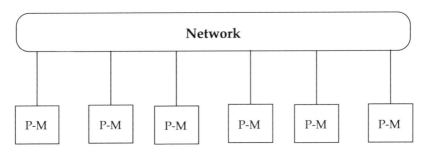

These two architectures look different—and they are at present programmed using two different programming-styles. However, I believe that they have been converging over a number of years, and I expect this to continue. For example, in all current common-memory machines the processors have local memories; this is needed to reduce the loading on the interconnection network. I will return to discuss this convergence later. I believe it to be important as it gives rise to some hope that a single MIMD architecture—able to support both programming-styles—will emerge.

Parallel programming-styles

Experience with existing parallel machines has given rise to a number of programming-styles. Per Brinch Hansen has already discussed one style for MIMD machines. I am going to show three techniques already in widespread use on transputer-based machines—and on other distributed-memory multiprocessors. They all involve expressing an application as a collection of communicating processes. In most transputer systems, the programmer then explicitly allocates the processes to processing-elements. Some typical applications of these techniques can be found in (Hey 1987).

The first—and in many ways the simplest—is *pipelining*. In a pipeline, data flows through a number of pipeline-stages, each one performing an operation on each incoming data-item before forwarding it to the next stage.

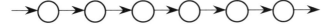

Pipelines have been used in many application-areas—and have been implemented in both hardware and software. Hardware pipelines are often found in signal-processing applications.

Software pipelines are often used in high-speed graphics (animation) where a series of transformations converts an abstract world-model into an image on a screen. Pipelining provides only limited parallelism (up to about ten parallel operations) because it is difficult to find applications which can exploit a large number of pipeline-stages. Another difficulty is that one stage of the pipeline may be a bottleneck - causing other stages to idle.

A technique which can provide large-scale parallelism is *farming*. In a farm, a *controller*-process hands out tasks to a number of independent *worker*-processes.

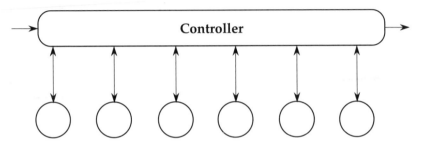

Data-items flow into the controller. As each data-item arrives, the controller allocates it to a free worker-process; when the worker-process has completed its operation on the data, it returns the result to the controller for output. In this way, it is possible to keep all of the worker-processes busy, regardless of the time taken to process individual data-items—the farm is load-balanced. Farms of hundreds of worker-processes have been used successfully. In such cases, it may be necessary to use a hierarchy of controllers to avoid the controller itself becoming a bottleneck.

A further technique which can also provide large-scale parallelism is *array-processing*. This involves using a regular array of processes to perform a correspondingly regular computation.

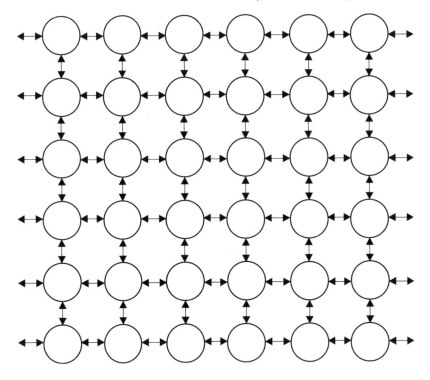

Process   [i, j]

computes   a[i, j]

A typical application is the processing of a two-dimensional image using a two-dimensional array of processes. Typically, each process stores and processes a representation of a small portion of the image. Each process needs to communicate with only its nearest neighbors.

Many applications use a predetermined combination of these techniques. However, as with sequential programs, there are cases where the technique used for one part of a computation should be selected according to characteristics of the input data— or of data produced by an earlier stage of the computation. This requires a general-purpose computer which can support all of the different techniques. It must have the ability to allocate newly-created processes to processing-elements dynamically—and the ability to implement the dynamic communication-patterns between them.

Unlike our current parallel computers, a general-purpose machine must be *optimized* for *generality*: it must achieve an effective balance of computation, memory and communication appropriate to a broad range of programming-styles. We shall see that this requires a substantial communications capability.

Balancing computation and communication

The importance of achieving a good balance between computation and communication can be understood by considering the previous array-processing example. Having expressed the algorithm as a collection of communicating processes, we have to map the processes on to the processors of the parallel machine.

Assuming that the machine is a two-dimensional array of processing-elements, the following illustration (in which square boxes represent processing-elements) shows a possible allocation:

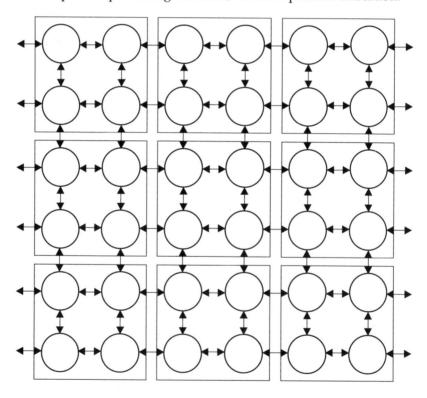

Process   [i, j]

computes a[i, j]

In this decomposition, we can see that every processor performs the processing-operations of four processes and that data-items flow between adjacent processing-elements. To achieve high efficiency, we must carefully map the processes onto the processing-elements in such a way that communication and computation requirements are consistent with the capabilities of the processing-elements. As an illustration of how this can be done, consider the following simple example.

We assume that at every step of the computation, every element of the array $a[i, j]$ is to be updated to

$f (a[i, j], a[i-1, j], a[i+1, j], a[i, j-1], a[i, j+1])$

and that the function f involves four operations. The following table shows the operations performed for each item.

processes/processor	operations/communication
1	1
4	2
16	4
256	16

If we chose a mapping which allocates one process to each processing-element, we need a machine which can perform one operation in the same time that it can communicate one data-item. This is often referred to as *fine-grain* processing. If, on the other hand, we allocate a large number of processes to each processing-element, the communications requirements are small. This is often referred to as *coarse-grain* processing. It can be seen from the example that as the grain is decreased, the communications capability becomes the limiting factor. This is why scale-up is easier to achieve than speed-up.

Machines such as transputers are well-balanced provided that the structure of the algorithm matches the structure of the machine—as in the example above. This can often be arranged where the transputer-network is designed for a particular application, or where a reconfigurable machine is used. However, for some algorithms, local communication is inadequate and it is necessary to communicate via a number of intermediate processing-elements. In such cases, the communication-rate becomes much too slow for fine-grain processing. This difficulty can also arise when mapping algorithms onto non-configurable machines. In order to support a wide range of algorithms, and to allow automatic allocation of processes to processors, a general-purpose machine must support a high rate of *non-local* communication.

Another important factor affecting the performance of parallel computers is the *delay* in communication. A processor may be idle, awaiting data from another processor, even though the communication-rate between the processors is adequate. A technique which overcomes this difficulty by *hiding* communication delays has been known for some time; I believe it was first used for hiding memory-access delays in the Denelcor processor (Smith 1978).

The most interesting observation is that hiding communication-delays involves the use of yet more parallelism in the algorithms. Instead of executing one process on each processor, we provide each processing-element with a scheduler allowing it to share its time between several processes.

Distributed memory MIMD machine

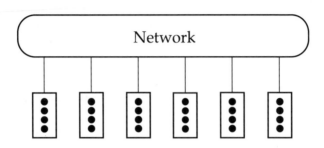

Excess concurrency in the
algorithm can hide
interconnect delays

Hiding communication-delays is then accomplished as follows: whenever a process is delayed as a result of a communication, it is descheduled and the processor activates another process. This in turn will eventually become descheduled as a result of a communication. Execution proceeds in this way through several processes. Whenever a communication completes, the corresponding process is rescheduled ready for subsequent execution. Provided that there are sufficient processes, the processor will never idle as a result of communication-delays. Exactly the same technique can be used to hide delays in common-memory machines—in this case a process is descheduled each time it attempts a read- or write-operation to the common memory.

To understand the use of excess parallelism, consider the following simple *worker*-process suitable for use in a processor-farm. In a typical farm a controller-process would hand out packets of work to many such processes.

```
local data, result
loop
{ input ? data
  result := compute (data)
  output ! result
}
```

This process performs input (?) to a local variable, computation, and output (!) from a local variable sequentially. Any delay in performing communication will be directly reflected in the time taken for each iteration of the loop.

Provided that the result output at each iteration of the loop is not used (by the controller) to produce input for the next two iterations, this process could be replaced by the following version which allows input, computation and output to take place in parallel.

```
local data, nextdata, result, nextresult
loop
{ parallel
  { input ? nextdata
    nextresult := compute (data)
    output ! result
  }
  data, result := nextdata, nextresult
}
```

Here, delays in communication will affect the total time taken for the loop only if one of the communications takes longer than the computation. Even larger delays in communication can be tolerated by executing several such processes in each processor, as in the following version. The n processes are all independent of each other, and each operates on its own local variables (data, nextdata, result).

```
parallel i = 1 to n
{ local data, nextdata, result, nextresult
  loop
  { parallel
    { input[i] ? nextdata
      nextresult := compute (data)
      output[i] ! result
    }
    data, result := nextdata, nextresult
  }
}
```

Here, every communication can be delayed by up to n computation-steps. An algorithm of this kind can be efficiently executed even in the presence of long communication-delays.

This leads directly to the conclusion that algorithms must contain large-scale parallelism. Provided that there is sufficient parallelism, we can hide delays in store-access or communication. There are, therefore, two requirements of the network. Firstly, it must be predictable in the sense that there is a known upper bound on the delay—otherwise it will not be possible to determine how many processes should be executed on each processor. Secondly, it must provide adequate capacity in relation to the processing-speed of the processing-nodes.

The concept of a universal parallel machine

We have drawn on the experiences of designing and using parallel machines in an attempt to understand how to construct general-purpose parallel machines. We now outline some recent theoretical work which establishes the concept of a universal parallel computer in the same way that the work of Alan Turing and his successors established the concept of a universal sequential computer. The results described here are due to Valiant and can be found in (Valiant 1989a).

The concept of a universal sequential computer is well understood. Firstly, Turing demonstrated the universality of the sequential (Turing-) machine. Secondly, it was shown that there is a single general-purpose Turing machine which can simulate in time $O(T log T)$ every special-purpose time-T Turing-machine. Finally, for a random-access machine the $log T$ overhead can be reduced to a constant (Cook 1973).

These results show that a general-purpose sequential machine can simulate any specialized sequential machine with constant overheads. In a well-engineered machine, the constant will be very small. This is the reason why sequential computers can use a standard architecture ensuring portability of software and making performance predictable. If a sequential computer is not designed to optimize general-purpose performance, the machine becomes much less predictable. This is particularly noticeable where random memory-access is compromised. A machine with a virtual-memory system delivers acceptable performance for simple programs which manipulate arrays (objects easily supported by paging-systems) but performs badly on list-processing.

Our theory of universal sequential computers corresponds closely to our experience of designing and using such machines. Can a similar theory be developed to guide the development of universal parallel computers? Yes! It has recently been shown (Valiant 1989a) that there is an efficient general-purpose architecture for parallel computers. We call the product pT the *operation count* corresponding to executing an algorithm in time T on a specialized p-processor machine. Then, with operation count $O(pT)$, a general-purpose machine can simulate all specialized machines provided that the algorithm to be executed has excess parallelism. The excess parallelism is needed to hide the communication-delays within the machine. In order to ensure that an algorithm can be executed efficiently on a p-processor general-purpose machine, it must have $log(p)$ excess parallelism—in other words it could be executed on a specialized machine with $plog(p)$ processors.

The need for $log(p)$ excess parallelism means that if we want to provide algorithms which can be used on machines with up to a thousand processors, they will need to have ten thousand concurrent processes. Such algorithms will run on machines with less than a thousand processors with performance scaling with the number of processors.

The excess concurrency is the price to be paid for the ability to use implementable communication-networks. Networks in which every processor is connected to every other processor have minimal delay but are not implementable for realistic numbers of processors. However, there are several networks with delay $O(log(p))$ which are implementable for large numbers of processors in current technology. One of these (the binary n-cube, or *hypercube*) also meets the requirements of overall communication capacity—this must grow as $plog(p)$. Maintaining this overall capacity requires that all of the links in the network must operate concurrently.

A binary n-cube network is formed by linking corresponding nodes of two binary $(n - 1)$-cubes. The binary 3-cube network can be thought of as a cube with nodes at each corner and links along its edges:

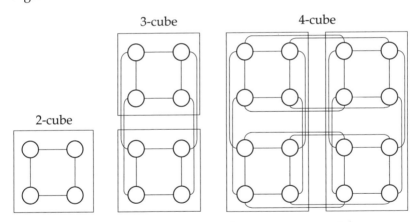

The binary n-cube network has 2^n nodes and $n \times 2^{n-1}$ links; the longest distance between any two nodes (the network 'diameter') is n links. Another way to express this is to say that a p-processor cube has diameter $log(p)$.

General-purpose parallel architectures

We have shown that there are three requirements of a general-purpose parallel machine. Firstly, there must be efficient multiprocessing within the processing-element to hide communication or memory-access delays. Secondly, there must be concurrent communication on all of the communication-links. Thirdly, the interconnection-network must support communication with *bounded* delay—otherwise it is impossible to determine the amount of excess parallelism needed to hide it.

There is also a requirement for general-purpose parallel algorithms with large-scale parallelism. I believe that the languages and algorithms for these machines will take longer to produce than the machines themselves. In fact, I believe that the machines could be built with current technology—but I doubt that there is very much software ready to exploit them.

I have not yet explained how to construct a network with bounded delay of $O(log(p))$. The p-processor hypercube has a delay of $O(log(p))$ if there are no collisions between messages. This is an unreasonable assumption, however, as all of the processors will be communicating via the network simultaneously. An important case of communication is that of performing a *permutation* in which every processor simultaneously transmits a message and no two messages head for the same destination. Valiant's proof (Valiant 1989a) demonstrates constructively that permutation-routing is possible in time $O(log(p))$ on a sparse p-node network even at maximal communication-load.

To eliminate the network hot-spots which arise commonly when messages from many different sources collide at a link in a sparse network, random routing is employed. Every message is first dispatched to a randomly-chosen intermediate destination; from the intermediate destination it continues to its final destination. This is a distributed algorithm—it does not require any central co-ordination—so it is straightforward to implement and scales easily. Randomization does not, in fact, guarantee a worst-case delivery-time of $O(log(p))$—but it does so with sufficiently high probability to achieve the universality result. The processors will occasionally be held up for a late message—but not often enough to affect performance noticeably. For example, in a 1024-node hypercube performing a permutation, the probability that all messages will have been delivered within 70 time units is 1 minus 10^{-9}. (1 time unit is the time to transmit data between two processors).

It is not clear that random routing is the only suitable technique. For example, there are several adaptive routing-schemes which attempt to route messages around hot-spots. These have the difficulty that it does not seem possible to predict their behavior. In view of the substantial effort being expended to develop high-performance networks, it is to be expected that there will be many future developments in this area. The important point is that the aim is to maximize capacity and minimize delay under heavy-load conditions—a *parallel* communications-network is a vital component of a parallel computer.

Parallel random-access machines (PRAMS)

Much of the theoretical work on universal parallel computers is based on an idealized abstract machine: the parallel random-access machine, or PRAM. A PRAM is a synchronous parallel machine in which, at each step of the computation, every processor can make an access to a common memory. However, many of the theoretical results obtained for PRAMs can be applied to machines which are not synchronous—and to machines based on message-passing rather than common-memory access. It is useful to distinguish three different types of PRAM.

In a *seclusive* PRAM, no two processors access the same memory-module in the same 'step' of the computation. The universality result applies directly to this case.

In an *exclusive* PRAM, no two processors access the same memory-location in the same step, but more than one processor may access the same memory-module. The universality result still holds, but requires that data is randomly distributed throughout the memory-modules. Certain address-hash functions can be proved to distribute data effectively enough to achieve the universality result in this case.

In a *concurrent* PRAM, more than one processor may access the same memory-location in the same step (indeed, *all* of the processors may access the same memory-location). Again, the universality result holds, but in this case the communications network must be enhanced by a *combining* capability. This combines multiple accesses to the same memory-location into a single access. This operation can also be viewed as a sorting-operation: the simultaneous accesses from all of the processors are sorted in order of their addresses with the result that accesses to the same location are grouped together. It is known that sorting the requests from p processors can be performed in $log(p)$ steps—but only at the cost of $plog(p)$ sorting elements. This is an expensive hardware-function and there have been few attempts to implement such machines; one proposal for a VLSI concurrent PRAM can be found in (Ranade 1988). An interesting recent development is the demonstration that a concurrent PRAM can be efficiently simulated by a bulk-synchronized seclusive PRAM with combining software (Valiant 1989b). A bulk-synchronized machine is one in which the processors are synchronized every few operations.

Although formulated for common-memory machines, it seems likely that many of the universality results can also be applied to message-passing machines. The seclusive PRAM is a machine in which, at every step, each processor accesses only one memory module: this is closely related to a message-passing machine in which each processor sends data to only one other processor. The exclusive PRAM allows several processors to access the same memory module in every step: this is similar to a message-passing machine in which several processors are allowed to send data to a single destination-processor. Just as data is randomly distributed to avoid collisions in an exclusive PRAM, processes can be randomly distributed in a message-passing machine. Finally, it is clear that one of the important practical uses of the concurrent PRAM is its ability to implement a broadcast operation: this is also a desirable property of a message-passing machine and requires similar implementation-techniques.

We have discussed some similarities between PRAMs and message-passing machines: what of the differences? The most important is that message-passing machines do not provide high-speed synchronization between all of the processing-elements. This means that algorithms which rely on such synchronization cannot be efficiently implemented on message-passing machines. As the technology makes it impractical to synchronize the processing-elements for every operation, it seems likely that a good compromise is to synchronize the processors every few operations; this is the *bulk-synchronized* machine proposed in (Valiant 1989b). These issues are an important topic for further research.

Before leaving this discussion of universal machines, I should point out that many existing machines—equipped with appropriate software—could be used as 'coarse-grain' universal machines. This would provide software portability between the machines *now*. As the machines evolve towards universal machines, the efficiency will increase. I believe that this would be useful in bringing together the development of general-purpose architectures, programming languages and algorithms.

Memory-access and message-passing

I have already mentioned the convergence between the common-memory machines and the distributed-memory machines. I believe that general-purpose machines must directly support *both* message-passing and common-memory-access. There are two reasons for this.

Firstly, synchronization and message-passing between processes cannot be efficiently implemented by memory read- and write-operations. Implementing the synchronization needed to detect that a message has arrived using read- and write-operations involves continually reading a location which will eventually change state to indicate that the message has arrived. This requires an unbounded number of read operations—to perform an operation which can be implemented directly in a small fixed number of operations! Transputers already provide this capability at negligible cost in hardware.

Secondly, remote memory-operations cannot be efficiently implemented by message-passing. To read or write some remote data, it should not be necessary to send a message to a remote process executed by the processor where the data is stored. Both communication and remote store-access require the existence of an efficient communication-network: a simple addition to the processing-elements would allow incoming read- and write-requests to be handled by hardware.

Can general-purpose machines be constructed in VLSI technology?

I have already described the main characteristics of VLSI technology. A wide variety of high-performance processors is already available. These include the transputer, a device which also supports on-chip multi-processing and concurrent communications. Transputers demonstrate that concurrency and communication can be efficiently implemented. A process can be created and terminated in about one microsecond—a small-enough time for a process to perform only a few operations. Interprocess communication has fixed overhead of 1.5 microseconds and a data-transfer rate of 40 megabytes per second within a transputer and 1.5 megabytes per second between transputers.

Current transputer communication-architecture provides communication between two processes on directly-connected devices. Communication between remote nodes must be implemented by software. Such software takes between ten microseconds and one millisecond for each message and takes processor-time in the intermediate transputers. Some architectures already attempt to avoid this problem by including hardware routing-chips. One example is the torus routing-chip (Dally 1988). So far, these chips are of little use, however, as they have been used with conventional sequential microprocessors which do not support efficient multiprocessing and have a high cost of message-initiation. An additional difficulty is that the routing algorithms used can give rise to network 'hot-spots'.

It is important to note that optimizing a processing-element for a parallel machine is not the same as optimizing a sequential processor. For example, most sequential processors have a large number of registers in order to optimize sequential performance. As the time taken to save and restore these registers is large, such machines do not sustain a high-enough rate of process-scheduling to hide communication and memory-access delays. Clearly, if we are trying to execute a sequential algorithm, it is reasonable to spend four times the silicon to obtain twice the sequential performance. However, if we are trying to execute a parallel algorithm, it makes more sense to spend four times the silicon on four processors—achieving four times the performance.

VLSI communications architecture

An important development for parallel computers is a VLSI implementation of a scalable communications-network with bounded delay. An obvious possibility arising from the theoretical considerations is a hypercube with randomization.

Communication-networks are discussed extensively in the literature. Network-delays can be minimized by *wormhole* routing (Dally 1988), in which a message can start to leave a network node whilst it is still entering. Another important issue is whether or not the routing algorithm can *deadlock* with messages blocking each other. Efficient deadlock-free routing algorithms are now known for a wide variety of regular networks (Dally 1987). These networks and routing algorithms are equally applicable to both processor-processor communications and processor-memory communications.

The importance of this work is easily appreciated when we consider the major purpose of parallel processing. When we use parallelism to achieve speed-up, we do so by breaking the computation into smaller sequential segments and using more processors. This increases the communication-rate needed to support the processing-rate. In VLSI, communication is relatively expensive. The result is that *communication becomes the limiting factor* determining the performance of parallel machines.

I have already remarked that, for general-purpose concurrent computers, the interconnect-capacity must grow faster than the number of processors ($p \log(p)$ for p processors). The reason for this is that in a p-processor hypercube a message typically travels to its destination via $log(p)$ communication-links. As we scale up the network, the messages are in flight longer. This means that the capacity of the network must grow as $p log(p)$. The hypercube achieves this—and its delay with randomized routing scales as $log(p)$.

At Inmos, we have recently been studying the design of VLSI communication-networks, and we have obtained some simulation results. In these, we have assumed a point-to-point link-speed of about a hundred megabits per second, giving rise to an effective data-rate of eight megabytes per second. We have also assumed a delay through a routing chip of about 250 nanoseconds. These are reasonable assumptions if the device were to be implemented in 1990.

The total rate through the network with randomized routing is shown in the graph below. The solid line shows ideal, linear scaling. The simulation shows a result only slightly less than this; it arises because the typical distance travelled differs slightly from $log(p)$.

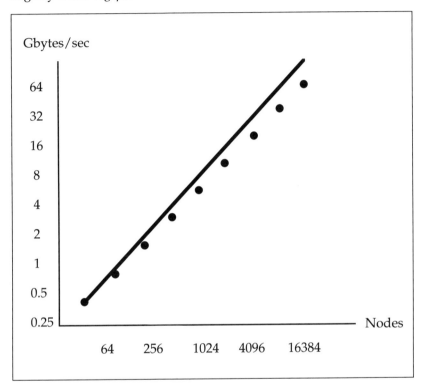

This shows that with 1024 processing-nodes, the network allows each processing-element to communicate data via the network at eight megabytes per second (in each direction). As the number of nodes scales up, the rate for each processing-element is (nearly) sustained. Furthermore, as the theory predicts, and as the next graph shows, the delay scales up logarithmically.

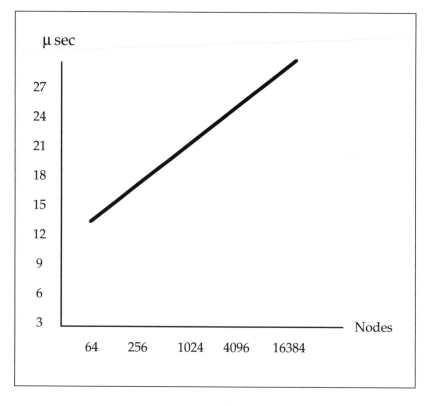

This confirms that we can use *log(p)* excess parallelism in the algorithms to hide interconnect-delay. The following graph shows the distribution of message-delay at full network load:

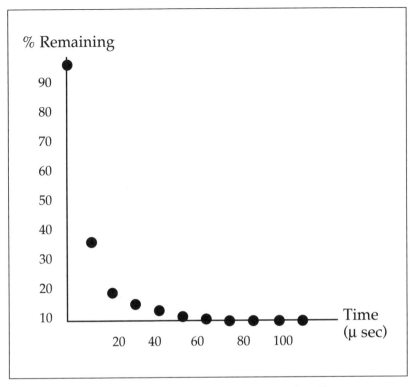

This shows the effect of randomization: nearly all messages are delivered within the first twenty microseconds; the remaining ones are delivered within sixty microseconds. With very low probability, some may take longer than this.

Scaling a VLSI hypercube

There has been some debate about whether large hypercubes are efficiently implementable in VLSI (Dally 1988). To implement the hypercube in VLSI requires it to be implemented using two-dimensional interconnections as shown in the following diagram:

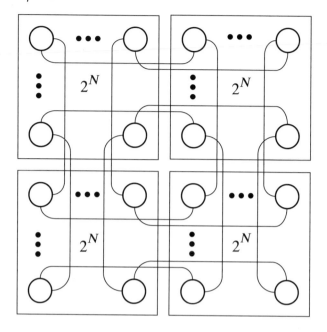

$$W = \text{width of node}$$

$$\text{wire length} = W \times \sqrt{2^N}$$

$$\text{total wire} = 4 \times W \times 2^N \times \sqrt{2^N}$$

The obvious problem is that some of the wires are very long. Long wires implemented on silicon have significant signal-propagation delays; this limits their transmission-rate. However, it is likely that the long wires would be implemented between chips (or boards) rather than on silicon. This means that they could be implemented using transmission lines which are much faster. If the signal-propagation speed in a hypercube becomes a limiting factor, there are several alternatives.

One possibility is a two- (or three-) dimensional grid. In this case, scaling can be achieved by extending the grid and simultaneously increasing the width and/or speed of the links between adjacent network nodes. This eliminates the long wires of the hypercube, minimizes the number of points in the network where wires cross each other, and results in a constant wire density throughout the interconnect. It has been shown that the randomization techniques used to eliminate network hot-spots in hypercubes can also be applied to grids (Valiant 1981).

Can we build general-purpose machines now?

Even in 1990 VLSI technology, a parallel computer capable of sustaining, say, 10^9 operations per second on a wide range of algorithms could be constructed from 1024 processing-elements connected in a hypercube. In addition to the 1024 processing elements, 1024 network-routing chips would be needed. Every processing-element would sustain about a million operations per second, and communicate (with arbitrary destinations) at about ten megabytes per second. I believe that this would be a well-balanced machine able to deliver high performance across a wide range of parallel algorithms—in contrast to, say, a vector processor which sustains high performance only on a very small range of algorithms. It is time to exploit our technology to build machines optimized for general-purpose performance rather than yet another generation of specialized machines with high performance peaks—and correspondingly deep valleys!

It is commercial, rather than technological, factors which impede the construction of general-purpose parallel computers. The first problem is that commodity processors continue to be optimized for sequential performance—and customers still expect to evaluate processors primarily on the basis of their sequential performance. The second problem is the absence of commodity message-routing chips—machines will need as many of these as processors. These factors impede the construction even of *experimental* machines—without commodity devices a 1024-processor machine is very expensive. But without the experimental machines we cannot develop the programming tools needed for a large-scale parallel computing industry.

Future problems

Although I have argued that effective general-purpose machines could be constructed now, many issues remain open. I would like to conclude by mentioning a few of them.

I have ignored developments in basic technology, and I have assumed that these machines will be constructed in commodity VLSI technology. This is deliberate: I believe that this technology will remain the dominant technology for many years. In particular, I do not expect to see computers based on superconductivity or optics in the immediate future. However, it might be attractive to use a mixed technology: perhaps using VLSI processors together with optical interconnections. Optical interconnection is rapidly becoming a commodity technology because of its use in high-speed telecommunications.

I have not discussed machines based on caches. I do not believe that machines should be designed to *rely* on cache behavior. Caches can be designed only by examining the cache behavior on a set of 'typical' algorithms. The obvious danger is that the resulting machine is good for these applications—and not very good for anything else! Caches have been very effective in providing small performance-improvements for existing sequential architectures. It is not at all clear how effective they will be in massively parallel processors.

I have stressed the importance of algorithm-development. In many application-areas, I believe that the algorithmic flexibility of general-purpose machines will enable them to outperform specialized machines. I would like to see a convincing demonstration of this.

A great deal of work on languages remains to be done. In a very short time we will have some good parallel machines. We will also have some good highly-parallel algorithms—and no general-purpose parallel language to implement them in. Five years ago, Inmos had to introduce a new language—occam—to enable specialized parallel machines to be designed and programmed. This had to be followed by proprietary extensions of C and FORTRAN. Occam could be used more generally—it can be implemented efficiently on most MIMD machines. In some respects, it is surprising that there is so little activity in producing new general-purpose languages—or extensions of standard languages—for general-purpose parallel computers.

A related issue concerning languages is the extent to which parallelizing compilers will allow existing programs to be executed on general-purpose parallel computers. I have been amazed at the developments in optimizing and parallelizing compilers over the last ten years. Such compilers are not at present effective for distributed-memory multiprocessors—perhaps they will be more effective for parallel machines with much faster communications. However, it seems to me unlikely that parallelization will ever enable us to program massively parallel machines effectively.

Finally, more theoretical work is needed. The PRAM model has provided important insights into the analysis of the behavior of parallel algorithms and parallel machines. It enables us to understand how 'general-purpose' our machines are by analyzing how effectively one machine can simulate another. However, the theoretical relationships between the PRAM model and other parallel programming-styles—such as the message-passing model—needs to be more fully explored.

References

Cook, S.A., and Reckhow, R.A.   Time-bounded random-access machine, *JCSS* 7, 354-375, 1973.

Dally, W.J. *A VLSI Architecture for Concurrent Data Structures*, Kluwer Academic, 1988.

Dally, W.J., and Seitz, C.L.   Deadlock-Free Routing in Multiprocessor Interconnection Networks, *IEEE Transactions on Computers* Vol. C-36 No. 5, 1987.

Hey, A.J.G., Pritchard, D.J., and Whitby-Strevens, C.   Multi-paradigm Parallel Programming, *Twenty-second Hawaii International Conference on System Sciences*, Vol 2, 716-725, IEEE Computer Society Press, 1987.

Hillis, W.D. *The Connection Machine*, MIT Press, 1985.

Hoare, C.A.R. Communicating Sequential Processes, *Communications of the ACM* 21 (8), 666-677, 1978.

Homewood, M., May, D., Shepherd, D., and Shepherd, R.   The IMS T800 Transputer, *IEEE Micro*, Volume 7, Number 5, October 1987.

INMOS Ltd., *Transputer reference manual*, Prentice Hall, 1988.

INMOS Ltd., *occam2 reference manual*, Prentice Hall, 1988.

Nicole, D.A. Reconfigurable Transputer Processor Architectures, *Twenty-second Hawaii International Conference on System Sciences*, Vol 1, 365-374, IEEE Computer Society Press, 1987.

Reddaway, S.F.   DAP - A Distributed Array Processor, *First Annual Symposium on Computer Architecture*, 61-65, 1973.

Ranade, A.G., Bhatt, S.N., and Johnsson, S.L. The Fluent Abstract Machine, in: *Advanced Research in VLSI*, ed. J. Allen, MIT Press, 1988.

Smith, B.J.   A Pipelined, Shared Resource MIMD Computer, *1978 International Conference on Parallel Processing*, 1978.

Valiant, L.G. *General-purpose Parallel Architectures*, TR-07-89, Aiken Computation Laboratory, Harvard University, 1989.

Valiant, L.G. *Bulk-Synchronous Parallel Computers*, TR-08-89, Aiken Computation Laboratory, Harvard University, 1989.

Valiant, L.G., and Brebner, G.J.   Universal Schemes for Parallel Communication, *ACM STOC*, 263-277, 1981.

III

PARALLELISM IN THE BRAIN

Chapter 6

COOPERATIVE COMPUTATION IN BRAINS AND COMPUTERS

MICHAEL A. ARBIB

Rana computatrix—a biological robot

In computational neurobiology, our goal is to understand a biological system, the brain, using the methodology of computer science to model the data. In neural computing—also known as neural engineering—our goal is to show how the lessons learned from the brain can guide the evolution of new computing technology. By studying brain-mechanisms which enable an animal to interact with its world, we get ideas for the design of sensorially-guided, perceptual robots. Looking at how a number of different brain-regions work together, we gain concepts to aid the design of distributed architectures for intelligent machines.

To introduce computational neurobiology, I will focus on frogs and toads as examples of 'biological robots', *i.e.*, living creatures whose behavior has properties which will suggest new ideas for the technology of robot-design. In our study of these animals, experimental analysis has been combined with computational modelling to develop *Rana computatrix* (Latin for 'the frog that computes'). As a counterpoint to this biological emphasis, the section ends with a brief example of how *Rana computatrix* has stimulated work in neural engineering.

Figure 1 gives an example of the animal's repertoire of behavior. A toad is excited by a mealworm, but in between it and the mealworm is a barrier that it can see through. What challenges our work is that the toad is able not only to recognize the mealworm as prey, but also to recognize the barrier as an obstacle, recognize the spatial relationships between them, and come up with a detour-trajectory that will carry it around the barrier to get the worm. Figure 2 samples just some of the

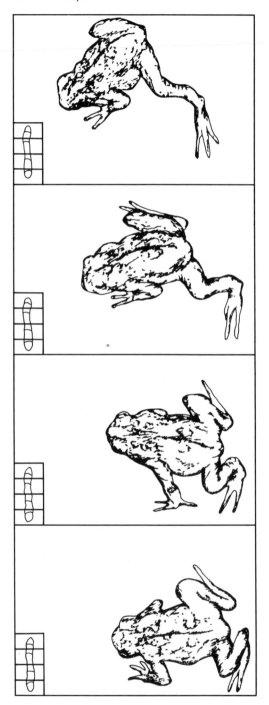

Figure 1. When a toad sees a worm behind a barrier, it will detour rather than snapping directly (Ingle 1976).

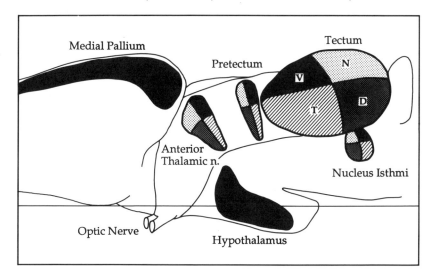

Figure 2. An anatomical overview of retinotopic projections from the left retina to the tectum, pretectum, and nucleus isthmi of the right half of the frog brain. The anterior thalamic nucleus, medial pallium and hypothalamus are implicated in habituation.

anatomical regions which subserve this behavior. We show the right eye of the frog reporting to the left brain, the most notable region of which, in this figure, is the tectum. This key area of the visual system is in the mid-brain of the animal. Noting that the forward direction of the left brain is to the left of the figure, we see a region called the pretectum in front of ('pre-') the tectum. The nucleus isthmi enters into the study of depth perception; while the hypothalamus, anterior thalamus, and medial pallium are part of the circuitry of habituation, a simple form of learning. But these are beyond the scope of this Chapter. In what follows, I will outline the analysis of the interaction between retina, tectum, and pretectum—showing both how many different parts of the brain cooperate, and how the brain cells, the neurons, interact within each part of the brain.

When we study the brain, we probe its physiology, anatomy, and neurochemistry, with some questions in mind. Believing that a part of the brain is involved in vision, we might flash visual stimuli at the animal, and use microelectrodes to measure activity of neurons in that part of the brain, and try to find correlations between stimulus and response. However, we must aim not so much to understand responses in a single region of the brain as to try to understand how many different parts of the brain cooperate to subserve a task. Therefore, we need a vocabulary in which to express the interactions between many parts of the brain at a high-level, so that we may then formulate the more detailed hypotheses about how the functions of individual neurons fit into those constituent activities.

Over the years I have thus developed a two-level methodology of modelling, complementing neural networks with functional entities called schemas, which describe basic subcomponents of some overall computation. Since my emphasis in studying *Rana computatrix* is on visuomotor coordination, the exposition will start with perceptual and motor schemas and how they interact, and then turn to work on neural networks which can implement particular schemas. This work will be constrained by two types of data: hypotheses about how schemas are played out over one or more regions of the brain are constrained by lesion data showing how the behavior of animals changes when one or more brain regions are missing. Similarly, neural network models are constrained by detailed studies of anatomy and physiology.

We start with an example of how lesion experiments can test a schema model of a simple behavior. Frogs and toads snap at small moving objects and jump away from large moving objects. Thus, our first theory of the frog brain at the level of schemas might look something like Figure 3a. One perceptual schema recognizes small moving objects, another recognizes large moving objects. The first schema activates a motor schema for approaching the prey; the latter activates a motor schema for avoiding the enemy. And these, in turn, feed the motor apparatus.

Lesion experiments can put such a model to the test. It was thought that perhaps the pretectum (that region in front of the tectum) was the locus for recognizing large moving objects. Peter Ewert lesioned pretectum and discovered that while this claim about the role of tectum may be true, the model of Figure 3a is wrong. That model would predict that an animal with lesioned pretectum would be unresponsive to large objects, but would respond normally to small objects. However, the facts are quite different. The pretectum-lesioned toad will approach any moving object at all, and does not exhibit avoidance behavior. This leads to the new schema model of Figure 3b. The perceptual schema in the pretectum does recognize large moving objects, but the tectum contains a schema not for small moving objects, but one which will recognize any moving object. We then add that activity of the pretectal schema not only triggers the avoid motor schema but also inhibits approach. This new schema model does fit the lesion data, since removal of the pretectum removes inhibition, and so the animal will now approach any moving object.

Is it the real frog that has schemas in it, or just the artificial frog-models? My claim is that schemas are as real as any theoretical entity, such as gravity and electrons. But just as

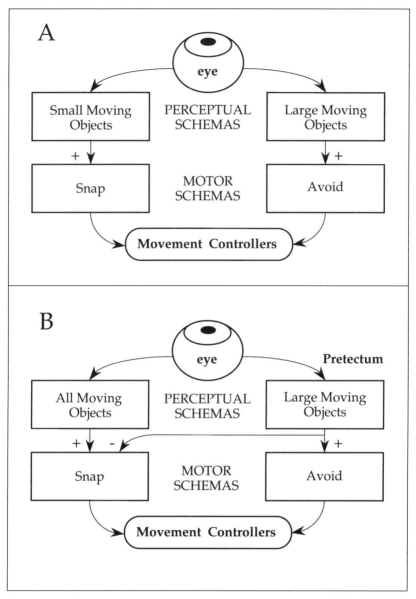

Figure 3 . (a) The 'naive' schema program for the toad's snapping and avoidance behavior.   (b) The schema program revised in light of data on the effect of lesioning the pretectum.

physical theory has evolved over the years so that our notion of what is real changes accordingly, so too will our theory of schemas as meaningful units of functional analysis change over the years.   What makes this more than a game of 'artificial realities' is that our scientific concepts evolve under the pressure of the pragmatic criterion in which models expressed in theory-language are brought as far as possible into a harmonious whole with observations expressed in observation-language (Hesse 1980; Arbib and Hesse 1986). Both these languages may evolve in the process. The brain is as real at the level of interacting schemas and brain regions as it is in terms of the fine details of interacting neural networks. But having said that, let me give a sample of interacting neural networks.

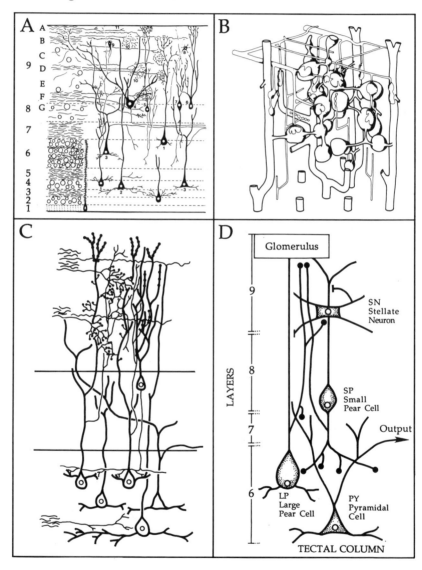

Figure 4a is not meant to be comprehensible at a glance. It is a classic picture from the Hungarian neuroanatomists Székely and Lázár (1976), of the neuroanatomy of the frog tectum. It uses a method called Golgi anatomy which stains only a random subset of neurons in the tissue, but does let us visualize all the ramifications of each stained cell. All we need note here is that neurons have intricate shapes. Surely a goal of computational neurobiology must be to understand how those shapes allow these cells to play distinctive roles in the economy of the tectum. But this light-microscope anatomy is not detailed enough to tell us about the fine details of connections between the neurons. For this we might turn to Figure 4b, reconstructed from the electron microscope. What might have at first seemed a little process coming out of a cell in Figure 4a is seen to have branches, wonderful shapes, invaginations, splashes and splotches. What do the fine details of these synapses, these cellular connection-points, mean?

This is where you make a career decision. You either say: 'I am going to devote the rest of my life to synaptology, and try to understand what's going on here, and I will never think about behavior or thought again', or you say 'I really want to understand how brains allow animals to behave, humans to think', and you backtrack—seeking ways to simplify this picture, rather than complicate it, to begin to model how it is that the various pieces might fit together. This is the path I have chosen. In judicious consultation with anatomists and physiologists, my colleagues and I pick just a few of the cells for inclusion in our

---

Figure 4   (left)
(a) Diagrammatic representation of the lamination and the representative types of neurons of the optic tectum. Numbers on the left indicate the different tectal layers. The numbered cell-types included in the model of part (d) are: (1) SP, the large pear-shaped neuron with dendritic appendages and ascending axon; (3) PY: the large pyramidal neuron with efferent axon; (6) SP: small pear-shaped neurons with ascending axons; and (8) SN: stellate neurons. Cell types omitted in (d) are (2) the large pear-shaped neuron with dendritic collaterals; (4) the large tectal ganglionic neuron with efferent axon; (5) small pear-shaped neurons with descending axons; (7) bipolar neuron; (9) amacrine cell; (10) optic terminals; and (11) assumed evidence of diencephalic fibers.
(b) Details of synaptic interaction of dendritic appendages, which exceed current models in intricacy.
(c) Schematic for a tectal column.
(d) Neurons and synaptology of the model of the tectal column. The numbers at the left indicate the different tectal layers. The glomerulus comprises the LP and SP dendrites and recurrent axons as well as optic and diencephalic terminals. The LP excites the PY, the SN, and the GL, and is inhibited by the SN. The SP excites the LP and PY cells, and it sends recurrent axons to the glomerulus; it is inhibited by the SN. The SN is excited by LP neurons and diencephalic fibres and it inhibits the LP and SP cells. The PY is activated by the LP, SP, and optic fibres, and is the efferent neuron of the tectum.
Figures a,b,c are from Székely and Lázár 1976; while d is after Lara, Arbib and Cromarty (1982).

basic circuitry, throw away much of the beautiful geometry (not without regret, not without a whispered promise to return to it when the time seems ripe to extend the details of our model), and set up differential equations to describe the cellular dynamics— and show that, yes, certain basic properties of animal behavior can be explained with these simplified neural networks.

Our strategy is to maintain models at a level which aids us in understanding behavior. Sometimes these models are simply in terms of interacting schemas; in other cases those schemas will be explicated in terms of relatively simple neural networks. Then as the years go by, and our computing power becomes greater, we can expand the number of schemas to explain a richer range of behavior, and expand the detail of the neurons to catch more subtleties of the schemas' internal processing.

With this background, we will briefly examine a two-part example of how we capture some interesting behavioral properties in simple neural networks. Figure 4d (Lara, Arbib and Cromarty 1982) shows our tectal column: a simplified network (suggested by the choice of essential elements as pictured in 4c by Székely and Lázár) which represents a sample of the cells found in a vertical penetration of the frog tectum. The glomerulus is a twining together of neural fibers. Both the large pear cell (LP) and small pear cell (SP) send excitatory signals back to the glomerulus, to engage in a pattern of self-excitation where their own activity is fed back to increase that activity even further. Left to itself, this recurrent excitation would build up excitation to the point that eventually the conjoint activity of LP and SP can trigger an output from the pyramidal cell (PY). However, this can be blocked by the 'villain of the piece', the stellate neuron (SN). This inhibitory neuron can gain sustenance from the excitatory loop and try to reduce, try to inhibit, the recurrent activity. With parametric analysis, we were able to set the time constants and connection strengths to obtain a network that underlies the behavior of facilitation observed in real frogs by Ingle (1975). If you show a worm to a frog for a third of a second, there is no response, but presentation for two thirds of a second would be enough to yield a response. However, if you present the worm for a third of a second, take it away for two or three seconds, then show it again for another third of a second, the animal will respond the second time. The first subthreshold stimulation facilitates a response to the second. Build-up of activity within the network provides the short-term memory for two or three seconds that can allow that new brief presentation of the stimulus to yield a different response.

To proceed further, we develop the idea that the tectum (like many other parts of the brain) can, at least to a first approximation, be represented as an array or tiling of local units.

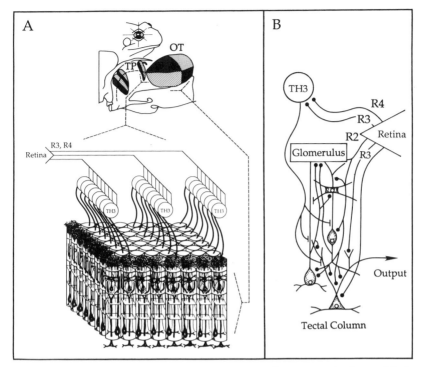

Figure 5. Interactions among retina, optic tectum and pretectum in the model of Cervantes-Perez, Lara and Arbib 1985. The retina sends fibres in a retinotopical fashion to both optic tectum (class R2, R3 and R4), and pretectum (class R3 and R4). (A) TH3 neurons also project retinotopically to the optic tectum. For simplicity we only show the projection of three rows of TH3 cells projecting upon the tectal columns. (B) A closer look at the interactions among retinal, tectal and pretectal cells. The TH3 cell of the pretectal column inhibits LP, SP and PY of the tectal column corresponding to its retinotopic projection.

To model such an array, then, we complement the description of the unit by specifying the interactions between the units, and then try to understand how processes are spread out over the architecture. The second (and last) neural network model of *Rana computatrix* that I will present here models the tectum by an 8.x.8 array of the tectal columns of Figure 4d, augmented by a very simple model of the pretectum (Figure 5; Cervantes-Perez, Lara, and Arbib, 1985). To see what the model explains, we look at further data of Peter Ewert (Figure 6). He exposed the toad to three types of stimulus: 'worms' (rectangles moving along their long axis), 'antiworms' (rectangles moving orthogonal to their long axis), and squares. The result was a parametric description of the animal's behavior. It responds better and better to longer and longer worms, it does not snap at any but the shortest antiworms, and there is a 'tug of war' between the two dimensions in determining the response to the square. We were able to show that the model of Figure 5 could be so tuned that the tectum could mediate response to movement extended in either direction, while the pretectal cells would respond best to objects elongated in the antiworm direction (antiworms or squares) and inhibit the tectum accordingly to exhibit pyramidal cell output whose firing rate correlated well with the rate of behavioral response shown in Figure 6.

Our study of *Rana computatrix* exemplifies two levels of modelling of brains: one at the functional level of interacting schemas which eventually makes contact with anatomical

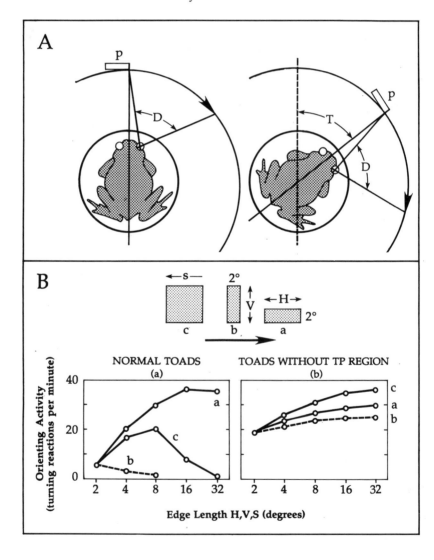

A

B

NORMAL TOADS
(a)

TOADS WITHOUT TP REGION
(b)

Orienting Activity
(turning reactions per minute)

Edge Length H,V,S (degrees)

hypotheses that can be tested by lesions; the other shows how particular pieces of brain can carry out their functions in terms of neural networks which often have a regular structure, as shown in the last example. Let me just mention one of the many other examples (for a full selection of data and models, see Ewert and Arbib 1989). Arbib and House (1987) gave a model of detour behavior which provides a quasi-neural network which explains how the animal can detour around a fence. Ron Arkin (1989) used this 'toad brain', essentially, as part of the controller for a mobile robot. Conventional AI techniques enabled the robot to plan its path, using a map of its environment. However, if an obstacle such as a graduate student would appear as the robot was navigating along this path, it would use the parallel computing algorithm we had from the toad brain to detour around the obstacle and then get back on the path afterwards. This provides an interesting case-study of how thinking about brain-modelling may help us in developing artificial intelligence.

Cooperative computation

Rather than think of computation as serial—here's the next step, here's the next step, do a test to decide what to do next—we are concerned now with a new paradigm in which computation is distributed across the interaction of many systems. In this approach—which I shall call cooperative computation—the key question is how local interaction of systems can be integrated to yield some overall result without explicit executive control. Here, the term 'cooperative computation' is really a shorthand for 'computation based on the competition and cooperation of concurrently-active agents'. It is the pattern of 'strengthened alliances' between mutually consistent hypotheses about aspects of a problem that represent the overall solution to a problem, as hypotheses which do not meet the evolving (data-guided) consensus lose activity. We shall see many examples of this interplay between cooperation and competition as we explore a variety of examples of cooperative computation in the following pages.

Our study of *Rana computatrix* gives us two grains of cooperative

---

Figure 6.   Prey-catching orienting behavior to different configurations of the stimulus.   A) Turning reaction to the stimulus presentation.   Note that D, the effective angular displacement of the stimulus, differs from T, the angle of turning movements.   B) Orienting activity to three stimulus-configurations, horizontal ('worm': type a) and perpendicular ('anti-worm': type b) rectangles, and squares (type c).   B(a) A normal animal's response becomes more frequent when we increase the dimension (H) of a stimulus of type a, whereas response-frequency rapidly drops to zero when we increase the dimension (V) of a type b stimulus, and a combination of these two responses is obtained when we increase both dimensions of stimulus type c.   B(b) This discrimination is lost in toads with pretectal lesions (from Ewert 1976).

computation: the fine-grain style in which many processes work in parallel to process some array of information; and a coarse-grain style, where relatively diverse systems—our schemas—interact. Incidentally, schema theory has much in common with what is now being done under the headings of concurrent object-oriented programming (Yonezawa and Tokoro 1987) and distributed artificial intelligence (Gasser and Huhns, 1989). What gives our approach its special flavor is that when we think about the brain, we want to understand to what extent the schemas can be localized in the brain or implemented in neural networks. With this, we turn to a crucial analogy between cooperative computation in neural networks and 'cooperative phenomena' as studied by physicists, in which the statistical properties of atoms or molecules 'cooperate' to yield properties of bulk matter which appear quite novel in terms of the properties of a few atoms considered in isolation.

Back in the 1950s, Cragg and Temperley (1954), a neuroanatomist and a physicist, observed that the formation of patterns across the cerebral cortex might well be compared to the formation of domains of magnetization in a magnet—regions in which the atomic magnets line up with one predominant direction of the magnetization. Perhaps the first person to really develop this analogy was Bela Julesz, who offered a cooperative computation model of depth perception. Figure 7a (from his beautiful book, *Foundations of Cyclopean Perception*, 1971) shows two arrays of spring-coupled magnets. One array of magnets is driven by the left eye, the other by the right. The orientation of each magnet encodes the depth of the corresponding point in the visual field. Julesz showed how to couple the magnets both within and across the two arrays to have the resultant orientation constitute a coherent hypothesis for the actual depths of the objects which stimulated the two retinas. It is not my point here to go into the explanation of this, but simply to exhibit it as the first concrete attempt to take some of the notions of statistical mechanics and carry them in to the modelling of an interesting perceptual phenomenon. This was carried even further by the effect of hysteresis (Figure 7b). If you are looking at two points, one projecting to each eye, they have to be very close in where they project before you can fuse them and see them as one. However, once you fuse them, if you now move them apart, you will see them as one for a much longer range. This is hysteresis: there is no single-valued function from separation of stimuli on the two eyes to whether or not fusion is achieved. Rather, there is a history-dependent curve. In the ensuing years, a number of people, such as Parvati Dev (1975) in my group and Marr and Poggio (1977) at MIT, began to build neural models that rationalized the

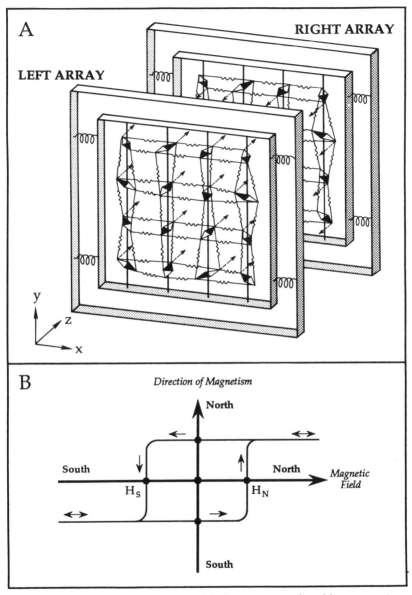

Figure 7. (a) Julesz's imaginative model of stereopsis mediated by cooperative computation in two arrays of spring-linked magnetic dipoles. Interaction between magnets may solve the correspondence problem by forming regions of coherent orientation to encode segments at a given depth.
(b) An example of a hysteresis cycle, plotting the direction of magnetization of a piece of iron against the magnitude of an external magnetic field. Because the magnetic field must flip each atomic magnet against the cooperative effect of interaction with those that remain unflipped, the field which induces a South-North transition, HN, is much larger than the reversal field HS.

rather fanciful interactions of Figure 7a; while, Erich Harth and his colleagues (*e.g.*, Harth, Csermely, Beek, and Lindsay, 1970) developed neural-net models that explicitly exhibited hysteresis. Now in the 80s, we see a large number of physicists moving into this area, to use sophisticated methods, from the study of what are called spin glasses, to further analyze neural networks.

However, rather than pursue models of depth perception and related types of functioning, I want to briefly give an example of learning—briefly, because in the chapter by Edelman and Reeke, and also in that by Merzenich, we will be given a superb view of what we know about synaptic plasticity and how we can use it in interesting computations. The example I will give is a classic model of development of feature-detectors developed by Christoph von der Malsburg back in 1973. Hubel and Wiesel had discovered that there were cells in the visual cortex that seemed to be tuned for the orientation of a visual stimulus. In other words, a cell would respond best to a bar stimulus only if it were presented in a particular place in the visual field and with a particular orientation. A nearby cell would respond better to a somewhat different orientation. How could that come about?

Hubel and Wiesel worked with monocular occlusion, covering up one eye of an animal, and then found that later no cells could be driven by edges viewed through the eye that had been covered up during this critical period of development. One hypothesis consistent with this was that while there is a genetic program that wires up everything correctly, if you don't use it, you lose it. However, Hirsch and Spinelli showed that the situation was more subtle than this. They gave a kitten different inputs through the two eyes. The animal wore goggles with patterns on a translucent background. One eye saw a bulls-eye pattern, the other saw three stripes. After the animal had lived awhile with only this restricted visual experience, Hirsch and Spinelli measured the activity of brain cells, and found essentially no edge detectors—but there were bulls-eye detectors driven by one eye, and three-bar detectors driven by the other. That got rid of the genetic pre-programming notion. However, as so often happens in neuroscience, each hypothesis turns out to be part of the truth. The finding by Imbert and Buisseret (1975) that certain visual neurons of the immature kitten are aspecific, some immature and some already specific in their receptive fields (see also Frégnac and Imbert, 1978) shows that genetics gives a rough sketch of the connectivity, and then experience tunes it, and in some cases greatly modifies it.

Synaptic competition and plasticity play a crucial role in this experiential tuning. Figure 8 shows the ideas of Christoph von der Malsburg (1973). Donald Hebb (1949) gave, in his book *The Organization of Behavior*, one of the key concepts of theoretical

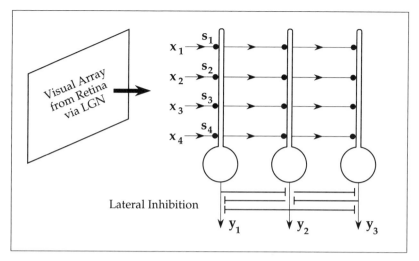

Figure 8. Hebbian synapses are augmented by normalization and lateral inhibition in the adaptive feature detectors of von der Malsburg 1973.

neurophysiology, now called the Hebb synapse: his idea was that learning would occur if synapses could automatically strengthen themselves to record associations, strengthening a connection on to a cell whenever that input helps fire the cell. In other words, if input x_i is positive (there is an active input on the ith line), and output y is positive (the cell is responding), Hebb's rule is to strengthen the corresponding connection, *i.e.*, increase the synaptic weight s_i. The trouble with this original Hebb model is that every synapse will eventually get stronger and stronger till they all saturate, thus destroying any selectivity of association. Von der Malsburg's solution was to normalize the synapses impinging on a given neuron. First compute the Hebbian contribution, and then you divide this by the total of putative synaptic weights to get the final result, *i.e.*, if Hebb would say Δs_i should equal $k x_i y$, then the normalization rule replaces s_i by

$$(s_i + \Delta s_i) / \Sigma_j (s_j + \Delta s_j)$$

where the summation j extends over all inputs to the neuron. Thus this new rule not only increases the strength of those synapses whose inputs were most strongly correlated with the cell's activity, it also decreases the synaptic strengths of other connections to these cells in which such correlations did not arise.

However, another problem is that a lot of nearby cells may, just by chance, all have initial random connectivity which makes them easily persuadable by the same stimulus. Or the same pattern might occur many times before a new pattern was experienced by the network. In either case, many cells would become tuned to the same pattern, with not enough cells left to learn important and distinctive patterns. To solve this von der Malsburg introduced lateral inhibition into his model of cortical plasticity. This is the connectivity pattern in which activity in any one cell is distributed laterally (*i.e.*, to all sides) to reduce (partially inhibit) the activity of nearby cells. This ensures that if one cell—call it A—were active, its connections to nearby cells would make them less active, and so make them less likely to learn, by Hebbian synaptic adjustment, those patterns that most excite A.

In summary: initially, the inputs are pretty much randomly connected to the cells of the processing layer. As a result, none of these cells is particularly good at pattern-recognition. However, by sheer statistical fluctuation of the synaptic connections, one will be slightly better at responding to a pattern than others were; it will thus slightly strengthen those synapses which allow it to fire for that pattern; through lateral inhibition, this will make it less easy for cells initially less well-tuned for that pattern to become tuned to it. Thus, without any teacher, this network automatically organizes itself so that each cell becomes tuned for an important cluster of information in the sensory inflow.

In this early paper of von der Malsburg's, one can see the ideas of Edelman's *Neural Darwinism* in miniature. The cortical cells form a repertoire of feature detectors. The one that is initially the best (but still a poor) detector for a cluster of patterns has its synapses tuned, by a process of Hebbian learning plus normalization, by repeated exposure to these patterns so that it becomes a finely-tuned feature-detector responding vigorously to patterns in or near that cluster. Edelman would emphasize the initial predisposition and so speak of the learning process as one of selection; others would note that the process of synaptic adjustment changes the cell so much that we cannot think of a detector that is already adequate being simply selected from a pre-existing repertoire. Whatever the terminological choice, these ideas play an important role in our understanding of development and learning in natural and artificial networks. Rumelhart and Zipser (1985) give a useful overview of this topic under the title *Feature Discovery by Competitive Learning*.

Learning in neural networks

I defer further discussion of synaptic plasticity to the Chapters by Edelman and Reeke and by Merzenich. Here I want simply to acknowledge the fact that the current immense excitement about neural networks as a technology is driven, in no small part, by the notion that we can make neural networks learn things 'by themselves'. The Hebb synapse and its refinements provide a way for getting a neural network to organize itself without a teacher so that particular neurons will learn salient features of the environment. Other approaches are needed for learning with a teacher. To learn to recognize a letter A, the network must be shown many patterns and told by a 'teacher' which is a letter A, and which is not a letter A.

The *perceptron* was introduced by Rosenblatt (1962) as a way to use error-correction to train a neural network to respond to a specific set of patterns. Much of the original work focused on the 'simple perceptron'. It had just one output neuron that sampled the results of preprocessing to come up with its classification (Figure 9). If the output neuron gave the right response, the synaptic connections were to remain unchanged. If it gave the wrong response, the error-correction rule would modify the synapses to make the neuron more likely to respond correctly to that pattern. But if there are many different pattern-examples, adjustment for the current pattern might mess up the learning for the previous patterns.

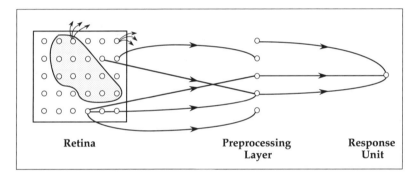

Figure 9. A simple perceptron

All that could be recognized by a simple perceptron were patterns that were *linearly separable* in terms of the preprocessing units. More formally, if a pattern on the retina is transformed into an array $(x_1, x_2, ..., x_d)$ of 'feature values' by the array of preprocessing units, then a simple perceptron could discriminate two sets of patterns only if there exist weights $w_1, w_2, ..., w_d$ and threshold q for the perceptron's output unit such that

$$w_1x_1 + w_2x_2 + ... + w_dx_d \geq q$$

for patterns in the first class, and

$$w_1x_1 + w_2x_2 + ... + w_dx_d < q$$

for patterns in the second class. The Perceptron Convergence Theorem said that *if* there is a setting of the synaptic weights and threshold that will make a simple perceptron correctly classify a given training set of patterns, *then* the perceptron error-correction rule will, after repeated presentation of all the patterns, finally converge on a setting of weights in which all the patterns in the training set are correctly classified.

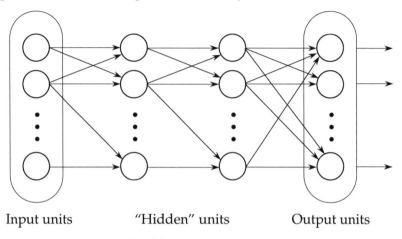

Input units   "Hidden" units   Output units

Figure 10. A network with hidden units.

The catch was the 'if'. If the training set of patterns is linearly separable, a simple perceptron can be trained to classify the patterns correctly. Minsky and Papert (1969) gave a number of elegant theorems showing how complex the preprocessing layer would have to be if a simple perceptron were to linearly separate members of a class of patterns from non-members. In recent years, various techniques, such as the Boltzmann machine (Hinton, Sejnowski, and Ackley 1984) and the back-propagation algorithm, have been devised for taking multi-layered networks of perceptrons (Figure 10) and finding ways of not only correcting the output units in terms of the observed error between their actual output and their desired output, but also of apportioning blame back into the network to train the hidden units. For example, back-propagation (Rumelhart, Hinton, and Williams 1986) is based on the discovery that gradient descent on an error-function defined as a function of all the adjustable synaptic weights in the networks is essentially equivalent to having each neuron pass back to those that provide its input a message saying 'If I'm wrong and you have a strong input to me, then you're greatly in error too; whereas, if I am wrong and you only have a weak input to me, then your error is so much the less'. In this way, error-messages propagate back to correct units further and further from the outputs. There are no rigorous convergence theorems for back-propagation, just the empirical finding that training of multi-layer nets can be carried out in many interesting cases, at least for small problems.

Such results on trainability of a far larger class of networks than the simple perceptrons—thus automating the recognition of classes of patterns that are not linearly separable—have been the source of much of the excitement over neural computing since the mid-1980s, and some people talk as if this is the end of computer science as we know it—suggesting that, in the future, we will not have to write explicit programs to get computers to do what we want. Instead, we will simply build a neural net, show it a few examples, and let it form the right connections to automatically solve the problem! I am skeptical of this claim. Consider the idea of a 'Shakespeare detector'. You provide 'to be or not to be' as input and train the network so that its output will be 'Shakespeare'. You give it a hundred lines from different poets, and see if thereafter it can classify other lines of all these poets correctly. Even if a setting of the weights in a network exists to do the job (our human brain's network of 10^{15} connections may provide the existence proof) there is no guarantee that the learning rule will find them quickly enough to be of practical use—'If you want a sweetheart in the spring, don't get an amoeba and wait for it to evolve' (McCulloch, Arbib and Cowan 1962). To get the system to converge under appropriate feedback to the desired solution will often require that it have initial structure that enables learning to tune a solution in a limited time, rather than creating it from an unlimited search space.

My dismissal of inflated claims for neural networks should not be seen as denigrating attempts to find applications of neural networks in more restricted areas of visual preprocessing, speech recognition, robot control, and so on. The study of neural networks has a long tradition, and while its 'rediscovery' around 1984 was accompanied by much hyperbole, the community that has since evolved has shown its willingness to learn from the earlier literature, and to incorporate into its thinking the lessons of a number of cognate disciplines such as control theory, statistical pattern-recognition theory, complexity theory, and statistical mechanics, as well as learning how to build hybrid systems which can exploit neural networks in tandem with, say, other techniques of artificial intelligence. It is in this spirit that I advocate the language of schemas to provide a top-down specification language to complement the use of adaptive neural networks. All my talk about schemas and interacting brain regions is meant to motivate a view which positions learning within a network of structured systems. While there are many technical applications where one stand-alone network can do the job, such as fingerprint- or voice-recognition, for complex problems we are going to have to program a network of interacting schemas, and program the initial structure of those schemas we build as neural nets.

Schemas for vision

This kind of network underlies the architecture of the VISIONS system developed by Hanson and Riseman and their colleagues at the University of Massachusetts. At the low level are processes of the kind that we can now implement in highly parallel hardware that embodies algorithms very much in the spirit of neural networks. Such processes as depth perception, motion perception, texture segmentation, shape-from-shading and so on, take the image and extract and describe regions which, because of their movement or depth or distinctive texture, are candidates for interpretation as meaningful surfaces in the scene represented by that image. But the meaning of the objects which underlie those surfaces does not enter into this low-level processing. The intermediate level provides a symbolic representation of the fruits of low-level vision, describing each region in terms of such features as shape, size, color, motion, and position in the image. Where low-level vision has a relatively close correspondence between neurons and pixels (picture elements), the intermediate representation provides symbolic 'hooks' for high-level processes. It is in high-level vision that knowledge of the objects of the world is brought to bear—the interacting schemas which encode recognition routines for houses and walls and trees and roadways and motor-cars, providing the processes to grab the different regions and come up with the overall interpretation of the image. I want to make three points about this architecture.

The first point is that different sources of information have different strengths and weaknesses, so that a successful system must be able to exploit cooperation between different sources. For example, depth is one good cue for separating figure from ground, but motion (when it is available) is a better cue. If you are in the forest, a sudden movement can make an animal visible—thus enabling a deer hunter to shoot other deer hunters, for example. One recent example of such cooperative mechanisms is given by Poggio, Little and Gamble (1988), using the Connection Machine described in Chapter 10 by David Waltz. Color, texture, edge extraction, motion and stereo, are all powerful cues for segmenting an image. For each such cue, they implement a neural-net-like structure, a Markov random field, to conduct segmentation on the Connection Machine, which will take the local cue. As many of us have noted (Arbib 1981a, Geman and Geman 1984), it is desirable to design cooperation between processes using nearest-neighbor interactions to grow regions and processes that line up nearby candidates for edges. Poggio *et al.* (Figure 11) couple the different segmentation estimates indirectly by coupling each of them to a network computing brightness-edges to coordinate the use of the different cues to segment the image.

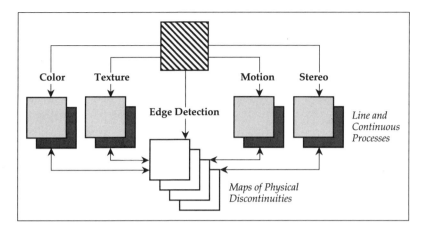

Figure 11. Cooperation with brightness-based edge estimates can improve the accuracy of diverse networks for region-growing each based on its own distinctive cue. (Poggio, Little and Gamble 1988).

The second point is that this type of thinking about low-level machine vision is now entering the vocabulary of neuroscience. Progress in machine vision is changing the way the neuro-physiologist thinks about brain-mechanisms. A notable example of this is a review paper in *Trends in Neuroscience* by DeYoe and Van Essen (1988; see also Arbib and Hanson 1987). We now understand there are many visual systems in the primate brain (compare the analysis of the brain given in Goldman-Rakic's Chapter), with distinguishable pathways—but, of course, with some cooperation between them—feeding into the parietal areas, which seem to be involved in the 'where' of things, and feeding into the inferotemporal areas, which are involved in the 'what' of things (Figure 12). We see many specialized regions. In some cases, two processors may be implemented as two subregions interdigitated within one chunk of brain. In other cases, different processors will be implemented in distinct regions of brain with their own specialization. Thus, there is *not* one place in the brain holding the intermediate visual representation. Rather, we have a network of specialized representations which must cooperate with each other. This leads me to emphasize again what sort of computer the brain is: it is a network of specialized subsystems forming distinguishable subnetworks which pass messages to one

INFEROTEMPORAL AREAS   PARIETAL AREAS
"What"   "Where"

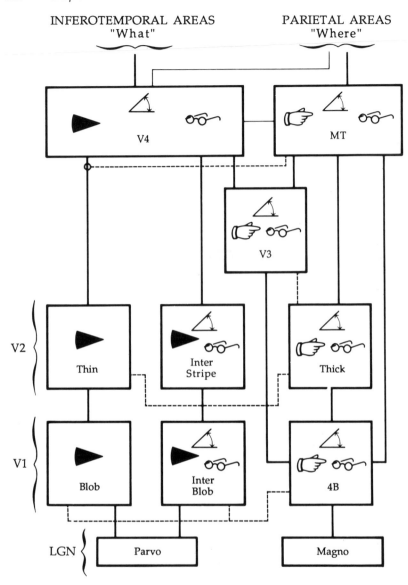

Figure 12 (left). The parvocellular cells of LGN feed two streams, the P-B (parvo-blob) stream at left, and P-I (parvo-interblob) stream in the middle. The magnocellular cells of LGN feed the M (magno) stream shown at right. Among the cues for the 'what' system (inferotemporal areas) are those of three-dimensional form—shape, size and rigidity—and of intrinsic surface properties—color, shininess, texture, and transparency. Cues for 'where' (parietal areas) include both static spatial relations—location and orientation relative to the observer and other objects—and the way in which the object is moving. These different properties can cooperate. Various cortical areas are marked with icons which denote sensitivities of cells in the region. Solid cone: At least 40% of cells have tuned and or opponent wavelength selectivity; angle: at least 20% of cells have orientation selectivity; spectacles: at least 20% of cells have binocular disparity selectivity and/or strong binocular interactions; hand: at least 20% of cells have selectivity for direction of motion. Thick lines indicate robust primary connections; thin lines indicate weaker, more variable connections; while dashed lines indicate connections that have been observed but need additional verification. (After DeYoe and Van Essen, 1988.)

---

another so that overall they can cooperate to find the right solution.[*] In one particular situation, color may be the most salient cue so that one particular subsystem of the brain will be very active, with other parts of the brain relatively quiet. In other cases, different cues, and thus brain regions, will predominate. It will probably be only when we are pushing the limits of our perception that activity of all these regions will be invoked together.

My last point about vision takes us from the orchestration of parallel neural net processing of specialized parts of low-level vision to high-level vision. Here insights come from the neurological clinic (Marshall 1987) but here let me look at clues that come from computer vision. Figure 13a shows a segmentation of a house scene highlighting a region that was given a high confidence value by an instance of the sky schema. Unfortunately the segmentation missed an edge so that when the wall schema looked for a region beneath the roof with rectangular cutouts, it classified that same region as a wall. In the particular system implemented in 1984, the solution was to resegment the region in contention at a finer grain. Figure 13b shows the finer segmentation. Instances of the sky and wall schemas can now compete

---

[*] One of the most persuasive current proponents of this view is Minsky (1985) who espouses a 'Society of Mind' analogy in which the 'members of society' play a role analogous to my schemas. Intriguingly, after his Ph.D. thesis on neural networks (Minsky, 1956 is based on Chapter II), Minsky became one of the strongest proponents of the 'intelligence must be serial' approach to artificial intelligence (Minsky and Papert 1969 did much to suggest a rigorous foundation for this view) and my paper (Arbib 1977) was based on a conference presentation in which I argued against the ideas on seriality presented in a talk by Minsky at that same conference. Yet within a year of that conference, Minsky was publicly espousing the ideas on distributed computing that culminated in his 1985 volume.

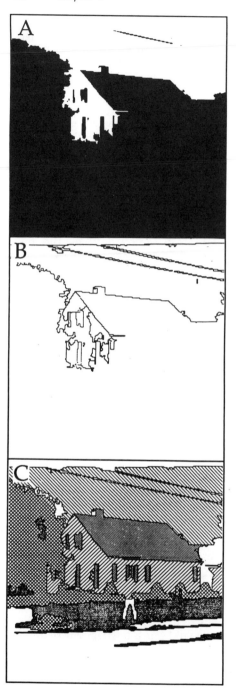

Figure 13 After segmentation of a house scene, the region shown in (a) can be interpreted as either wall or sky. When it is segmented more finely as in (b), the new segments are easily assignable to one or other of these two categories, yielding the correct interpretation. This is shown in (c) where different shading codes for sky, roof, wall, shutters, foliage and grass.

over just these regions (recall that cooperative computation involves competition as well as cooperation), and quickly yield their contribution to the final interpretation shown in Figure 13c.

There is no simple one-way flow of information from low-level to high-level. Rather, there is continual feedback from high to low as requests from the high-level adjust low-level processing to meet the current demands of scene interpretation. Harth (1988) is among those offering models of the analogous situation in real brains, trying to make sense of the fact that there are more fibers in the brain going down from visual cortex to the way-station in the thalamus than come up from thalamus carrying messages from retina to cortex.

Sixth generation computers

Part I of this volume provides an appreciation of how computer scientists are looking at parallel computation. It shows what can be done with transputers, hypercubes, and supercomputers. However, the ideas presented in this Chapter point beyond a uniform architecture for a general-purpose parallel machine to a new, Sixth Generation, (Arbib 1987a), architecture based on networks of specialized machines interacting in diverse ways to solve very complex problems of interacting with the world, in the style of the brain. The Japanese defined the Fifth Generation in terms of logic programming using semi-parallel inference machines, marrying the 'state of the art' in AI software (*e.g.*, expert systems) to appropriately-engineered hardware (*e.g.*, MIMD hypercubes). The development of Sixth Generation systems will be heavily influenced by discoveries concerning information-processing in the brain.

Since billions of human brains already exist, the goals of such computer design must be to develop computers that complement brain-function, rather than simply emulate it. Thus the field of neural computing must seek not to copy the brain, but to look for promising contributions from neural nets, physics, and 'classic' computer science. There is no ready-made body of wisdom in neuroscience waiting to be applied. Thus we cannot simply follow the 'neural blueprint' to build a better computer. Rather, fundamental research in neuroscience must continue, but now structured to extract key principles of information-processing that can enter into the design of the next generation of computers, building, for example, on the interaction between neuroscientists and AI workers in vision, sketched in the previous section.

I argue that Sixth Generation systems will be characterized by:

(1) Cooperative computation (the computer will be a heterogeneous network of special-purpose and general-purpose subsystems);

(2) Perceptual robotics (increasingly, computers will have intelligent perceptual and motor interfaces with the surrounding world); and

(3) Learning (any of the subsystems will be implemented as adaptive 'neural style' networks).

Let me address each of these points in turn.

Cooperative computation. Inspiration from the brain leads away from emphasis on a single universal machine towards a device composed of different structures, just as the brain may be divided into cerebellum, hippocampus, motor cortex, etc. Thus we can expect to contribute to neural computing as we come to better chart the special power of each structure. Subsystems will include general-purpose engines and special-purpose machines some of which (such as the front ends for perceptual processors, and devices for matrix manipulation) will be highly parallel.

Perceptual robotics. Just as the interface to computers has progressed from bits to symbols to interactive graphics, the next generation will be more 'action-oriented' with computers including robotic actuators and multi-modal intelligent interfaces among their subsystems. Such computers will 'grow' with the design of new subsystems using, *e.g.*, silicon compilers to specify new chips, and mechotronics for integrated design of robotic subsystems and their controllers. The design of these perceptual robotic systems will be heavily influenced by the analysis of neural mechanisms for perception and the control of movement.

Learning. Sixth Generation computers will be machines that learn, with principles of adaptive programming that incorporate lessons from brain theory and AI. Much of the resurgent enthusiasm for neural-network technology is based on the excitement over a variety of learning-rules for neural networks, especially those that address the problem of training hidden units. In addition, extrapolating research that is now beginning in intelligent computer-assisted instruction, a Sixth Generation computer will develop models that allow it to adapt itself to each individual user. However, learning is not the sole key to neural computing, and much is to be learned from the explicit design of networks for cooperative computation and perceptual robotics, and other intelligent functions.

Note the blurring of the line between hardware and software. For many applications, we may take an existing Sixth Generation machine and program it or—appealing to the power of neural networks—adapt it to a new application. However, for many applications, the design of a new architecture, the specification of physical systems and their relationships, will be an integral part of tackling that application. The computer scientist of the future will see hardware and software issues, as well as learning components and robotic interfaces, as integral parts of the overall design process. Such a view leads to the apparently paradoxical claim: 'neural computing is not restricted to neural networks'. This is because, as preceding sections have made abundantly clear, the design of Sixth Generation systems must embrace both 'coarse-grain' analysis of the overall system as a network of interacting schemas and 'fine-grain' neural analysis using artificial neural networks to build many of these subsystems.

References

Amari, S. and Arbib, M.A. Competition and cooperation in neural nets. *Systems Neuroscience* (J. Metzler, editor), 119-165. Academic Press, 1977.

Amari, S. and Arbib, M.A. (editors). Competition and Cooperation in Neural Nets. *Lecture Notes in Biomathematics*, Vol. 45, Springer-Verlag, 1982.

Anderson, J.A., and Rosenfeld, E. (editors). Neurocomputing: Foundations of Research, The MIT Press, 1988.

Arbib, M.A. The Metaphorical Brain: An Introduction to Cybernetics as Artificial Intelligence and Brain Theory. Wiley Interscience, 1972.

Arbib, M. A. Artificial intelligence and brain theory: unities and diversities. *Ann. Biomed. Eng.* 3, 238-274, 1975.

Arbib, M.A. Parallelism, Slides, Schemas and Frames. In *Systems: Approaches, Theories, Applications* (W.E.Hartnett, editor), 27-43, Dordrecht-Holland: D. Reidel Publishing Co., 1977.

Arbib, M.A. Perceptual structures and distributed motor control. *Handbook of Physiology—The Nervous System II. Motor Control* (V.B. Brooks, editor), 1449-1480. American Physiological Society. Bethesda, MD 1981.

Arbib, M.A. Visuomotor coordination: from neural nets to schema theory. *Cognition and Brain Theory*, 4, 23-39, 1981a.

Arbib, M.A. *Rana Computatrix*, An Evolving Model of Visuomotor Coordination in Frog and Toad. *Machine Intelligence 10*, (J. Hayes and D. Michie, editors) 501-517, Ellis Horwood, 1982.

Arbib, M.A. Neural Computing: The Challenge of the Sixth Generation. *EDUCOM Bulletin*, 23(1), 2-12, 1987a.

Arbib, M.A. Levels of modelling of mechanisms of visually guided behavior (with commentaries and author's response). *The Behavioral and Brain Sciences*, 10, 407-465, 1987b.

Arbib, M.A. *Brains, Machines, and Mathematics*, 2nd Edition, Springer-Verlag , 1987b.

Arbib, M.A. *The Metaphorical Brain 2: Neural Networks and Beyond*. Wiley Interscience, 1989a.

Arbib, M.A. Programs, schemas, and neural networks for control of hand movements: Beyond the RS framework. In *Attention and Performance XIII* (M. Jeannerod, editor), 1989b.

Arbib, M.A., Conklin, E.J., and Hill, J.C. *From Schema Theory to Language*. Oxford University Press, 1986.

Arbib, M.A., and Hanson, A.R., editors. *Vision, Brain, and Cooperative Computation*. A Bradford Book/MIT Press, 1987.

Arbib, M.A., and Hesse, M.B. *The Construction of Reality*. Cambridge University Press, 1986.

Arbib, M.A., and House, D.H. Depth and Detours: an Essay on Visually Guided Behavior. *Vision, Brain, and Cooperative Computation* (M.A. Arbib and A.R. Hanson, editors), 129-163. A Bradford Book/The MIT Press, 1987.

Arbib, M.A., Iberall, T., and Lyons, D. Coordinated Control Programs for Control of the Hands. *Hand Function and the Neocortex* (A.W. Goodwin and I. Darian-Smith, editors). Exp. Brain Res. Suppl. 10, 111-129, 1985.

Arkin, R.C. Neuroscience in motion: the application of schema theory to mobile robotics. *Visuomotor Coordination: Amphibians, Comparisons, Models, and Robots* (J.-P. Ewert and M.A. Arbib, editors), 649-671. Plenum Press, 1989.

Block, H.D. The Perceptron: A Model for Brain Functioning, I. *Rev. Mod. Phys.*, 34, 123-135, 1962.

Cervantes-Perez, F., Lara, R., and Arbib, M.A. A neural model of interactions subserving prey-predator discrimination and size preference in anuran amphibia. *J. Theoretical Biology* 113, 117-152, 1985.

Cragg, B.G. and Temperley, H.N.V. The organization of neurones: a cooperative analogy. *EEG Clin. Neurophysiol* 6, 85-92, 1954.

Dev, P. Perception of Depth Surfaces in Random-dot Stereograms: A Neural Model. *Int. J. Man-Machine Studies*, 7, 511-528, 1975.

Ewert, J.-P. The visual system of the toad: behavioral and physiological studies on a pattern recognition system. *The Amphibian Visual System* (Fite, K.V., editor), 142-202. Academic Press, New York, 1976.

Ewert, J.-P. Neuroethology of Releasing Mechanisms. *The Behavioral and Brain Sciences*, 10, 337-405, 1987.

Ewert, J.-P., and Arbib, M.A., editors. Visuomotor Coordination: Amphibians, Comparisons, Models, and Robots. Plenum Press, 1989.

Ewert, J.-P., and von Seelen, W. Neurobiologie and System-Theorie eines visuellen Muster-Erkennungsmechanismus bei Kroten. *Kybernetik* 14, 167-183, 1974.

Fite, K.V., and Scalia, F. Central visual pathways in the frog. *The Amphibian Visual System: A Multidisciplinary Approach* (K. Fite, editor), 87-118. Academic Press, New York, 1976.

Frégnac, Y., and Imbert, M. Early development of visual cortical cells in normal and dark-reared kittens. Relationship between orientation selectivity and ocular dominance. *J. Physiol.* (London), 278, 27-44, 1978.

Gasser, L., and Huhns, M.N., editors. *Distributed Artificial Intelligence*, Vol. II, Pitman/Morgan Kaufmann Publishers, 1989.

Geman, S., and Geman, D. Stochastic relaxation, Gibbs distributions, and the Bayesian restoration of images. *IEEE Transactions in Pattern Analysis and Machine Intelligence* 6, 721-741, 1984.

Harth, E.M., Csermely, T.J., Beek, B. and Lindsay, R.D. Brain functions and neural dynamics. *J. Theor. Biol.* 26, 93-120, 1970.

Harth, E.M., Unnikrishnan, K.P., and Pandya, A.S. The inversion of sensory processing by feedback pathways: A model of visual cognitive functions. *Science*, 237, 184-187, 1987.

Hesse, M.B. Theory and observation. *Revolutions and Reconstructions in the Philosophy of Science*, 63-110. Indiana University Press, 1980.

Hinton, G.E., Sejnowski, T.J., and Ackley, D.H. Boltzmann Machines: Constraint Satisfaction Networks that Learn. *Cognitive Science*, 9, 147-169, 1984.

House, D.H. *Neural Models of Depth Perception in Frog and Toad.* Ph.D. Dissertation, Department of Computer and Information Science, University of Massachusetts at Amherst, 1984.

Huhns, M.N., editor. *Distributed Artificial Intelligence*, Pitman Publishing/Morgan Kaufmann Publishers, 1987.

Iberall, T., Bingham, G., and Arbib, M.A. Opposition Space as a Structuring Concept for the Analysis of Skilled Hand Movements. *Experimental Brain Research Series*, 15, 158-173, 1986.

Imbert, M., and Buisseret, P. Receptive field characteristics and plastic properties of visual cortical cells in kittens reared with or without visual experience. *Exp. Brain. Res.*, 22, 2-36, 1975.

Ingle, D. Focal attention in the frog: behavioral and physiological correlates. *Science* 188, 1033-1035, 1975.

Ingle, D. Spatial visions in anurans. *The Amphibian Visual System: A Multidisciplinary Approach* (K. Fite, editor), 119-140. Academic Press: New York, 1976.

Jeannerod M., and Biguer, B. Visuomotor mechanisms in reaching within extra-personal space. *Advances in the Analysis of Visual Behavior* (D.J. Ingle, R.J.W. Mansfield and M.A. Goodale, editors), 387-409. The MIT Press, 1982.

Julesz, B. *Foundations of Cyclopean Perception.* University of Chicago Press, 1971.

Lara, R., Arbib, M.A. and Cromarty, A.S. The role of the tectal column in facilitation of amphibian prey-catching behavior: a neural model. *J. Neuroscience* 2, 521-530, 1982.

Lettvin, J. Y., Maturana, H., McCulloch, W.S. and Pitts, W.H. What the frog's eye tells the frog brain. *Proc. IRE*, 1940-1951, 1959.

Marr, D. and Poggio, T. Cooperative computation of stereo disparity. *Science* 194, 283-287, 1977.

Marshall, J.C. Eye of Toad, and toe of Frog? *Behavioral and Brain Sciences* 10, 444-445, 1987.

McCulloch, W.S., Arbib, M.A., and Cowan, J.D. Neurological Models and Integrative Processes. *Self-Organizing Systems*, (M.C. Yovits, G.T. Jacobi and G.D. Goldstein, editors) 49-59. Spartan Books, 1962.

McCulloch, W.S., and Pitts, W.H. A logical calculus of the ideas immanent in nervous activity. *Bull. Math. Biophys.* 5, 115-133, 1943.

Minsky, M.L. Some Universal Elements for Finite Automata. *Automata Studies* (C.E. Shannon and J. McCarthy, editors) 117-128. Princeton University Press, 1956.

Minsky, M.L. *The Society of Mind.* Simon and Schuster, 1985.

Minsky, M.L., and Papert, S. *Perceptrons, An Essay in Computational Geometry.* The MIT Press, 1969.

Paillard, J. Basic neurophysiological structures of eye-hand coordination. In *Development of eye-hand coordination across the lifespan*, (C. Bard, M. Fleury and L. Hay, editors). University of North Carolina Press, 1989.

Poggio, T., Gamble, E.B., and Little, J.J. Parallel integration of visual modules. *Science* 242, 436-440, 1988.

Riseman, E.M., and Hanson, A.R. A Methodology for the Development of General Knowledge-Based Vision Systems. *Vision, Brain and Cooperative Computation*, (M.A. Arbib and A.R. Hanson, editors), 285-328. A Bradford Book/The MIT Press, 1987.

Rosenblatt, F. *Principles of Neurodynamics.* Spartan, 1962.

Rumelhart, D.E., Hinton, G.E., and Williams, R.J. Learning Internal Representations by Error Propagation. *Parallel Distributed Processing: Explorations in the Microstructure of Cognition*, (Rumelhart, D.E., and McClelland, J.L., editors). Volume 1, 318-362. The MIT Press/Bradford Books, 1986.

Rumelhart, D.E., and Zipser, D. Feature Discovery by Competitive Learning. *Cognitive Science* 9, 75-112, 1985.

Székely, G. and Lázár, G. Cellular and synaptic architecture of the optic tectum. *Frog Neurobiology* (Llinás, R. and Precht, W., editors) 407-434. Springer-Verlag, 1976.

von der Malsburg, C. Self-organization of orientation-sensitive cells in the striate cortex. *Kybernetik* 14, 85-100, 1973.

Weems, C.C., Levitan, S.P., Hanson, A.R., Riseman, E.M., Nash, J.G., and Shu, D.B. The image understanding architecture, *COINS Technical Report* 87-76, University of Massachusetts, Amherst, 1987.

Weymouth, T.E. *Using object descriptions in a schema network for machine vision.* Ph.D. Dissertation and COINS Technical Report 86-24, Department of Computer and Information Science, University of Massachusetts at Amherst, 1986.

Widrow, B., and Hoff, M. E. Adaptive switching circuits. 1960 IRE WESCON Convention Record 4, 96-104, 1960.

Yonezawa, A., and Tokoro, M., editors. *Object-Oriented Concurrent Programming*. The MIT Press, 1987.

Zeki, S. Anatomical guides to the functional organization of the visual cortex. *Neurobiology of Neocortex* (P. Goldman-Rakic and W. Singer, editors), 241-251. Wiley, 1988.

Chapter 7

PARALLEL SYSTEMS IN THE CEREBRAL CORTEX: THE TOPOGRAPHY OF COGNITION

PATRICIA GOLDMAN-RAKIC

Beyond the traditional view of cerebral cortex organization

The cerebral cortex has captured the attention of numerous scientists and clinicians throughout this century but its complexity has also daunted quite a few. The cortex has been divided into many anatomically distinct areas with different functions. The best-studied and best-understood areas are the primary sensory areas, so-called because they are directly innervated by the senses of vision, audition, somatic sensation or olfaction. In addition, the primary motor cortex is that area with direct (but not exclusive) output to the motor neurons of the spinal cord. We do not know all the regions of cerebral cortex nor their ultimate boundaries nor the functions of all these different regions, but it is clear that most of the cerebral cortex falls into the category of association cortex. It has been estimated that the association cortex occupies almost 90% of the cerebral cortical surface (Eccles 1984).

Traditional models of the cerebral cortex emphasize information-flow in the feed-forward direction from sensory to motor cortices. Such models hold that convergence increases at each stage such that the areas furthest removed from the sensory receptors and closer to the motor controllers receive the most information and serve executive monitoring and command functions. However, without denying that some convergence occurs in association cortical regions, considerations discussed in the present chapter lead toward a different view of the cerebral cortex based on the organization of its extrinsic circuitry that may be relevant not only to models of higher cortical function but useful also to applications that employ distribution of function in parallel systems with largely independent functions. A similar position is taken in this volume by Edelman (1990).

Strategy for examining cortical function

Because so much of the cortex is association cortex, it is particularly challenging to interpret its many functions, and one has to have some kind of strategy for approaching this formidable task. In our laboratory we study the rhesus monkey because its brain is quite similar to that of humans and has a similarly-long ontogenetic development, making this non-human primate unexcelled as a model for human function. It thus plays a central role in our studies of the *neurobiology of cognition* or *cognitive neuroscience*.

For most of this century, the large 'polymodal' association cortical regions of the frontal, temporal and parietal lobes of the neocortex have often been treated as more or less homogeneous regions. However, closer scrutiny by modern anatomical and physiological techniques has revealed a relatively high degree of compartmentalization in these areas. Further, the most recent data do not fully support the classical concept of association cortical areas as zones of increasing intersensory convergence. In fact, the large association areas, at least in nonhuman primates, can be divided into smaller specialized information centers that retain a large measure of modality specificity, both as interpreted from anatomical considerations (Cavada and Goldman-Rakic 1989a; Pandya and Selzer 1982) and physiological studies (Mountcastle 1957; Hyvarinen 1981).

To focus our study further we have paid particular attention to Area 46, the functional anatomic entity of the principal sulcus region in the prefrontal cortex. We emphasize Area 46 because we are convinced that it functions like a special-purpose machine devoted to *working memory* (to be described below) and because, as we shall see later, it has important and intriguing connections with multiple cortical areas. Our hope is that if we can understand the organization and principles of functioning of this region, then we will be in a good position to extend our understanding to other regions, which we suspect to be very similar in their organization and to be special-purpose machines with analogous functions.

Working memory

In the last decade or so it has become clear to cognitive psychologists that memory is not a unitary concept or a unitary mechanism, but that there are various forms of memory. A useful and conceptually meaningful distinction is the one between

Delayed Spatial Response

Visual Pattern Discrimination

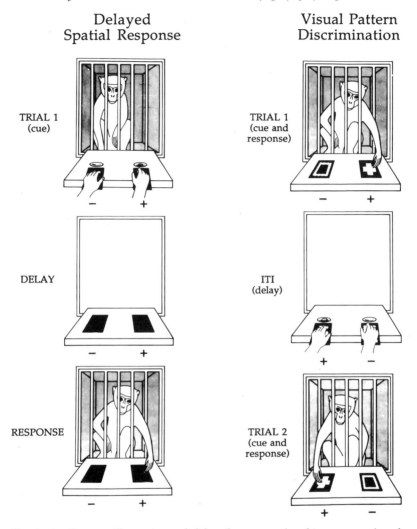

Figure 1. Cartoon illustrations of delayed-response (working memory) and visual discrimination (associative memory) tasks. In the delayed-response task, the monkey observes as the experimenter 'hides' a food morsel in one of two food wells (top panel). The wells are then covered with identical plaques, the screen is lowered (middle panel) and, after a delay of several seconds, the screen is raised (lower panel) and the monkey selects one of the wells. Note that, at the time of the response, there is no cue in the test situation to guide the animal's choice: it must be guided by its memory of the baiting event, only seconds before. On the other hand, in conventional learning paradigms, illustrated by a visual discrimination problem, choice is elicited by external cues (trial 2) that have been consistently rewarded in the past (trial 1). Monkeys with prefrontal lesions are profoundly impaired on delayed-response tasks, but perform as well as unoperated controls on simple and conditional discrimination problems.

associative memory and working memory. I shall argue that working memory is the essential process underlying our ability to guide behavior by mental representations (internal signals and ideas) rather than by immediate stimuli in the outside world.

In contrast, the associative process is that process by which repetition of stimuli and responses stamps in an association for long-term storage. An example from the laboratory is the acquisition of a visual discrimination problem. The monkey is given a choice of two panels to press, one marked with a plus and one marked with a square. He is rewarded every time he selects the plus sign, and gets no reward when he selects the square. With repeated trials, he learns more and more reliably to choose the plus over the square. This is not an extraordinary feat for the animal. A rat can do this—it is just trial-and-error learning in which a particular stimulus is consistently associated with reward (or punishment). Such associative conditioning underlies our knowledge of facts, symbols (including words), and various skills.

However, *working memory* is an entirely different process that can be measured in animals by delayed-response paradigms. In such tests, an animal sees a food morsel placed in one of two food wells; the food wells are covered; a screen is lowered to block the view of the wells from the animal; and a delay is imposed. After the screen comes up, the animal is allowed to select one of the two food wells. The major difference between this type of paradigm and the associative paradigm is that in this instance when the animal has to select his response, to the left or to the right, there is no distinguishing stimulus present to guide his choice. Rather, the information guiding the response must be provided by an internal signal, based on internalized information or the memorandum of what happened a few seconds previously. Furthermore, the information is relevant only transiently and is useful only for the trial at hand. On subsequent trials, new information becomes relevant as the location of the reward is randomly shifted from one location to another.

Association memory and working memory are cooperative processes. Association memory is important because this is the way we acquire knowledge about the outside world. Working memory utilizes that knowledge. Association memory is long-term, stable, and, for all practical purposes, permanent. For example, an apple is always a round object with a shiny surface. But, in working memory, it is what is true for the moment that is important. Working memory is the glue of our experience, connecting one moment to another, allowing us to have goals, plans, and ideas that govern behavior, allowing us to transcend obligatory responsiveness to stimuli in the outside world. Considering the implications of working memory to the utterance of a sentence, to programming, to chess, and to all the other cognitive operations that are so impressive in human behaviors, we have been inspired to examine its neural underpinnings.

The role of area 46

The distinction between working memory and association memory is a dichotomy that the brain obeys! If we remove area 46 of the principal sulcus region bilaterally in rhesus monkeys, the animal is unable to perform working-memory tasks, even though it is capable of any of a whole host of associative tasks. Animals with this lesion can see the stimuli, and they remember to select one of the two food wells, but they simply choose at chance level. Note that on different trials the stimulus might be in one well, or it might be in the other. Since each trial is a new event, information must be continually updated. So, after each trial the animal has to *erase* what he just learned because it would interfere with the information that becomes relevant for the next trial. Working memory, in brief, is the ability to keep a bit of information in mind for a few seconds in order to guide behavior in the absence of relevant information in the outside world.

The covered-well experiment has proven to be a useful way of testing working memory, but more exacting methods have recently been developed.   With the aid of technology that allows continuous monitoring of eye position, monkeys can be trained to fixate, *i.e.* to keep their eyes focused on a central spot on a TV monitor (Funahashi *et al.*, 1989, 1990). After the animal fixates for a certain period of time to assure that the conditions of the trial are met, a target is briefly presented (for five seconds) in a specified location of the visual field. After the target goes off, a delay commences, lasting for one to six seconds. At the end of the delay the fixation spot goes off, and its offset provides the instruction to the animal to move its eyes to where the target *had* been.

In a control version of this oculomotor task, the target remains on during the delay and is present at the time of the response. So we have two versions of this task—the latter is the *sensory-guided* version, and the former is the *memory-guided* version. Small lesions in prefrontal cortex produce deficits only on the memory-guided task leaving performance on the sensory-guided version unaffected.

The oculomotor delayed-response task described above has proven especially useful for correlating neuronal activity and behavioral events. Therefore, single-unit recordings are obtained from normal animals. Several different classes of neuronal activity have been found in the principal sulcus (Figure 2). One class of cells responds phasically to the onset of the target, *i.e.*, it increases firing when the target comes on and sustains this as long

PFC

CUE-SELECTIVE

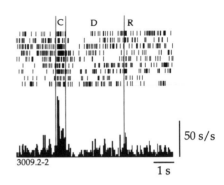

DELAY SELECTIVE

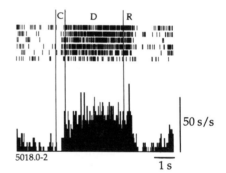

RESPONSE SELECTIVE

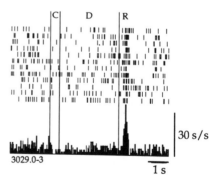

as the target is on; neuronal discharge returns to baseline when the target disappears (Funahashi *et al.*, 1990). This type of neuronal activity is stimulus-bound or stimulus-related. Another type of neuronal activity is response-related, occurring around the time the response is initiated (Funahashi *et al.*, in preparation). Yet another neuron fires once the cue goes off as if following the dictum 'out of sight, in mind'. Such a cell continues firing throughout the delay, and returns to baseline abruptly as soon as the response is initiated (Funahashi *et al.*, 1989). This extraordinary type of cell is thus activated both when no stimulus is present and when no response is occurring, and maintains that activity until a response is executed. We believe that such a cell is a *cellular correlate of working memory* and that its firing constitutes information which the animal uses, *i.e.* that the neuronal activity reflects, in essence, a transient memory-trace. Strong support for this view comes from our evidence that delay-period activity is directionally specific, *i.e.* occurs only for particular target locations and not for all others. Furthermore, if the length of the delay is increased, the activity is prolonged, and if it is foreshortened, the activity is also foreshortened. The target location which induces the greatest delay-period activation can be considered the *memory field* of that neuron, in analogy to the sensory receptive field of visual or somatosensory cortical neurons or the directional fields of motor neurons. We have shown that different neurons code memories for different locations, so that, within area 46 of the prefrontal cortex, there appears to be

---

Figure 2. (left) Examples of three major types of neuronal processing exhibited by different prefrontal neurons, while a monkey performed an oculomotor delayed-response task (see text for full description of the task).
Top. This cell exhibits a phasic response that is time-locked to the presentation of a specific cue in the visual field. Over 95% of cue-related neurons are directional; *i.e.*, they increase their rate of firing to cues in specific parts of the visual field only; other neurons code other target locations.
Middle. This is an example of a neuron that is activated in the delay period, when the to-be-remembered stimulus is no longer in view and the response has yet to be executed. The monkey is fixating during the delay, but the neuron responds directionally; *i.e.*, it increases its rate of discharge only for specific cue locations. The tuning and 'best directions' of the delay-period activity are highly similar to those of the cue-related activity for the cue-activated cells. We presume that these classes of neurons are synaptically related (Funahashi *et al.*, 1990).
Bottom. This cell has pre-saccadic activity; *i.e.*, it discharges in a directionally-specific manner after the fixation point disappears, but before the initiation of the required saccade. Such neurons presumably participate in the initiation of the oculomotor response. Possibly they are prefrontal neurons with direct connections to the deep layers of the superior colliculus (Goldman and Nauta 1976). Other neurons (not shown) are also related to the response, but exhibit post-saccadic activity. The post-saccadic activity may serve as a signal from other centers to terminate the delay-period activity of synaptically-linked prefrontal neurons. (Funahashi, Bruce and Goldman-Rakic, in preparation). PFC = prefrontal cortex; C= one period; D = delay period; R = response period; 50 s/s = 50 spikes per second.

a place map in which different neurons access visuospatial information and hold that information on line during a delay period to guide the response in the absence of external cues. The prefrontal cortex appears to operate as an 'open loop'.

It is of interest that once animals learn to perform the oculomotor delayed-response task, they rarely make errors. But the occasional errors are instructive. When neuronal activity of cells with memory-fields are retrospectively analyzed, it can be shown that the delay-period activity had not been sustained during the entire delay. We found a highly significant difference between neuronal activity on error trials and that when the animal has made the correct response. All these results support the thesis that the neuronal activity of prefrontal neurons represents information that guides the response and forms part of the intentional memory-code to the animals.

The reader may be aware that the traditional view of cerebral cortex is closely linked with an emphasis on association memory as the key to the mind: sensory cortex relays stimuli to association cortex, a vast storehouse of associations, where the stimulus is matched to an appropriate response, the command for which is issued through motor cortex. However, considerations raised here based on studies of prefrontal cortex lead to a different view. The prefrontal cortex, part of what is traditionally called association cortex, is not cortically involved in association memory, but is instead crucial for working memory. Working memory, indeed, may override associative responses, to allow an organism to base responses on stored representations rather than directly on the sensory stimuli they represent.

Figure 3. (right) A. Retrogradely labeled neurons mainly in layers III and V of cerebral cortex. The terminals of these cells are in the HRP injection-site at some distant cortical area; the HRP molecules are transported *retrogradely*—from terminals *back* to cell bodies; the biochemical reaction product in the cytoplasm of the cell body could have taken place only if the enzyme HRP were present in the cell. The section also contains some heavy anterograde label in the outer part of layer I as well as lighter anterograde label intermixed in a 'column' of retrogradely-labeled neurons because HRP also travels anterogradely.
B. Anterograde tracing experiment. Triteated amino acids and/or HRP travel *anterogradely* from the cell bodies at the site of the injection to the terminal regions of the neurons. Sections processed for autoradiography (coated with emulsion and developed) or enzymatically, as in the case of HRP, reveal a fine-grain dust-like product (silver grains in overlying emulsion of autoradiograms/reaction product in biochemically-processed HRP sections) which represents the terminal fields of neurons lying in the injection-site.

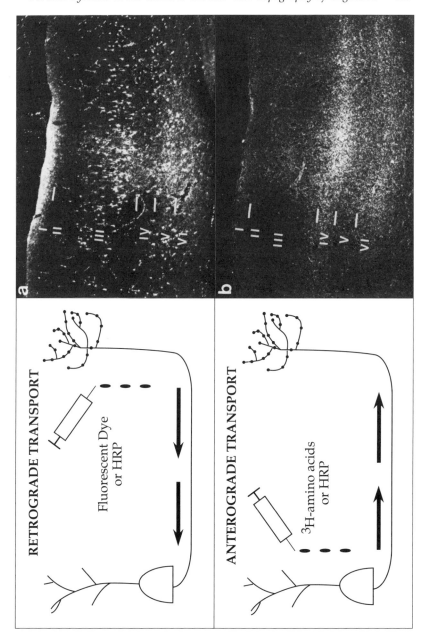

Feed-back and feed-forward

Given the evidence that prefrontal cortex is important for working memory, how does it do it? We have turned to anatomy to determine how the neurons in this region are connected with the rest of the brain, in hopes that this will provide some clue.

The neocortex is a six-layered structure. The cortical layers provide a stratified organization of the cortical circuits with cells in the different layers projecting to layer-specific targets. The connections of the prefrontal cortex have been elucidated by modern tract-tracing methods. Certain radionuclides, amino acids for example, can be injected anterogradely into the cortex, where they are taken up by the cell-bodies of neurons and transported anterogradely from the cell-body along the axon to the terminal destination of that cell, appearing in the histological section as a fine grain 'dust' (Figure 3). In a complementary pattern, other substances (such as horseradish peroxidase, HRP) are injected into regions of the cortex, and these substances are transported *retrogradely*, from terminals back to the cell-body of the neuron, filling and labeling the cell-body (Figure 3). From such studies we have been able to develop an understanding of given specific connectivity of different cell-groups in different layers.

Area 46 in the principal sulcus of the prefrontal cortex, which we believe is essential to the regulation of behavior by ideas, is connected to many major motor-centers in the brain. In particular, the principal sulcus issues direct projections to the superior colliculus, the deep layers of which are known to be the final common pathway for controlling eye-movements. Neurons in the principal sulcus project as well to the caudate nucleus, which is also part of the motor output system and is thought to organize complex motor skills. In addition, connections to premotor cortical areas have been demonstrated which are part of the brain's motor control system. In short, Area 46 has access to several motor outputs.

Recall the 'working-memory neuron' in area 46 that is able to retain information about the location of a target in space. This neuron is far removed from the retina and from the visual centers of the brain. How does that neuron access information about space? We, and others, have found that area 46 receives its main cortical input from the posterior parietal cortex. Moreover these parietal projections terminate in a 'feed-forward' pattern in layers I, IV and VI of prefrontal cortex (Schwartz and Goldman-Rakic 1984). Prefrontal neurons also project back to parietal cortex; these axons in parietal cortex terminate in a 'feed-back' pattern in layers I and VI (Goldman-Rakic, unpublished observations). On the basis of these studies we can state that the connections between prefrontal and parietal association areas are characterized

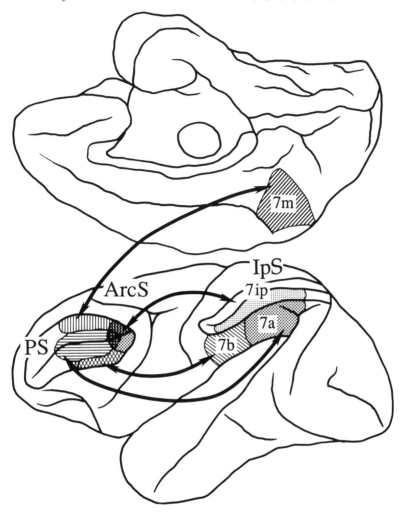

Figure 4. Diagram of the lateral view of the macaque brain illustrating topography, parallelism, and reciprocity of connections between four subdivisions of posterior parietal cortex and four distinguishable targets in the principal sulcus. Thus areas 7m, 7a, and 7b project to the dorsal rim, lower half of both banks, and ventral rim of the principal sulcus respectively. Area 7ip projects to the caudal end of the sulcus (Goldman-Rakic 1987a).

by reciprocity (Figure 4). Moreover, we find a number of parallel sets of pathways from the posterior parietal area to the prefrontal area that do not overlap (Figure 4). Thus, the principal sulcus is itself not a homogeneous area, but is a structure that can be parcellated into at least four subdivisions, each subdivision innervated by a different part of the parietal cortex. For

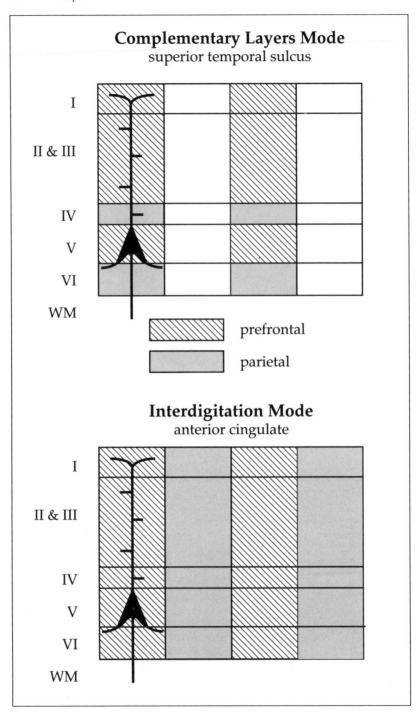

example, area 7b projects to the rim of the sulcus and area 7a to the bottom of the sulcus. For each area that projects forward to a subset of cells in prefrontal cortex, we see a selective return-pro-jection—a feed-forward projection, and a feed-back projection. The density of fibers projecting backward appears to be as great as the number projecting forward, suggesting a potential mechanism whereby the frontal lobe could gate its own input from the parietal lobe.

These studies are leading to the new view of association cortex as a number of subareas specialized for information-processing in particular representational domains rather than as large pluripotential complexes designed especially for cross-modal associations.

Interconnected networks: revelations of a double-labeling paradigm

In the study of connections, as in other areas of research, the results and the overview or conception of brain organization that they generate are greatly dependent on the methods and strategies used.   We have employed a strategy of double anterograde (from cell to terminal) labeling to trace connections simultaneously from two cortical areas that are connected to each other in the same monkey.   We asked the question whether two cortical areas that project to each other (*e.g.*, posterior parietal and principal sulcus) also project to other cortical areas in the same hemisphere.   If they do, are the connections divergent or convergent?   If convergent, do they overlap totally or partially and what is their relationship to the columnar architecture of the target-structures?   We injected one tracer (HRP) into the parietal cortex of a monkey while another tracer (tritiated amino acid) was injected into the principal sulcus of the same monkey. It was necessary to do this in the same animal because when anatomy is done, as it usually is, one site at a time, each in a different animal, it is impossible to identify the exact same point in two different brains.   We processed alternate sections through the same brain by two different methods and then superimposed pairs of adjacent sections to determine the location of the two labels in virtually the same spot in the brain.

The results of our double-label study revealed that posterior parietal and dorsolateral prefrontal cortex project in common to

Figure 5. (left) Modes of distribution of area 7a and area 46 terminals in 'third' party targets.   In anterior cingulate (and other medially situated) cortex, parietal and prefrontal fibers terminated in the same layers of adjacent columns; in the superior temporal sulcus, and also the frontoparietal operculum, the two areas of cortex project to different layers of the same columns—prefrontal cortex mainly to layer I and less densely to layers III and IV.

virtually the same targets in at least a dozen distinct cytoarchitectonic areas, none of which are primary sensory (Figure 5; modified from Selemon and Goldman-Rakic 1988). Moreover, the prefrontal and parietal axons within these 'third-party' targets terminate in one of two characteristic modes; either as tangentially alternating fiber columns (interdigitating mode) or in a stacking pattern within a single column or set of columns (the complementary mode described above) (Figure 6). In some cases, anterior and posterior cingulate cortices, for example, the mode of termination is an interdigitated pattern, *i.e.,* prefrontal and parietal terminals formed adjacent cortical columns; whereas in other cases, the parietal operculum and superior temporal sulcus, the pattern is a complementary one. In the latter, parietal axons terminate predominantly in layers IV and VI across a 0.5 – 1.0 mm wide zone, and prefrontal projections are highly concentrated in layer I and much less densely in layers III and V/VI of the same column. The two different patterns of cortical termination suggest that the integration of prefrontal and parietal information differs accordingly. In the cingulate regions, for example, parietal and prefrontal afferents probably terminate on different sets of cells, whereas in temporal lobe and parietal operculum it is possible that prefrontal and parietal afferents terminate upon different parts of the dendritic arbor of the very same cells, much as hippocampal inputs are distributed on proximal and distal dendritic segments of pyramidal neurons in Ammon's horn. These anatomical findings open up new issues and possibilities for physiological analysis of cortical networks.

This, then, is an anatomist's distributed network involving a large number of interconnected cortical regions. Such a re-entrant network lies literally in-between sensory input and motor output and is a candidate structure for 'hidden units' that have been posited on the basis of computational modelling. More importantly, the neural network we have described appears to be a dedicated system in that it is activated during cortical operations in the sphere of spatially-guided behavior. Studies from this laboratory support the idea that each node in the network contributes some specialized subfunction in visuospatial information-processing. We have proposed that there may be other networks similarly organized to carry out cognitive operations for other information-processing domains.

To close this section, consider the linkages between the two cerebral hemispheres. The cerebral cortices of the two hemispheres are interconnected mainly through the fibers of the corpus callosum. The less sensitive silver degeneration methods employed for many years indicated that each cortical area was connected with its counterpart area in the opposite hemisphere

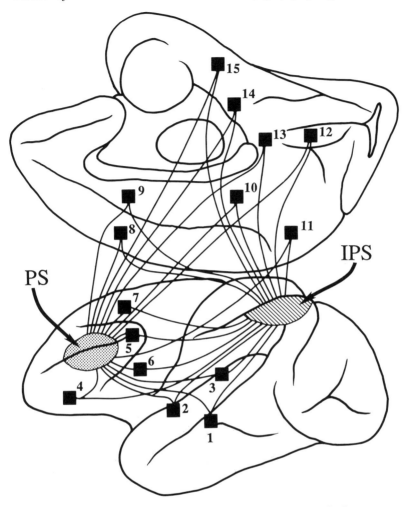

Figure 6. Diagram of lateral and medial views of the cerebral cortex illustrating the location of injections (3H-AA, tritiated amino acids or HRP horseradish peroxidase) in the posterior parietal and prefrontal cortex and the fifteen cytoarchitectonic regions (marked 1-15) that were sites of double anterograde labeling, *i.e.*, the sites interconnected with both injected areas. The numbers on the figure correspond to the following target structures: (1) the superior temporal sulcus; (2) the insular cortex; (3) the frontoparietal operculum; (4) the orbital prefrontal cortex; (5) the anterior arcuate cortex; (6 and 7) the ventral and dorsal subdivisions of premotor cortex; (8) the supplementary motor cortex; (9) the anterior cingulate cortex; (10) the posterior cingulate cortex; (11) the medial parietal cortex; (12) the parieto-occipital sulcus; (13) the presubiculum; (14) the parahippocampal gyrus; and (15) the caudomedial lobule. The location of some of the target areas (*e.g.*, 1, 2, 3, and 13) are indicated only roughly because the projections are buried in the depths of sulci and cannot be seen on the surface view. PS, principal sulcus; IPS, intraparietal sulcus.

and with little else (*e.g.*, Pandya and Vignolo 1971). With the advent of more sensitive axonal-transport techniques, we have learned that an area of one hemisphere, while mainly interconnected with the homotopic area of the contralateral hemisphere, has widespread 'heterotopic' connections. For example, several studies in my laboratory have shown that area 46 in the prefrontal cortex of one hemisphere connects to area 8, 9 and 46 of the opposite hemisphere (McGuire and Goldman-Rakic 1990; Schwartz and Goldman-Rakic 1984). Likewise, area 7a of the posterior parietal cortex projects to both medial and lateral aspects of the temporal lobe, to prestriate areas in the occipital lobe, and to the posterior cingulate cortex as well as to other areas of the parietal lobe (Cavada and Goldman-Rakic 1989a). Thus, a cortical area in one hemisphere has connections with a subset of the areas in the opposite hemisphere that it is connected to in the ipsilateral hemisphere. This pattern reveals that interhemispheric as well as intrahemispheric connections are embedded in complex networks.

We have seen that neurons in over a dozen target-areas are interconnected with the prefrontal and parietal cortex. These interconnected areas are, in turn, unified by their input from the medial pulvinar nucleus of the thalamus (*e.g.*, Baleydier and Mauguiere 1985; Giguere and Goldman-Rakic 1987). The medial pulvinar is the latest-evolved nuclear subdivision of the thalamus. It projects to the anterior and posterior cingulate and retrosplenial cortices—the paralimbic areas—and also to the superior temporal and fronto-parietal operculum and to most of the nodes delimited in Figure 5 as well as to the principal sulcus and parietal area 7a. This thalamic nucleus, which is particularly prominent in primates, is thereby in position to recruit an entire neural system defined by cortico-cortical connectivity and possibly by common dedication to the complex function of being oriented in time and space.

Dedicated network: spatial cognition

Both prefrontal and posterior parietal areas have been associated with spatial abilities, and physiological studies in these areas suggest possible functional collaborations between them. Neurons in the principal sulcus and those on the parietal convexity in area 7a behave in a similar way in delay paradigms (Funahashi *et al.*, 1989; Gnadt *et al.* 1989; Chaffee *et al.* 1989). Thus, we can conclude that the similar profiles of activation in parietal and prefrontal cortex indicate a commonality of function and shared circuitry. We may speculate that the parietal contribution is presumably to form and maintain the spatial coordinates of an object in space and the prefrontal contribution is to access and use that knowledge to guide either a manual or saccadic response. The behavioral contributions of other cortical components of the neural networks defined in anatomical studies are much less obvious and more difficult to infer. Neuronal recording in behaving monkeys has not been attempted in many of the cortical areas connected to prefrontal and parietal cortex, *e.g.,* the anterior or posterior cingulate cortex or parahippocampal cortex. Further, in cortical regions, like the superior temporal sulcus, that have been studied physiologically, delay-tasks have not generally been employed. However, it must be noted that delay-enhanced discharge during delayed-response tasks has been reported in several key structures with which posterior parietal areas, the principal sulcus and frontal eye fields are connected, *e.g.,* the hippocampus (Watanabe and Niki 1985), the head of the caudate nucleus (Hikosaka and Wurtz 1983) and the mediodorsal nucleus of the thalamus (Alexander and Fuster 1973), though not from the cholinergic system of basal forebrain nuclei (Richardson and DeLong 1986).

Results from ^{14}C-2-deoxyglucose studies of monkeys performing delayed-response tasks show elevated metabolic activity in prefrontal cortex (Bugbee and Goldman-Rakic 1981), in the hippocampus proper (Friedman and Goldman-Rakic 1988) and mediodorsal nucleus of the thalamus (Friedman *et al.* 1990) compared with animals performing other types of memory-tasks. In fact, all the parts of the network that we have examined quantitatively so far show that they are driven by this task, suggesting that the network does indeed behave as a network, and that all the areas are simultaneously activated when the animal does the task.

While not necessarily revealing the functional specialization of each structure in the network, these physiological and metabolic studies are consistent with the supposition of a distributed richly-interconnected system of neural structures engaged in spatial information-processing. In such systems, integrative functions may emerge from the dynamics of the entire network and from its interactions with similarly-constructed networks rather than from linear computations performed at each nodal point in the circuit.

If parallel systems of circuits subserve various distinct information-processing tasks, it is appropriate to raise the issue of integration across cortical networks. The field of cortical-systems research will have to address the mechanisms by which knowledge of the color or form of an object is integrated with knowledge of its position in space, as such knowledge would appear to involve cross-talk between two different functional systems. It is possible that the mechanism of the prefrontal cortex, postulated by some cognitive studies in humans (Shallice

1982; 1989) may ultimately be explained by the nature of the interconnections between independent parallel neural networks. This could take the form of local cortico-cortical connections between, for example, subdivisions (*e.g.*, areas 7a, 7b, 7ip) of posterior parietal and those of prefrontal cortex, or possibly the multiple innervation of all components of a network by a thalamic nucleus. It is my conviction that anatomical and physiological data are both necessary to solve the perplexing riddle of complex brain-function.

References

Alexander, G.E., and Fuster, J.M. Effects of cooling prefrontal cortex on cell firing in the nucleus medialis dorsalis. *Brain Res.*, 61, 93-105, 1973.

Baleydier, C., and Mauguiere, F. Anatomical evidence for medial pulvinar connections with the posterior cingulate cortex, the retrosplenial area, and the posterior parahippocampal gyrus in monkeys. *J. Comp. Neurol.*, 232, 219-228, 1985.

Barbas, H., and Mesulam, M.M. Organization of afferent input to subdivisions of area 8 in rhesus monkey. *J. Comp. Neurol.* 232, 407-431, 1981.

Bruce, C.J., and Goldberg, M.E. Primate frontal eye fields I. Single neurons discharging before saccades. *J. Neurophysiol.* 53, 603-635, 1985.

Bugbee, N.M., and Goldman-Rakic, P.S. Columnar organization of cortico-cortical projections in squirrel and rhesus monkeys: similarity of column width in species differing in cortical volume. *J. Comp. Neurol.* 220, 355-364, 1983.

Bugbee, N.M., and Goldman-Rakic, P.S. Functional 2-deoxyglucose mapping in association cortex: Prefrontal activation in monkeys performing a cognitive task. *Society for Neuroscience Abstracts* 7, 416, 1981.

Cavada, C., and Goldman-Rakic, P.S. Posterior parietal cortex in rhesus monkey: I. Parcellation of areas based on distinctive limbic and sensory cortico-cortical connections. *J. Comp. Neurol.* 287, 393-421, 1989a.

Cavada, C., and Goldman-Rakic, P.S. Posterior parietal cortex in rhesus monkey: II. Evidence for segregated corticocortical networks linking sensory and limbic areas with the frontal lobe. *J. Comp. Neurol.* 287, 422-445, 1989b.

Chaffee, M., Funahashi, S., and Goldman-Rakic, P.S. Unit activity in the primate posterior parietal cortex during an oculomotor delayed response task. *Society for Neuroscience Abstracts* 15 (1), 786, 1989.

Edelman, G.M., Chapter 9 of this book.

Eccles, J.C. The cerebral neocortex. A theory of its operation. In *Cerebral Cortex*, Volume 2, 1984.

Friedman, H.R., Bruce, C.J., and Goldman-Rakic, P.S. Interdigitating and coincident metabolic columns in cortical areas Vl and V2 after sequential monocular stimulation of both eyes in the macaque monkey revealed by a double label 2-DG technique. *Experimental Brain Research*, in press, 1989.

Friedman, H.R., Bruce, C.J., and Goldman-Rakic, P.S. A sequential double-label 14C- and 3H-2-DG technique: Validation by double-dissociation of functional states. *Experimental Brain Research*, in press, 1989.

Friedman, H.R., and Goldman-Rakic, P.S. Activation of the hippocampus by working memory: a 2-deoxyglucose study of behaving rhesus monkeys. *J. Neuroscience* 8, 4693-4706, 1988.

Friedman, H.R., Bruce, C.J., and Goldman-Rakic, P.S. Double-label 3H-l4C-2DG method for mapping brain activity underlying two experimental conditions in the same animal. *Methods in Neurosciences*, Volume 3 (ed. P. Conn), Academic Press, 1990.

Funahashi, S., Bruce, C.J., and Goldman-Rakic, P.S. Mnemonic coding of visual space in the monkey's dorsolateral prefrontal cortex. *J. Neurophysiology* 61, 1-19, 1989.

Funahashi, S., Bruce, C.J., and Goldman-Rakic, P.S. Visuospatial coding in primate prefrontal neurons revealed by oculomotor paradigms. *J. Neurophysiology* 63, 814-831, 1990.

Funahashi, S., Bruce, C.J., and Goldman-Rakic, P.S. Neuronal activity related to saccadic eye movements in the monkey's dorsolateral prefrontal cortex. *In preparation.*

Fuster, J.M. Unit activity in prefrontal cortex during delayed-response performance: Neuronal correlates of transient memory. *J. Neurophysiology* 36, 61-78, 1973.

Fuster, J.M. *The Prefrontal Cortex*. Raven Press, 1980.

Giguere, M., and Goldman-Rakic, P.S. The primate medial pulvinar (MP) and its connections with the frontal lobes and other cortical areas. *Neuroscience Abstracts* 13, 1098, 1987.

Gnadt, J.W., and Anderson, R.A. Memory related motor planning activity in the posterior parietal cortex of macaque. *Exp. Brain Res.* 70, 216-220, 1989.

Goldman-Rakic, P.S., and Schwartz, M.L.   Interdigitation of contralateral and ipsilateral columnar projections to frontal association cortex in primates. *Science* 216, 755-757, 1982.

Goldman-Rakic, P.S.   The frontal lobes: Uncharted provinces of the brain. *Trends in Neuroscience* 7, 425-429, 1984.

Goldman-Rakic, P.S.   Modular organization of prefrontal cortex. *Trends in Neuroscience* 7, 419-424, 1984.

Goldman-Rakic, P.S.   Circuitry of the primate prefrontal cortex and the regulation of behavior by representational knowledge. *Handbook of Physiology: The Nervous System. Higher Functions of the Brain*, (F. Plum, Ed.) Bethesda, Maryland, American Physiology Society, Section I, Volume V, Part 1, Chapter 9, 373-417, 1987a.

Goldman-Rakic, P.S.   Topography of cognition: parallel distributed networks in primate association cortex. *Annual Review of Neuroscience* 11, 1987b.

Goldman, P.S., and Nauta, W.J.H.   Autoradiographic demonstration of a projection from prefrontal association cortex to the superior colliculus in the rhesus monkey. *Brain Research* 116, 145-149, 1976.

Goldman, P.S., and Nauta, W.J.H.   Columnar organization of association and motor cortex: autoradiographic evidence for cortico-cortical and commissural columns in the frontal lobe of the newborn rhesus monkey. *Brain Research* 122, 369-385, 1977.

Goldman, P.S., and Nauta, W.J.H.   An intricately patterned prefronto-caudate projection in the rhesus monkey. *J. Comp. Neurol.* 171, 369-386, 1977.

Hikosaka, O., and Sakamoto, M.   Cell activity in monkey caudate nucleus preceding saccadic eye movements. *Exp. Brain Res.* 63, 659-62, 1986.

Hikosaka, O., and Wurtz, R.H.   Visual and oculomotor functions of monkey substantia nigra pars reticulata. III. Memory-contingent visual and saccade responses. *J. Neurophysiology* 49, 1268-1284, 1983.

Hubel, D.H., and Wiesel, T.N.   Anatomic demonstration of columns in the monkey striate cortex. *Neuroscience* 221, 747-750, 1969.

Hyvarinen, J.   Regional distribution of functions in parietal association area 7 of the monkey. *Brain Research* 206, 287-303, 1981.

Isseroff, A., Schwartz, M.L., Dekker, J.J., and Goldman-Rakic, P.S. Columnar organization of callosal and associational projections from rat frontal cortex. *Brain Research* 293, 213-223, 1984.

Jones, E.G., and Powell, T.P.S. An anatomical study of converging sensory pathways within the cerebral cortex of the monkey. *Brain Research* 93, 793-820, 1970.

McGuire, P., and Goldman-Rakic, P.S. Homotopic regions of the principal sulcus and of the supplementary motor area. II. Ipsi- and contralateral neostriatal connections and their convergence in common targets. Submitted to *J. Comp. Neurol.* 1990.

Mesulam, M.M. A cortical network for directed attention and unilateral neglect. *Annals of Neurol.* 10, 309-325, 1981.

Mountcastle, V.B. Modality and topographic properties of single neurons of cat's somatic sensory cortex. *J. Neurophys.* 20, 408-434, 1957.

Mountcastle, V.B. An organizing principle for cerebral function: The unit module and the distributed system. *The Neurosciences: Fourth Study Program*, (edited by F.0. Schmitt and F.G. Worden) pp. 21 ff. MIT Press, 1979.

Mountcastle, V.B., Lynch, J.C., Georgopoulos, A., Sakata, H., and Acuna, C. Posterior parietal association cortex of the monkey: command functions for operations with extrapersonal space. *J. Neurophys.* 37, 871-908, 1989.

Niki, H., and Watanabe, M. Prefrontal unit activity and delayed response: relation to cue location versus direction of response. *Brain Research* 105, 78-88, 1976.

Pandya, D.N., and Selzer, B. Intrinsic connections and architectonics of posterior parietal cortex in the rhesus monkey. *J. Comp. Neurol.* 204, 196-210, 1982.

Pandya, D.N., and Vignolo, L.A. Intra- and inter-hemispheric projections of the precentral, premotor and arcuate areas in the rhesus monkey. *Brain Research* 26, 217-233, 1971.

Posner, M.I. Neural systems underlying cognition. *J. Clin. Exp. Neuropsychol.* 7, 598, 1986.

Richardson, R.T., and DeLong, M.R. Nucleus basalis of Meynert neuronal activity during a delayed response task in monkey. *Brain Research* 399, 364-368, 1986.

Schwartz, M.L., and Goldman-Rakic, P.S. Callosal and intra-hemispheric connectivity of the prefrontal association cortex in rhesus monkey: relation between intraparietal and principal sulcal cortex. *J. Comp. Neurol.* 226, 403-420, 1984.

Selemon, L.D., and Goldman-Rakic, P.S. Common cortical and subcortical target areas of the dorsolateral prefrontal and posterior parietal cortices in the rhesus monkey: a double label study of distributed neural networks. *J. Neurosci.* 8, 4049-4068, 1988.

Selzer, B., and Pandya, D.N. Converging visual and somatic sensory cortical input to the intraparietal sulcus of the rhesus monkey. *Brain Research* 192, 339-351, 1980.

Shallice, T. Specific impairments in planning. *Philosophical Transactions of the Royal Society of London*, B, Biological Science 298, 199-209, 1982.

Shallice, T. *From Neuropsychology to Mental Structure.* Cambridge University Press, 1988.

Van Essen, D.C. Functional organization of primate visual cortex. *Cerebral Cortex*, Volume 3, (edited by A. Peters and E.G. Jones), pp. 259 ff. Plenum Press, 1985.

Van Essen, D.C., and Maunsell, J.H.R. Hierarchical organization and functional streams in the visual cortex. *Trends in Neuroscience* 6, 370-375, 1983.

Watanabe, T., and Niki, H. Hippocampal unit activity and delayed response in the monkey. *Brain Research* 325, 241-254, 1985.

Chapter 8

How the Brain Functionally Rewires Itself

MICHAEL M. MERZENICH, GREGG H. RECANZONE, WILLIAM M. JENKINS AND RANDOLPH J. NUDO

Introduction

Despite the substantial growth of experimental neuroscience, of the behavioral sciences and of theoretical neuroscience over the past several decades—that is, despite the intensive efforts of several tens of thousands of scientists generating thousands of volumes filled with detailed observations about molecules and synapses and neurons and neuronal circuits, animal and human behaviors, human neuropsychology in the dysfunctional or brain-injured patient, and a great panoply of theoretical models and arguments—we still understand surprisingly little about the origins of the 'higher' functions of the brain from the perspective of its complex neuronal ensembles.

Thus, while some fundamental mechanisms underlying molecular and cellular and connectional alterations driven by behaviors have been described and modeled, there is still no generally agreed-upon notion of how or where learning arises as a product of real neuronal networks of the mammalian nervous system. There is still no generally-accepted notion of the bases or origins of the great functional illnesses of the brain—for example, of madness, of childhood autism, of depression. There is still no clear understanding of the mechanisms by which we recover functionally from brain-injury, although recovery can occur on a remarkable scale, especially in the young. There is still no clear understanding of how our idiosyncratic human experiences can lead humankind into such completely different and specific operational forms; issues raised in thousands of studies of human child-development have, in fact, been little investigated by experimental neuroscientists.

Considered from another perspective, there is still no detailed and generally-accepted understanding of the neurological processes relevant to behavior attributable to the two-and-a-half-square-feet of cortical mantle, in large part because the cerebral cortex has almost never been investigated on an appropriate neuron-cell-assembly level of analysis during the acquisition of new behaviors. This is the case despite the fact that this great practical question has long been recognized as among the most important of issues to be addressed in our research field—and at the heart of relating the real operation of distributed neural networks to theoretical 'neural' networks.

In our own research, we are interested in the shaping of neural cell-assemblies—and thereby, behaviors—by experience that, with an undeniable contribution from genetics, marks us all as individuals. Again, from a second operational perspective, this constitutes a search for the basic general operations in the neocortex that underlie adaptive behaviors. We seek identification of these general dynamic neocortical processes with the recognition that their elucidation should bear important implications for understanding the origins of functional illnesses and modes of dysfunction of this dynamic machine, and for understanding processes accounting for often-remarkable recovery from brain-damage.

Experimental approach

These issues have been addressed by our research-group in large part by defining the topography of the selective response properties of neurons in areas in the cortical mantle that represent either the skin-surfaces or movements in adult monkeys. By reconstructing a sector of cortical skin-surface representations or cortical movement-representations in detail, we attempt to assay the specific, distributed-response properties of neurons over a significant part of the complexly-coupled cortical-cell network in a monkey that is acquiring or has acquired new perceptual abilities or motoric skills. We study these particular representations because they are relatively simple in form; we believe that they constitute reasonable general models for studying cortical-network plasticity. Our objective is to describe directly the neuron-response changes and cell-assembly changes that account for what the cortical fields under study contribute to this behavioral acquisition.

One basic technical approach employed in both the somatosensory and motor cortex is illustrated in Figure 1. In a somatosensory cortical field, the effective responses of neurons are defined over a small patch of cortex 2 or 3 or 4 millimeters across with a dense sampling, usually on a scale of about 100-150 microns. In this illustrative example, a patch of the somatosensory cortical area 3b, the true 'primary somatosensory cortex' (Merzenich 1978) in a normal adult monkey has been mapped. This is one of several cortical areas that we have studied that topographically represent the surfaces of the body of this monkey (Merzenich 1978, Merzenich 1981).

The New World owl monkey (*Aotus trivirgatus*) has been used in many of these experiments because it lacks major fissures in these brain-regions. It is far easier to define the details of cortical representational topographies in skin-surface- and movement-representational areas in this monkey as compared with most other primate species because in this species they are almost completely exposed out on the flat exterior surface of the forebrain.

In Figure 1B, the view is down on the surface of a small mapped cortical region in the hand-representation zone of area 3b in a typical adult monkey. Each symbol represents the surface location at which a recording microelectrode has penetrated the cortical mantle. At each sampled site, the skin on the surface of the hand was explored with fine probes to determine the specific skin-surfaces whose stimulation evoked discharges in neurons at that location in the cortical network. The sites marked by diamonds, stars and large filled circles represent the locations of those microelectrode-penetrations at which effective inputs were from the glabrous (hairless) surfaces of fingers 2, 3 and 4, respectively. With this grain of sampling, the estimation of the territory representing these fingers in the cerebral cortex is accurate (Stryker 1987). If we were to look internally within each small mapped digital representational zone, the distal fingertip skin below the fingernail would usually be represented in the extreme rostral aspect of these areas, toward the right in Figure 1B. The finger-surfaces along the margin of the palm would usually be represented in the most caudal aspect of these small zones. The surfaces of these fingers toward the thumb would usually be represented along the upper margin of each patch, and those toward the little finger along the lower margin.

In other words, *there is a single, simple, topographically-ordered pattern of representation of each functional hand-surface in this cortical zone*. The representational topography of this 'hand-representation' can be well defined by a 'map' constructed from this dense sample.

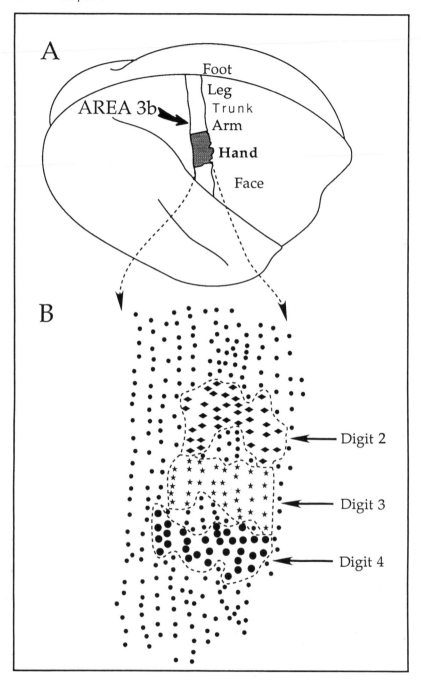

Figure 1. One strategy employed to assess the distributed, selective response properties of neurons in a small sector of the cortical network in one of the several model-regions chosen for study, the true primary somatosensory cortex, area 3b. Many of our experiments have been conducted in the cerebral cortex of the New World owl monkey, drawn from a lateral perspective at the top, because it lacks major fissures in the primary areas of representation of the skin surfaces and movements. The front of the cerebral hemisphere is toward the right.

In this typical response 'mapping' experiment, several hundred microelectrode penetrations, represented by dots, diamonds and stars in the lower panel, have been introduced into the cortical mantle over a roughly 2 x 4.5 mm region. At each of these sites, skin-surfaces are explored using fine probes (and often, computer-controlled temporally modulated skin-stimulation) to determine the specific skin 'receptive fields' (and other response characteristics) effective for evoking cortical-neuron discharges at each sampled site. The cortical-network sites sampled that are marked by diamonds, stars and large filled circles represent those at which cutaneous receptive fields were located on the glabrous surfaces of fingers 2, 3 and 4, respectively. The overall mapped region illustrated in this case represents the approximate zone of representation of the surfaces of the hand in this monkey. With this grain of sampling, the territory in the cortex dedicated to the representation of any given skin-surface, like a finger-segment or palmar pad or arm-ector—and their internal representational topographies—can be accurately estimated. There is a single, simple, topologically-ordered representation of the surfaces of the hand in adult owl monkeys.

Most of our experiments are directed toward determining how the selective, distributed-response properties across a limited cortical-network sector like this one are altered by the acquisition of new behaviors in adult monkeys.

Cortical representations of the skin surface are remodeled by use, throughout life

It had long been believed that cortical representations like those of the skin-surfaces of the hands in area 3b are anatomical constructs, and are unalterable in adults. However, we and others have generated a large body of evidence that reveals that cortical representations are actually dynamic constructs, altered by experience (see Merzenich 1988 for review). *The details of cortical somatosensory representations can be shaped by behaviorally important skin-use, throughout life.*

One simple, exemplary experiment that illustrates the use-dependent alteration of a skin-surface representation is outlined in Figure 2 (see Jenkins 1990). In this experimental series, we trained monkeys to maintain contact of a fingertip or two on a rotating, grooved surface for ten or fifteen seconds for each food-reward (see Figure 2A). Why use a task like this one? First, it is relatively easy to initiate this behavior in an adult monkey; a monkey can be trained to perform it successfully with only a few days of training. Second, with a task like this one, it is relatively easy to get the monkey to heavily differentially engage a very limited skin-surface region—in this case, a small skin-sector on two, and occasionally three, fingertips. Third, this task requires the monkey's full attention. We have no direct measure of attention in these experiments other than the monkeys' successful

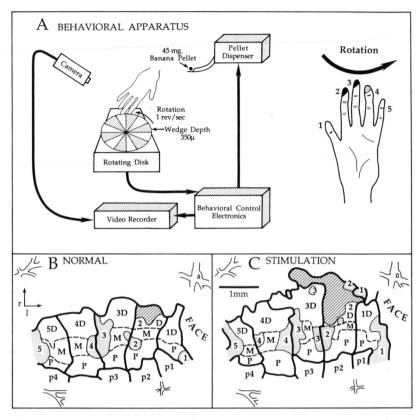

Figure 2. A representative case from one of several experimental series revealing that somatosensory cortical representations are altered by hand-use. In this study, the monkey was trained to maintain contact with the tip of two and occasionally three fingers (see hand drawing) for about 15 seconds for each 500-600 daily food-rewards.   The behavioral training system, which was mounted on the monkey's home-cage, is shown at the left. Surface-views of the area 3b cortical representations of the hand before and after a 7-week period of this training are shown schematically in B and C.   There, numbers 1-5 mark cortical zones in which all skin receptive fields for sampled neurons were on finger 1 (the thumb) to finger 5. Territories of representation of skin-surfaces on the back of the hand are shaded. D, M and P mark the zones of representation of distal, middle and proximal finger-segments, respectively.   Lower-case p marks palmar pad representations. The cross-hatched zones mark the cortical area excited by stimulation of fingertip surfaces on finger 2 that were engaged in this behavior before the behavior was initiated (B), and after performing this task for seven weeks (C).

See the text and Figure 1 for a further description of this experiment and these methods, and for a further description of the specific response-changes and topological changes generated by this perturbation of inputs into a small region in the cortical neural network. Modified from Jenkins, *et al.* (Jenkins 1990).

performance.   At the same time, *you* would have to focus your attention closely on this task to perform it successfully.   Contact pressure must be continually actively regulated by the subject, or the hand is thrown off the disk or breaks contact with its rotating, ridged surface.

From a map of hand-surfaces recorded in a monkey prior to such training, it is possible to determine just how the skin-surfaces of the hand are represented in a particular 'naive' monkey. One such control-map is shown in Figure 2B. There, outlined areas '1' to '5' mark the cortical territories representing fingers 1 (the thumb) to 5 (the little finger). That is, all sampling penetrations introduced into each of these outlined zones had cutaneous receptive fields restricted to the designated digits.

Following the derivation of this control-map under sterile surgical conditions, this monkey underwent a training regime in which it differentially self-stimulated the skin of two or occasionally three fingertips on a rotating disk (see the hand-drawing, Figure 2A, bottom), as described above. After seven weeks at this task, a fine-grained map of the cortical representation of this monkey's hand was again derived. In this post-behavior map (Figure 2C) as in all other post-behavior maps derived in this experimental series, there was a distortion in the cortical representation of the fingertips engaged in this behavioral task. In Figure 2C, the zone of representation of the struck surfaces of digit 2 are highlighted by cross-hatching. The cortical territory of representation of this skin-surface—and equally, the tip of digit 3, also consistently stimulated in the behavior in this monkey—was obviously greatly enlarged over this training period.

In addition to the enlargement of the representation of the differentially engaged fingertip-skin, two other aspects of the distributed representation of the fingers that underwent change in this cortical zone are worth noting: a) the details of the topologic map of the fingertip were altered substantially, and b) the differentially stimulated skin came to be represented by far smaller cutaneous receptive fields.

As we march in a caudal-to-rostral direction over this brain-area across the zone of representation of a single finger in a normal map, receptive fields of sequentially studied neurons march in an orderly, shifter-overlap progression from the base of the finger to the fingertip. By contrast, after this training, as we marched toward the border of the representation of the distal segment of the finger, receptive fields suddenly jumped discontinuously, to overlie closely the skin that was directly stimulated in the behavior. Indeed, the representation of the remainder of the distal finger-segment was substantially neglected in studied monkeys. After training, *every* neuron over a cortical zone hundreds of microns across specifically responded *only* to cutaneous stimulation over this small skin-surface region, comprising only a small fractional part (about 1/6th) of the skin surface of the distal finger-segment.

Another obvious change, illustrated in Figure 3, was in the sizes of the cutaneous receptive fields effective for exciting neurons over this altered cortical-network zone. Cutaneous receptive fields in the cortical region representing this exercised skin-surface were only a fraction of their normal size: *as a consequence of this behavioral experience, this skin-surface was represented in much finer spatial grain.*

To summarize, alterations of the cortical representation of the fingertips have been produced by behavioral training at a task that involved the differential engagement of restricted fingertip-surfaces in an attentive adult monkey. The fingertips were represented over a substantially larger cortical zone than before. The topology has been altered to exaggerate greatly that limited distal segment-skin-surface whose cutaneous receptors have been selectively activated in the behavior. And this over-represented skin-surface is now represented in much finer detail, by much smaller cutaneous receptive fields.

It is interesting to note that if we look elsewhere in these maps, *as a rule*, we find that the topography of the representation of the hand differs over these two slices of time in the life of these adult monkeys. Map differences are not limited to the differentially-activated region. Of course this monkey has very many other uses for his hand over this period. In Figure 2B and C, note, for example, the differences in the patterns of representation of the surfaces of the hairy dorsum of the hand (shaded) or the glabrous surfaces of the thumb ('1' in these figures), or of the fifth digit ('5'). On these two different days in the life of this monkey, separated by about three months, these hand surfaces are represented in detail in very different forms, even though they were not obviously involved in this particular behavior. In fact, with reference to constant vascular landmarks shown around the perimeter of the cartoons in Figures 2B and C, note that the border of the cortical representation of the hand with the face actually shifted rightward (lateralward) after behavioral training, in this—as in most other—trained monkeys. Many thousands of neurons that formerly responded overtly only to stimulation of the skin-surfaces of the face responded several months later only to stimulation of the surfaces of the thumbward side of the hand. One consequence of such long-distance representational shifts is that there appeared to be little net loss in the territory of representation of different hand-surfaces consequent upon a positive local increase in the territory of representation attributable to differentially heavy use of a limited hand-surface—like a fingertip or two—because territory

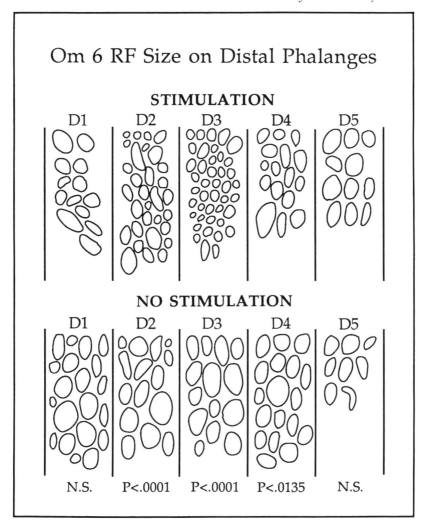

Om 6 RF Size on Distal Phalanges

STIMULATION

D1   D2   D3   D4   D5

NO STIMULATION

D1   D2   D3   D4   D5

N.S.   P<.0001   P<.0001   P<.0135   N.S.

Figure 3. Outlines of skin receptive fields on the distal finger-segments drawn from a second, representative experiment in this same fingertip-on-rotating-disk series. Note that as a consequence of this simple behavior (upper panel contrasted with lower panel), receptive fields were a fraction of their normal size. Changes were especially striking on finger 3, which underwent the most dramatic representational changes in this particular monkey. In this case, the second map—from which receptive fields were drawn in the bottom panel—was derived three months after the derivation of the post-behavior map. Over that three-month period, the behavioral apparatus was removed from the monkey's cage.

was borrowed progressively over relatively-long cortical distances (Jenkins 1990).

In fact, if we go to any clearly-marked site in this map, using blood-vessel-locations as a reference, for *most* locations the receptive field differed substantially at the second slice of time when compared with the first, and in a large percentage of paired comparisons, the receptive field derived at the same or almost the same location was completely non-overlapping with that defined in the first map. This evident dynamism of the details of cortical representations was first recorded in the 'primary motor cortex', cortical area 4, in long-forgotten double stimulation-mapping experiments of Karl Lashley, and were, in fact, the initial bases for his positing the concept of cortical 'equipotentiality' (Lashley 1923).[*]

Thus, a simple differential hand-use behavior results in a remodeling of the details of representation of the skin-surfaces of the hand in this primary somatosensory cortical field in an adult monkey. On the basis of this and a number of other similar and related experiments (Merzenich 1984b, 1987b, 1988; Clark 1986, 1988; Jenkins 1987), we conclude that *cortical sensory representations are remodeled by use throughout life.* There are countless possible detailed forms of cortical representations of the skin-surface.

It is not surprising, then, that if we look at detailed maps in a series of normal monkeys, they differ idiosyncratically in representational detail (Merzenich 1985, 1987a). Individually-different cortical area 3b hand-representation-maps derived in six adult monkeys are shown, for example, in Figure 4. There, again, the view is down onto the cortex in the area of the hand-representations in this 'primary' area 3b skin-surface-representation. Again, numbers designate the territories representing the skin-surfaces of the digits (1-5) or of the pads of the palm (P). The representation of the face bounds that of the hand at the left; the arm-representation, not drawn, is off the right margin. Cortical zones representing the surfaces on the back of the hand are shaded.

Note the individual differences, for example, in the territories of representation of the hairy skin on the back of the hands (shaded in the cartoon-panels in Figure 4) in these six monkeys; at the differences in the territories of representation of the thumb ('1') or forefinger ('2'); or of the identity or order of finger-surfaces represented along the border of the area 3b representation of the hand with that of the face. Again, we believe that idiosyncratic differences like these reflect predominant hand-uses of these individual monkeys.

---

[*]   In Lashley's words: 'The results suggest that ... the cortex may be equipotential for the production of all ... movement ... and ... the particular movements elicited in any test depend on the temporary physiological organization of the area, rather than upon any point-for-point correspondence between [cortical] pyramidal [cells] and spinal neurons.'

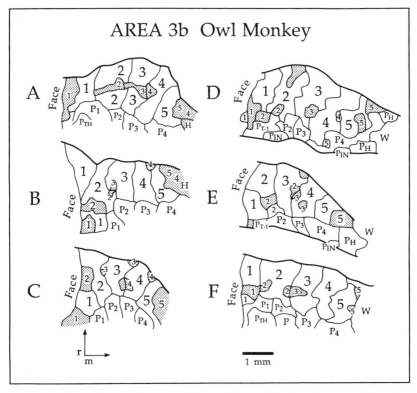

Figure 4. Cortical area 3b maps of the surfaces of the hand in six adult owl monkeys. The cortical zones representing the skin on the hairy dorsum of the fingers and palm are shaded. Numbers 1-5 designate those area 3b sectors representing the glabrous surfaces of the fingers. PTH, PH and PIN designate the hypothenar, thenar and insular palmar pads, respectively. P1-P4 designate the palmar pads at the base of the digits. H and W mark zones representing the palm dorsum and the wrist. The striking idiosyncratic differences in the sizes and topographies of representations of the skin-surfaces of the hand are, we believe, primarily attributable to predominant hand-uses in these adult monkeys (Merzenich 1985, 1987, 1988). See text for further description. Redrawn, from Merzenich 1987.

Cortical representational plasticity reflects *general* neocortical processes

This representational dynamism is presumably general in the neocortex. We have investigated that generalization by studying other somatosensory cortical fields, and by investigating experience-induced plasticity in auditory and motor cortical areas. *Topographic representations in all investigated cortical areas appear to be similarly altered by use.*

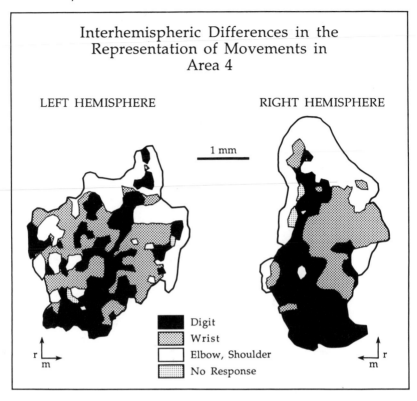

Figure 5. Surface-view of normal lowest-threshold movement-maps in the cortical zone of representation of movements of the fingers (cross-checked), wrist (shaded), and elbow and shoulder (clear background) in cortical area 4 in two hemispheres in an adult owl monkey. The more complicated representation at the left (with twelve discrete zones representing movements of the fingers) maps the movements of the preferred hand; the far simpler representation at the right (with two discrete zones representing movements of the fingers) is of the non-preferred hand. These maps were each reconstructed from more than six-hundred microelectrode-penetrations. In each of these penetrations, the movements evoked by low-current-level microstimulation (Asanuma 1972) were defined. See text for further description.

In cortical area 4, the primary motor cortex, movement-selective responses are evoked by intracortical microstimulation in a cortical output-layer populated by neurons whose axons project to the spinal cord and to special motor nuclei innervating the muscles of the face. These movement-representations have a definable topography, in any adult monkey (Sherrington 1906; Leyton 1917; Franz 1915; Woolsey 1958; Asanuma 1972; Strick 1982). Early investigators recognized that there were substantial individual differences in movement-representation topographies in different adult monkeys (Sherrington 1906; Leyton 1917; Franz 1915; Woolsey 1958). Gould and his colleagues have recently documented striking individual differences in adult owl monkeys (Gould 1986). We have extended their experiments by mapping these movement-representations in both hemispheres in a small series of animals (Nudo 1988). Two movement-maps from our series are shown in a highly-abbreviated form in Figure 5. There, cortical territories over which movements of the fingers, the wrist, and the elbow or shoulder can be elicited are distinguished. These two maps roughly represent the range of differences in movement-maps recorded in different adult monkeys in our experimental series. If we were to subdivide movement-representations further by categorizing movements more specifically, the differences between these representations would be more exaggerated.

In fact, these two 'maps' are not from different individuals. They are from two hemispheres of the same adult monkey. The more complex map on the left represents the movement-map of the preferred hand, as adjudged by a food-retrieval task (Nudo 1988). The less complex map on the right represents the hand that this monkey employed to maintain himself in balance posturally.

Is it likely that this variability reflects the consequences of different predominant hand-uses? To answer that question, we conducted studies in movement-cortex that paralleled those in somatosensory cortex, discussed earlier. That is, after derivation of movement-representations in adult monkeys, they were trained in a simple motoric task, to determine whether or not their movement-representations could be altered by hand-use. In one such task, monkeys were trained to retrieve food-pellets from a food-well in a modified Klüver board. The results of one of these experiments are illustrated in Figure 6. This monkey initially successfully retrieved a food-pellet on every 18th attempt. In any simple motoric behavior like this, this monkey—as you would— becomes more skillful day by day. With only eleven days of practice, this particular monkey could successfully retrieve a food-pellet on every attempt. When this 'perfect' motoric skill performance-level was attained, with a total of only eleven hours of training, the movement-representation was again reconstructed.

As in somatosensory-mapping experiments, there were clear differences in movement-representations induced by this limited behavioral practice, with an enlargement of the representation of movements critical to the successful performance of this motor task recorded in the anterior (in Figure 6, upward) aspect of the area 4 movement-representation. The majority of the acquired gains were in the representation of digit-extension, a movement that was clearly crucial for the performance of this food-retrieval task. Two other changes evident in the pre-training and post-training maps of Figure 6 are worth noting. First, after training, two movements—wrist-extension and digit-extension—were recording

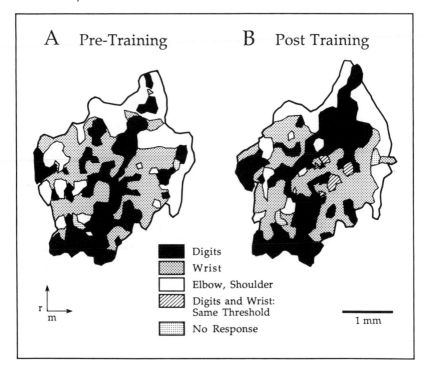

Figure 6. Surface view of area 4 movement-maps derived before and after a period of eleven hours of behavioral training in a simple food-retrieval task. Representational differences before and after training are most prominent in the rostral (upward) sector of this mapped region. They would be still more striking if movements of the thumb (not engaged in the task) were distinguished from movements of the other fingers (critical for performance of the task). A large part of the gains in territory in this rostral area 4 zone were for the representation of digit-extension, which was crucial for the performance of this simple skill. See text for further description.

at equal stimulation threshold at 13 cortical-map sites, within the small black zones in Figure 6B. *These were movements that co-occurred in the successful performance of this task.* No such sites were recorded in this animal prior to these few hours of practice. Second, paralleling findings in somatosensory cortical maps, the specific movements recorded at the same cortical sites changed over time all across these 'maps'. Indeed, in control-experiments, movements derived in a second map were found to involve a different joint at about half of the sampled area 4 sites, confirming earlier, double cortical-surface electrical-stimulation mapping results of Lashley (Lashley 1923).

Thus, these experiments reveal, preliminarily, that movement-representations, like sensory representations, are continually modified by use throughout adult life. With only a few hours of training in this practiced movement, there was a substantial increase in the territory of representation of specific task-related movements, and an indication of a topographic functional remapping that resulted in an alignment of movements that co-occurred in the task.

Taking these and other sensory and motor cortex representational plasticity experiments together, we conclude that *use-driven representational changes at least partly account for the improvement in discriminative performance and the acquisition of motoric skill with practice.* In any attentive behavior, sensory inputs alter the details of a substantial number of the more than a hundred cortical representations distributed across the human neocortex (Merzenich 1984a). By this view, this lifelong, distributed, experience-driven representational remodeling constitutes the principal cortical contribution to the nurture-based development of specific perceptual and motoric abilities that mark each of us as individual.

What do we know about mechanisms underlying these processes?

Many facets of this evident representational dynamism are consistent with the neuronal-group-selection theory, posited by Edelman (Edelman 1978, 1981, 1984; see also Chapter 9 of this volume).

1. *Representational plasticity manifests lifelong operation of cortical mechanisms of input-selection. Anatomical spreads of input required to support this input-selection are probably in place.* Many neural network models apply a distributed convergent/divergent input— termed a 'degenerate' input by Edelman (*op.cit.*). In the somatosensory cortex, direct evidence indicates that the anatomical map of the skin-surface in area 3b in a carnivore or primate is crude, relative to the functionally-defined representation of the skin-surface. Anatomical inputs delivered to any point in the cortical network actually represent much of the surface of the hand, and perhaps a significant part of the surfaces of the face or wrist as well (for different lines of evidence that support this conclusion, see Garraghty 1989; Landry 1981; Raussel 1989; Snow 1988; Hicks 1983; Alloway 1988; Recanzone 1990; Zarzecki 1982). Neurons at any given time in life overtly respond to a small *selected* subset—perhaps a hundredth or a thousandth— of that extensive input-repertoire. *All other inputs are suppressed.* From another perspective, input from any given point on the hand or arm or face is actually represented anatomically over a cortical zone at least two or three mm across in area 3b in this small monkey—which constitutes a large part of the cortical hand- or arm- or face-map sector.

2. *Input effectivenesses for driving cortical representational changes are modulated as a function of behavioral state.* If a monkey is trained at a task that involves heavy selective engagement of the surfaces of the hand and if that stimulation is behaviorally significant, relatively-large changes are produced in cortical maps. On the other hand, if virtually-identical inputs are delivered on a virtually-equivalent schedule *but are behaviorally insignificant,* no major input-dependent changes are created (Recanzone 1989). These somatosensory findings confirm earlier similar results drawn from classical conditioning studies of the selective-response properties of neurons in premotor cortex (Woody 1972; Disterhof 1976) and auditory cortex (Kitzes 1978; Diamond 1985, 1986, 1989; Weinberger 1988; Woody 1972). In both of those cortical regions, response properties of cortical neurons were selectively changed so that a larger neuron population responded differently—significantly more strongly, or significantly more weakly—to conditioning broad-band or tonal sound-stimuli as an animal was behaviorally conditioned. Induced changes were roughly reversed when this behavioral conditioning was extinguished.

3. *Cortical representations are shaped by input-time-structure. Considered in detail, cortical 'maps' are time-based constructs.* We have conducted five series of experiments that, collectively, convincingly demonstrate that the topographic details of cortical representations of the skin-surface are shaped by afferent input-time-structure. Results from two of these experimental series will be briefly described.

Representational changes follow digital syndactyly

When sampling microelectrode-penetrations march across the cortex on an axis that crosses the individual finger-representations of area 3b (for a reminder, see Figures 1 and 2), a representational discontinuity marks the separation of representation of adjacent fingers. That is, within the confines of the cortical-network representation of any given finger, receptive fields recorded in a medial-to-lateral penetration-sequence usually march across the width of the finger with a shifted-overlap skin-receptive-field sequence, but when the representation of the extreme outer margin of a finger is located, the next receptive fields in sequence suddenly jump to the bordering finger. With rare exception, there is a sharp representational break between the area 3b cortical representations of adjacent fingers. Nearly all neurons respond to stimulation of only one finger on one side of a given break, and nearly all neurons respond to stimulation of its neighbor across the break.

We know that these between-digit cortical representational discontinuities are *functional* constructs, because they *moved* in several cortical-plasticity experiments (Jenkins 1987, 1990; Merzenich 1984b). We hypothesize that they arise because the surfaces of adjacent fingers have—on the relevant time-scale for network-plasticity—largely temporally independent inputs. If that interpretation is correct—if the cortical representation locally reflects the quantities of behaviorally significant *coincident* inputs—then cortical-network models indicate that the delivery of a heavy schedule of non-coincident inputs from competing skin-surfaces into the network might create just such representational discontinuities.

These arguments can be tested by examining the consequences of fusing adjacent digits. This has been accomplished in an experimental series conducted in collaboration with a plastic- and reconstructive-hand-surgeon, Sharon Clark (Clark 1988; Allard 1990). In a small series of monkeys, employing a relatively harmless surgical procedure that is the reverse of that commonly applied in human children with congenital syndactylies, the skin along the margins of two adjacent fingers was cut, and the hairless and glabrous surfaces of these two adjacent fingers then sutured together to create a two-digit syndactyly.

Our hypothesis was that if cortical representations are normally time-based and if the normal discontinuity is a consequence of the fact that skin-surfaces have largely independent temporal-stimulation histories, then fusing two fingers together should destroy the discontinuity between their representations because it should result in strongly-temporally-dependent stimulation of the fused-digit skin. This prediction was borne out by the results of this study (Clark 1988; Allard 1990). After several weeks of digit-fusion, the two-digit syndactyly came to be represented like a normal single digit. Receptive fields recorded in penetration-sequences across this area simply marched across the fingers with a shifted-overlap sequence, as if the scar line was not there. Across a wide zone over the center of the territory of representation of the two fused fingers, *every* sampled neuron now had a receptive field that extended onto *both* of them.

To demonstrate that this representational remodeling was a consequence of central-nervous-system plasticity, the fingers were separated in these anesthetized monkeys at the end of each experiment and the cortex immediately remapped. After re-separating the fingers, whereas ordinarily glabrous digital receptive fields only occasionally extended onto two adjacent fingers, now nearly all neurons across a cortical zone several hundred microns in width had receptive-field components on both of these two adjacent, formerly-fused digits.

To summarize, temporarily fusing two adjacent digits resulted in a remapping of skin surfaces in the cortical network, consistent with the substantial change in spatiotemporal inputs induced by this minor surgical manipulation.

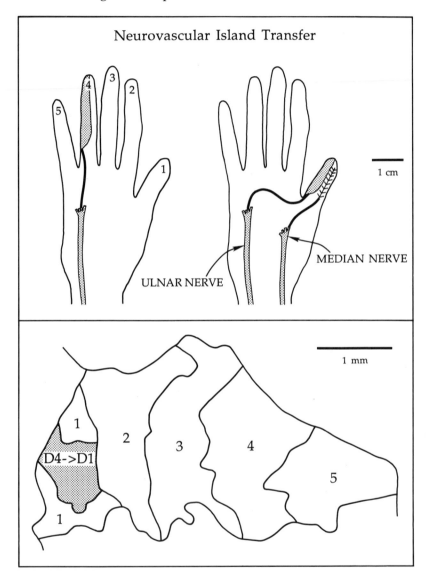

Cortical maps reorganize following a neurovascular-island skin-transfer

In a second test of the hypothesis that input timing contributes to the shaping of cortical maps, a 'neurovascular island'—an always-innervated, always-vascularized sector of skin—was moved to a new hand location (Merzenich 1988; Clark 1986). The innervated, vascularized skin-island in one such case (Figure 7) was comprised of the distal two-thirds of the skin-field of distribution of a digital cutaneous branch of the ulnar nerve, overlying the ulnar half of the middle and distal segments of the glabrous surface of the fourth digit (upper-left panel). This innervated skin island was inserted onto the ulnar half of the glabrous thumb (upper right). In turn, the ulnar thumb skin was used as a denervated graft to fill the fourth-finger skin-defect. This procedure again simulated a common human plastic-surgical procedure.

One objective of this experiment was to move always-innervated skin to a new location, while minimally disturbing peripheral skin-innervation. The excised skin was dissected along the margins of distribution of a single digital cutaneous nerve, which are relatively sharply demarcated on a human or simian finger. This transfer could be achieved with minimum disturbance of peripheral-nerve skin-destinations with respect to fixed central-nervous-system neurons. At the same time, by this simple procedure, a small, always-innervated peripheral skin-surface can be introduced into an entirely new skin-neighborhood. The distributed spatiotemporal inputs delivered to the brain from the skin are thereby radically altered with respect to their neighbors, in this case with fourth-digit skin now situated adjacent to first-digit skin, just across from the second digit.

Figure 7. (left) One of several experiments revealing that cortical-network representations are time-based constructs (Clark 1986). In this schematically illustrated case, a skin island (upper left) was dissected free from the fourth digit with its innervation and vasculature intact. It was then inserted onto the ulnar half of the glabrous surface of the thumb (upper right), using standard human plastic-surgery techniques. A cortical map derived six months later (bottom), again viewed from the surface of the cortical mantle, revealed that the representation of this neurovascular island skin (shaded) disappeared in the cortical sector in which it was formerly represented, *i.e.*, with the rest of digit 4. *It was now represented in entirety in the cortical zone of representation of the thumb.* In that cortical-network sector, the map of the half of the thumb innervated by the median nerve was represented in a topologically orderly way in relation to the emergent map of its new ulnar nerve-innervated neurovascular-island neighbor. Many receptive fields in this zone crossed the faint scar-line on the thumb, that is, had receptive fields comprised of skin formerly represented in zones two or three millimeters apart from each other across the cortical network. *Input co-selection based upon temporal coincidence* must account for this remapping.

When we examined the representation of the hand-surfaces in an adult monkey several months after this procedure, it was found to be completely reorganized.   If cortical maps were strictly anatomically based, then we would expect to see the neurovascular-island skin now inserted on the thumb to be represented permanently with the remainder of the fourth-digit skin in cortical representational maps.   In fact, in the two cases with this particular skin-transfer, *the representation of this fourth-digit skin completely disappeared from the area 3b territory of representation of the fourth digit—and re-emerged in the cortical territory of representation of the thumb* (see Figure 7, bottom).

There, it came to be represented in its entirety, and with an orderly relationship to the skin-surfaces covering the remainder of the thumb.   Many receptive fields in this cortical region came to overlap the faint scar-line that ran longitudinally down the central axis of the thumb.   For neurons at those cortical sites, part of their receptive fields were derived from island skin, which was innervated by an ulnar nerve branch, and part from the radial side of the thumb, which was innervated by a median nerve branch.   Control studies confirmed that these two sides of the finger received exclusive inputs from these two small cutaneous nerve branches.   In other words, *neurons in this network region unequivocally co-selected skin inputs that were formerly represented two or three or more millimeters apart from each other in this cortical field.*

The only plausible basis for that co-selection is input-coincidence.   Creation of this new topography—of this emergent fourth-digit skin-representation in topographic alignment with thumb-skin—*must* be attributed to the consequent reconfiguration of spatiotemporal inputs into the network.

Again, several other experimental series that we have conducted are also consistent with this interpretation (Allard 1988; Yun 1987; Wall 1986), *i.e.*, they represent other clear instances in which receptive fields and cortical representations are distorted by altering what peripheral skin inputs are delivered coincidentally into limited-map network-sectors.   From these studies taken together, we conclude that *the selected response properties of cortical neurons—and hence cortical representational topographies—are largely time-based.   Considered in detail, cortical topographic representations map TEMPORAL continua.*

4. *We hypothesize that the input selection underlying these cortical-map changes is achieved by coupled GROUPS of neurons.*   These neuronal groups (or 'minicolumns') are dynamic, functional entities, not static anatomical machines.   Input-coincidence underlies group formation and intergroup competition.   *As cortical maps change, these cortical-cell assemblies undergo virtually continual change.*

On the basis of detailed surface-mapping experiments, we believe that these functional neuronal groups are usually from a few tens of microns to more than a hundred microns across (see Mountcastle 1978; Eccles 1984). Edelman and his colleagues have hypothesized that neuronal groups are locally strongly positively coupled, with that coupling created dynamically by input-coincidence (Edelman 1978, 1981, 1984; Pearson 1987; see also von der Malsburg 1986; Grajski 1990a, 1990b). As a consequence of that positive coupling, the inputs that neurons come to respond to specifically—for example, their specific cutaneous receptive fields—are a product of this cooperative group of neurons, and all group members share the results of the group operation.

By extension, there would be on the order of a hundred million or more of these basic, parallel input-processing elements in the cerebral cortex of man. It should be emphasized that there appear to be significant differences in the dimensions of these groups, not just from place to place or group to group, but also from time to time, in the life of the animal under study. Thus, for example, we have recorded a number of instances in normal adult cats and monkeys in which relatively large neuronal groups—sometimes hundreds of microns across—have been encountered.

We have studied the mutability of these cell-assemblies in several ways. In one such experiment, stimulating microelectrodes have been introduced into the area 4 movement-representation, to deliver highly coincident stimulation into a small, local network-region. Such local network-perturbations result in a rapid distortion of the zone of representation of the movements evoked by stimulation at a given site, and were interpreted as representing a stimulus-evoked neuronal-group enlargement (Nudo 1987, 1990). Such distortions can be generated by stimulation at levels well below the threshold for directly evoking movements.

There is evidence that local intracortical microstimulation can alter the effective coupling of neurons in the local cortical network (Jankowska 1975). We have examined that possibility more completely by studying similar representational distortions generated by applying intracortical microstimulation in somatosensory cortical area 3b (Pearson 1987; see also von der Malsburg 1986; Grajski 1990a). Results of one series of such experiments are summarized schematically in Figure 8.

Normally, receptive fields derived for cortical neurons shift in an orderly way for sampling microelectrode penetrations that are moved across the cortex. Thus, for the five penetrations shown in Figure 8 (upper left), receptive fields for recorded neurons moved systematically down the finger. If the strength of non-stimulus-driven correlations were to be determined for neurons at sites 2, 3, 4 and 5 referenced to neurons at site 1, correlation would usually be observed at a nearby site (between sites 1 and 2 in our example),

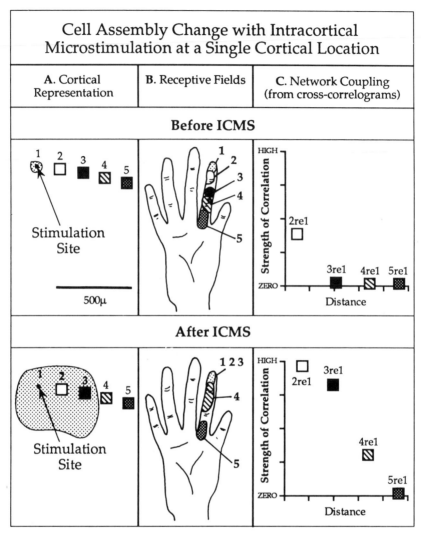

Figure 8. Schematic depiction of one strategy employed for perturbing a local network-region with highly coincident activity (see Recanzone 1988, 1990; Dinse 1989). Dramatic network changes including translocations and substitutions and/or enlargements of receptive fields, and up to a several-hundredfold growth in a coupled cortical-cell-assembly (a 'neuronal group' or 'minicolumn' = the shaded zones in the panels at the left) are produced by local intracortical microstimulation. In these enlarged groups, every neuron acquires response properties that initially applied only to the neurons in a small initial group around the site of the stimulating electrode. Changes over the spatial extent depicted would ordinarily require stimulation over a two- or three-hour period. At the same time, local network changes can be recorded with only a few minutes of such network-perturbing stimulation. These stimulus-induced changes are long-lasting. See the text for further description.

indicating that these neurons are positively coupled. However, no non-stimulus-driven correlation [= correlation during periods of spontaneous activity, when no peripheral stimulation was being applied] would usually be recorded for more-widely-separated locations (for example, between sites 1 and 3 or 1 and 4 or 1 and 5 in our example). This local network-region can be perturbed by a limited schedule (minutes to a few hours) of very-low-current-level intracortical microstimulation (ICMS), designed to excite all cortical elements synchronously within a network-region not more than 5-15 microns across. Such stimulation results in a remarkable reorganization of the cortical representation of the surfaces of the skin in this map-sector. After a period of stimulation, a number of cortical sites come to be excited by stimulation over the receptive field that was initially effective for exciting neurons *only* at the microstimulation-site. This enlargement—up to several hundred-fold—in the cortical zone over which a given cutaneous receptive field can be recorded is regarded as constituting a neuronal-group enlargement. That interpretation is supported by studies of non-stimulus-driven response-correlation after local ICMS, which reveal dramatic stimulation-induced changes. Now, strong correlation is recorded over a much larger cell-assembly. Neurons at the stimulus-site are now positively coupled to many hundreds or thousands more neighboring neurons than before the ICMS perturbation. *The limits of this zone of increased correlation-strength coincide with the cortical limits over which the cortical maps have been altered by the local stimulation.*

These experiments combined with related natural-stimulation studies indicate that *cortical-cell ASSEMBLIES are altered by experience.* As Edelman and others have hypothesized (Edelman 1978, 1981, 1984; Pearson 1987; Chapter 9 of this volume; see also von der Malsburg 1986; Grajski 1990a, 1990b), *the effective connections of the basic cortical machine are THEMSELVES altered by use.* In that sense, the cortex constitutes a complex machine that continually changes its effective local connections. This dynamic cortical 'group formation' and 'group competition', we conclude, largely accounts for the remodeling of cortical representations we observe in behaving animals.

It might be pointed out that these ICMS network-perturbation experiments are not completely original. They were conducted in another form by the great physiologist C. S. Sherrington in the first two decades of this century. When Sherrington mapped movement-representations by cortical-surface electrical-stimulation mapping in monkeys and apes, he realized that the heavy stimulation that he applied in the mapping procedure probably distorted his reconstructed movement-maps, such that the most heavily stimulated movements came to be represented over the largest cortical regions (Sherrington 1906; Leyton 1917). He and his colleagues further investigated this possibility in well-controlled experiments (Nudo 1990), demonstrating that the movements evoked at any given site could be altered by a conditioning period of stimulation at a second site up to more than a centimeter away from the first. In some instances, Sherrington and his colleagues recorded a substitution of the movement initially evoked only at the conditioning site at locations well away from it. It is reasonable to hypothesize that his restricted surface-stimulation, like our intracortical microstimulation, substantially altered the dimensions of cortical-cell-assemblies under and surrounding the zone directly activated by his stimulating electrodes.

5. *Cortical groups continually compete for the domination of neurons on their borders. In any given behavior, the details of cortical map changes reflect the predictable consequences of this competition.* As noted earlier, experiments have revealed that stimulation with moving stimuli results in an enlargement of representation, and in creation of a finer-grained representation of stimulated skin-surfaces. By contrast, stimulation with a coincident, spatially invariant stimulus results in very different representational changes (Recanzone 1989, 1990). There, receptive fields enlarge dramatically in size, and can be represented by very large cortical neuronal groups. To cite three examples:

Modification of a cortical map by a bar-press behavior.

In the experiment illustrated in Figure 9, an adult owl monkey performing a bar-press behavior was struck on the proximal segment of the third finger by the relatively sharp edge of the spring-loaded bar when the monkey released it. This resulted in the creation of a very large representation of this skin-surface by very large cutaneous receptive fields. The receptive fields over the majority of these sites, encompassing an area 1 cortical zone more than a millimeter across, were virtually indistinguishable.

Modification of receptive fields and creation of very large neuronal groups under a digital cast.

A second example of apparent cortical group modification by heavy, positionally invariant, coincident stimulation is illustrated in Figure 10. This monkey wore a hard-shell acrylic cast over digits 3 and 4 for a six-week period. This resulted in an expansion of the cortical zone of representation of these fingers (upper cartoon), presumably because the large, hard plastic cast was constantly and unavoidably stimulated, with virtually any stimulation conveyed effectively through the cast to all of the

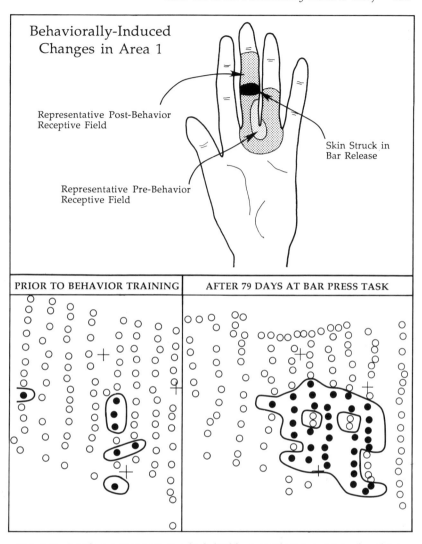

Figure 9. Another experiment in which highly coincident input introduced into the network from a constant skin-region resulted in enlargement of a local cortical group(s). In this case, a patch of skin on the surface of the third digit was consistently struck by the relatively sharp edge of a bar with each of about a hundred and fifty daily bar-presses. After eleven weeks at this behavior, receptive fields recorded in thirty-seven penetrations at sites marked by filled dots extended broadly over this skin-surface—as compared with seven that overlapped any part of it in the pre-behavior map. At the majority of penetrations, a virtually identical, large receptive field (illustrated in the hand drawing at the right) was recorded. This constituted a neuronal-group enlargement by comparison with the normal estimated average group-size of about 400x. *All* receptive fields recorded in this zone in the post-behavior map were larger than any recorded prior to behavioral training.

surfaces of both fingers. In several instances in these experiments, extraordinarily large neuronal groups marked by virtually identical receptive fields were recorded. Thus, for example, in the case illustrated in Figure 10, indistinguishable receptive fields extending over roughly half of the distal segment of digit 4 were recorded in twenty-five neighboring penetrations. We believe that this dramatic group-enlargement was attributable to the largely coincident and spatially invariant inputs delivered through this skin-sector through the hard-shell cast, *i.e.*, was due to the fact that a spatially constant skin-sector was stimulated coincidentally.

Enlargement of receptive fields in monkeys performing a frequency-discrimination task.

A more completely documented study of the changes in cortical networks induced by heavy coincident stimulation at an invariant location on the monkey's skin has been recently completed (Recanzone 1989, 1990). Again, these experiments reveal that when the cortical network is challenged by coincident inputs from an invariant skin-location, very large receptive fields and presumably enlarged coupled neuronal assemblies emerge in this map-sector.

Summary

These and other related experiments reveal that cortical representations and local cortical-cell-assemblies are shaped continually by our experiences. In any given cortical zone, such representational and neuronal-cell-assembly plasticity must be limited by the cortical field-specific identity of input sources and by the local, intrafield limits of divergences and convergences of delivered inputs. Thus, the cortex is locally 'equipotential', but, site by site, only for inputs from field- and site-specific, limited degenerate repertoires. The basic functional unit of the neocortex is a cooperative neuronal group or minicolumn. The dimensions of the basic cortical integrating machine—including the neuronal group and surrounding neuron populations within the potential range of its direct influence—is probably ordinarily relatively constant within the neocortex, on the order of 500-1000 microns in extent. Neurons collectively comprising strongly positively-coupled neuronal groups ordinarily subdivide these cortical zones into roughly one or two hundred cell-assemblies. These functional groups continually compete for the excitatory dominance of neurons along their mutual borders, and on a spatial scale limited by their spreads of primary network influences, are continually varying

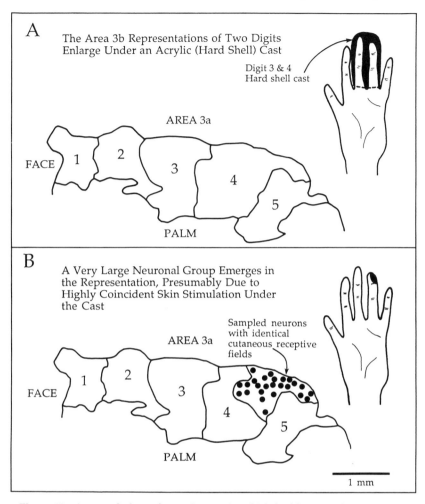

Figure 10. A second class of experiments in which highly coincident input—in this case imposed by the mechanical filtering of a hard-shell acrylic cast covering digits 3 and 4 for thirty days—into a limited cortical map sector appeared to result in creation of enormous cortical groups in which all neurons had virtually identical cutaneous receptive fields. For monkeys wearing digital casts, the overall size of the hand-representation appeared to shrink, while the territory of representation of the encased digits was proportionally larger than that of the other fingers. From wearing these casts on our own fingers and from observing these monkeys, we concluded that this was likely to be due to a neglect in the overall use of this hand, coupled with the fact that this large cast was invariably stimulated whenever the monkey attempted to use his hand, with virtually any stimulus conveyed to most or all digital surfaces through the cast. One of the large neuronal groups that we recorded in the cortical zone representing skin-surfaces under such casts is shown at the bottom. There, an indistinguishable receptive field was recorded in twenty-five microelectrode penetration samples (filled circles) across a cortical zone nearly a square-millimeter in area. This constitutes a neuronal-group enlargement relative to the normal estimated group-size of about 1000x.

their effective selected inputs and their neuronal memberships—
i.e., their sizes.

If we challenge a local network sector with differential heavy,
localized, moving or spatially variable inputs, the network
responds by expanding the cortical territory of representation of
the engaged skin-surface, and by representing it in finer and finer
grain. Why? Because each small skin-region drives a cortical
sector that thereby becomes a more effective competitor for
cortical territory. Intergroup competition assures that this cortical
zone will be competitively superior to the surrounding, more
weakly activated areas. On the one hand, group-size might be
expected to increase because of higher levels of locally correlated
activity. On the other hand, with heavy, spatially varying
stimulation, neuronal groups all across this engaged cortical
territory would be subject to proportionally stronger local network
competition, which would drive average group-sizes back
downward.

By contrast, when a network sector is perturbed by highly
correlated inputs that arise from a constant skin source, a specific
cortical group or groups will be competitively dominant. In
general, stronger local-network coupling from this competitively-
winning network-sector should result in larger receptive-field-sizes
and in larger coupled neuronal ensembles.

In the acquisition of any perceptual ability or motoric skill,
many of our more-than-one-hundred cortical representational areas
are engaged, and, within them, their field-specific representations
will be remodeled as many of their tens of millions of parallel
processing modules—and their individual, cooperative response
selectivities—are modified. These distributed experience-driven
changes collectively constitute the cortical contribution to learning
and memory.

Theoretical models of simple networks based on real cortical
network- and input-connections are consistent with these arguments
(see Pearson 1987; von der Malsburg 1986; Grajski 1990a, 1990b).
Indeed, they are a predictable consequence of a network model
with an appropriate coincidence-based learning-rule, with
appropriately convergent/divergent input-connections, and with
the learning-rule applied to both input effectivenesses and to
positive connections between excitatory—and if you like,
inhibitory—elements in the network.

Some general implications

First, these observations constitute a small part of the beginning
of a new science of the study of dynamic neuronal-cell-assemblies.
This subdiscipline should rapidly grow, as it is increasingly clear

that an understanding of the neural origins of higher brain-functions depends upon study of brain-circuits at this level of analysis.

Second, if we are to understand the operation of the dynamic cell-assemblies of the neocortex, we must study them more often with distributed neuronal sampling, and we must study them more often with the machine turned ON, *i.e.* through the acquisition of new perceptual experiences or abilities or motoric skills. A more substantial part of the effort of neuroscience should be turned to this enterprise, because such studies are crucial for addressing the great central issues of brain science—the origins of recognition and learning and memory, and their complex interplay in neuro-behavioral development.

Third, elucidation of the 'rules' or 'laws' of these dynamic, neural mechanisms constitutes a basis for *rapprochement* with the 'rules' or 'laws' of perceptual and cognitive science, and hence, a basis for initiating a merger of these great parallel scientific disciplines.

Fourth, from an understanding of the fundamental operations of cortical neuronal networks and distributed systems, we shall almost certainly gain an understanding of its modes of dysfunction and failure, and of the basis of its often-remarkable self-repair.

Finally, these studies constitute a small part of a rapidly expanding effort that is carrying a substantial branch of 'neural network' theory into the analysis of real neuronal circuits. Cross-disciplinary studies on this frontier will provide increasingly correct insights into how a particularly effective, very robustly constructed, remarkably adaptive, parallel processing machine—the human brain—accomplishes its manifold, rich and often-complicated enterprises. The endpoint of this line of study should be the general theory of the origin of higher brain-function.

Acknowledgements

This research was supported by NIH Grant NS-10414, Hearing Research, Inc., and the Coleman Fund. The authors thank their collaborators in this research, including Terry Allard, Sharon Clark, Hubert Dinse, Eliana Guic, Randy Nelson, Marleen Ochs, Jun-ti Yun and John Zook.

References

Allard, T.T., Clark, S.A., Jenkins, W.M., and Merzenich, M.M. Reorganization of somatosensory area 3b representation in adult owl monkeys following digital syndactyly. *J. Neurophysiology* (in press), 1990.

Allard, T.T., Clark, S.A., Grajski, K.A., and Merzenich, M.M. *Neuroscience Abstracts* 14, 844, 1988.

Alloway, K.D., Sinclair, R.J., and Burton, H. Responses of neurons in somatosensory cortical area II of cats to high-frequency vibratory stimulation during iontophoresis of a GABA antagonist and glutamate. *Somatosensory Motor Research* 6, 109-140, 1988.

Asanuma, H., and Rosen, I. Topographical organization of cortical efferent zones projecting to distal forelimb muscles in the monkey. *Experimental Brain Research* 14, 242-256, 1972.

Clark, S.A., Allard, T.T., Jenkins, W.M., and Merzenich, M.M. Syndactyly results in the emergence of double digit receptive fields in somatosensory cortex in adult owl monkeys. *Nature* 332, 444-445, 1988.

Clark, S.A., Allard, T.T., Jenkins, W.M., and Merzenich, M.M. Cortical map reorganization following neurovascular island skin transfers on the hands of adult owl monkeys. *Soc. Neurosci. Abstracts* 12, 391, 1986.

Diamond, D.M., and Weinberger, N.M. Role of context in the expression of learning-induced plasticity of single neurons in auditory cortex. *Behavioral Neuroscience* 103, 471-494, 1989.

Diamond, D.M. *Physiological Plasticity of Single Neurons in Auditory Cortex of the Cat during Learning.* Ph.D. thesis. University of California, Irvine, 1985.

Diamond, D.M., and Weinberger, N.M. Classical conditioning rapidly induces specific changes in frequency receptive fields of single neurons in secondary and ventral ectosylvian auditory cortical fields. *Brain Research* 372, 357-360, 1986.

Dinse, H.R., and Merzenich, M.M. Alterations in correlated activity parallel ICMS-induced representational plasticity. *Neuroscience Abstracts* 15, 1223, 1989.

Disterhof, J.F., and Stuart, D.K. Trial sequence of changed unit activity in auditory system of alert rat during conditioned response acquisition and extinction. *J. Neurophysiol.* 39, 266-281, 1976.

Eccles, J.C. The cerebral cortex: a theory of its operation. In *Cerebral Cortex* (Jones, E.G., and Peters, A., editors). Plenum Press, 1984.

Edelman, G.M. *The Mindful Brain* (with Mountcastle, V.B.). MIT Press, 1978.

Edelman, G.M.   Group selection as the basis for higher brain function.   In *Organization of the Cerebral Cortex* (Schmitt, F.O., Worden, F.G., Adelman, G., and Dennis, S.G., editors), 51-100. MIT Press, 1981.

Edelman, G.M., and Finkel, L.H.   Neuronal group selection in the cerebral cortex.   In *Dynamic Aspects of Neocortical Function* (Edelman, G.M., Gall, W.E., and Cowan, W.M., editors), 653-695. Wiley, 1984.

Franz, W.   *Psychological Review (monograph supplement)* 19, 80, 1915.

Garraghty, P.E., Pons, T.P., Sur, M., and Kaas, J.H.   The arbors of axons terminating in middle cortical layers of somatosensory area 3b in owl monkeys.   *Somatosensory Motor Research* 6, 410-411, 1989.

Gould, H.J., Cusick, C.G., Pons, T.P., and Kaas, J.H.   The relationship of corpus callosum connections to electrical stimulation maps of motor, supplementary motor, and frontal eye fields in owl monkeys.   *J. Comp. Neurol.* 247, 297-325, 1986.

Graham Brown, T., and Sherrington, C.S.   On the instability of a cortical point.   *Proceedings of the Royal Society of London* 85, 250-277, 1912.

Grajski, K.A., and Merzenich, M.M.   Hebb-type dynamics is sufficient to account for the inverse magnification rule in cortical somatotopy.   *Neural Computation*, 1990a (in press).

Grajski, K.A., and Merzenich, M.M.   Neural network simulation of somatosensory representational plasticity.   In *Advances in Neural Information Processing Systems 2* (Touretsky, D.L., editor). Morgan Kaufman, 1990b, (in press).

Hicks, T.P., and Dykes, R.W.   Receptive field size for certain neurons in somatosensory cortex is determined by GABA-mediated intracortical inhibition.   *Brain Research* 274, 160-164, 1983.

Jankowska, E., Padel, Y., and Tanaka, R.   The mode of activation of pyramidal tract cells by intracortical stimuli.   *J. Physiology* 249, 617-636, 1975.

Jenkins, W.M., Merzenich, M.M., Ochs, M.T., Allard, T.T., and Guic-Robles, E.   Functional reorganization of primary somatosensory cortex in adult owl monkeys after behaviorally controlled tactile stimulation.   *J. Neurophysiology* 63, 82-104, 1990.

Jenkins, W.M., and Merzenich, M.M.   Reorganization of neocortical representations after brain injury: a neurophysiological model of the basis of recovery from stroke.   *Progress in Brain Research* 71, 249-266, 1987.

Kitzes, L.M., Farley, G.R., and Starr, K.A.   Modulation of auditory cortex unit activity during the performance of a conditioned response. *Experimental Neurology* 2, 678-697, 1978.

Landry, P., and Deschenes, M.   Intracortical arborizations and receptive fields of identified ventrobasal thalamocortical afferents to the primary somatic sensory cortex in the cat. *J. Comp. Neurol.* 199, 345-371, 1981.

Lashley, K.   Temporal variation in the function of the gyrus precentralis in primates. *Amer. J. Physiology* 65, 585-602, 1923.

Leyton, A.S.F., and Sherrington, C.S.   Observations on the excitable cortex of the chimpanzee, orang-utan, and gorilla. *Quarterly Journal of Experimental Physiology* 11, 135-222, 1917.

Merzenich, M.M., Kaas, J.H., Sur, M. and Lin, C.S.   Double representation of the body surface within cytoarchitectonic areas 3b and 1 in SI in the owl monkey (*Aotus trivirgatus*). *J. Comp. Neurol.* 181, 41-74, 1978.

Merzenich, M.M., Sur, M., Nelson, R.J., and Kaas, J.H.   The organization of the SI cortex: multiple representations of the body in primates. In *Cortical Sensory Organization, Volume 2, Multiple Somatic Areas* (Woolsey, C.N., editor), 36-48.   Humana Press, Clifton NJ, 1981.

Merzenich, M.M., and Kaas, J.H.   Principles of organization of sensory-perceptual systems in animals. *Prog. Psychobiol. Physiol. Psych.* 9, 1-42, 1984a.

Merzenich, M.M., Nelson, R.J., Stryker, M.P., Cynader, M.S., Schoppmann, A., and Zook, J.M.   Somatosensory cortical map changes following digit amputation in adult monkeys. *J. Comp. Neurol.* 224, 591-605, 1984b.

Merzenich, M.M.   Sources of intraspecies and interspecies cortical map variability in mammals: conclusions and hypotheses.   In *Comparative neurobiology: modes of communication in the nervous system* (Cohen, M., and Strumwasser, F., editors), 138-157.   Wiley, 1985.

Merzenich, M.M., Nelson, R.J., Kaas, J.H., Stryker, M.P., Jenkins, W.M., Zook, J.M., Cynader, M.S., and Schoppmann, A.   Variability in hand surface representations in areas 3b and 1 in adult owl and squirrel monkeys. *J. Comp. Neurol.* 258, 281-297, 1987a.

Merzenich, M.M.   Dynamic neocortical processes and the origin of higher brain functions. *The Neural and Molecular Bases of Learning* (Changeux, J.-P., and Konishi, M., editors), 337-358.   Wiley, 1987b.

Merzenich, M.M., Recanzone, G.H., Jenkins, W.M., Allard, T.T., and Nudo, R.J. Cortical representational plasticity. In *Neurobiology of Neocortex* (Rakic, P., and Singer, W., editors), 41-67. Wiley, 1988.

Mountcastle, V.B. *The Mindful Brain* (with Edelman, G.M.). MIT Press, 1978.

Nudo, R.J., and Merzenich, M.M. Repetitive intracortical microstimulation alters the area 4 representation of movements. *Soc. Neuroscience Abstracts* 13, 1596, 1987.

Nudo, R.J., Jenkins, W.M., and Merzenich, M.M. Interhemispheric asymmetry in the area 4 representation of movements is correlated with hand preference. Neuroscience Abstracts 14, 598, 1988.

Nudo, R.J., Jenkins, W.M., and Merzenich, M.M. Repetitive microstimulation alters the cortical representation of movements in adult rats. *Somatosensory Motor Research* (submitted for publication) 1990.

Pearson, J.C., Finkel, L.H., and Edelman, G.M. Plasticity in the organization of adult cerebral cortical maps: a computer simulation based on neuronal group selection. *J. Neuroscience* 7, 4209-4223, 1987.

Raussel, E., and Jones, E.G. Modular organization of the thalamus VPM nucleus in monkeys. *Neuroscience Abstracts* 15, 311, 1989.

Recanzone, G.H., Allard, T.T., Jenkins, W.M., and Merzenich, M.M. Receptive field changes induced by peripheral nerve stimulation in SI of adult cats. *J. Neurophysiology* (in press), 1990.

Recanzone, G.H., Jenkins, W.M., Hradek, G.T., Schreiner, C.E., Grajski, K.A., and Merzenich, M.M. Frequency discrimination training alters topographical representations and distributed temporal response properties of neurons in SI cortex of adult owl monkeys. *Soc. Neurosci. Abstracts* 15, 1223, 1989.

Recanzone, G.H., Allard, T.T., Jenkins, W.M., and Merzenich, M.M. Receptive field changes induced by peripheral nerve stimulation in SI of adult cats. *J. Neurophysiology* (in press), 1990.

Recanzone, G.H., Merzenich, M.M. and Jenkins, W.M. Alterations in cortical area 3b representation of the hand induced by flutter-frequency discrimination behavior. *J. Neurophysiology* (to be submitted), 1990.

Recanzone, G.H., and Merzenich, M.M. Intracortical microstimulation in somatosensory cortex in adult rats and owl monkeys results in a large expansion of the cortical zone of representation of a specific cortical receptive field. *Soc. Neuroscience Abstracts* 14, 223, 1988.

Sherrington, C.S. *Integrative Action of the Nervous System.* Yale University Press, 1906.

Snow, P.J., Nudo, R.J., Rivers, W., Jenkins, W.M., and Merzenich, M.M. Somatotopically inappropriate projections from thalamo-cortical neurons to the SI cortex of the cat demonstrated by the use of intracortical microstimulation. *Somatosensory Research* 5, 349-372, 1988.

Strick, P.L., and Preston, J.B. Two representations of the hand in area 4 of a primate. I. Motor output organization. *J. Neurophysiology* 48, 139-149, 1982.

Stryker, M.P., Jenkins, W.M., and Merzenich, M.M. Anesthetic state does not affect the map of the hand representation within area 3b somatosensory cortex in owl monkey. *J. Comp. Neurol.* 258, 297-303, 1987.

von der Malsburg, C., and Schneider, W. A neural cocktail-party processor. *Biological Cybernetics* 54, 29-40, 1986.

Weinberger, N.M., and Diamond, D.M. Dynamic modulation of the auditory system by associative learning. In *Auditory Function: Neurobiological Bases of Hearing* (Edelman, G.M., Galland, W.E., and Cowan, W.M., editors), 485-512. Wiley, 1988.

Woody, C.D., and Engel, J. Changes in unit activity and thresholds to electrical microstimulation at coronal-pericruciate cortex of cat with classical conditioning of different facial movements. *J. Neurophysiology* 35, 230-241, 1972.

Woolsey, C.N. Organization of somatic sensory and motor areas of the cerebral cortex. In *Biological and Biochemical Bases of Behavior* (Harlow, H.F., and Woolsey, C.N., editors), 63-81. University of Wisconsin Press, 1958.

Yun, J.T., Merzenich, M.M., and Woodruff, T. Alteration of functional representations of vibrissae in the barrel field of adult rats. *Soc. Neuroscience Abstracts* 23, 1596, 1987.

Wall, J.T., Kaas, J.H., Sur, M., Nelson, R.J., Felleman, D.J. and Merzenich, M.M. Functional reorganization in somatosensory cortical areas 3b and 2 of adult monkeys after median nerve repair: possible relationships to sensory recovery in humans. J. Neuroscience 6, 218-233, 1986.

Zarzecki, P., and Wiggin, D.M. Convergence of sensory inputs upon projection neurons of somatosensory cortex. *Experimental Brain Research* 48, 28-42, 1982.

Chapter 9

NEURAL DARWINISM

GERALD M. EDELMAN AND GEORGE N. REEKE, JR.

In this chapter I discuss some work I have done with my colleagues, particularly George Reeke, on modeling the nervous system.[*]

Let me begin with some historical remarks. We are in a most remarkable period of scientific history. Many of the advances we see today are the outgrowth of an enormous surge in Western science that took place in the 17th century. Before addressing my subject proper, I would like to mention two major figures who contributed to that surge: Galileo and Descartes.

Galileo invented mathematical physics. In a sense he removed the mind from nature so that nature could be subjected to impartial experimentation and mathematical modelling. Descartes, on the other hand, in his radical scepticism, decided that in considering the mind he should distrust even experimentation, and reason only from introspection. He concluded that the world is divided into two kinds of material: *res extensa* (extended matter), which physicists like Galileo could investigate, and *res cogitans* (thinking matter), which was in fact inaccessible to the methods of such science.

We have come a long way since then. Alfred North Whitehead, in his *Science in the Modern World*, makes the comment that, as a result of the enormous rise of physiology in the latter part of the 19th Century including, of course, physiological psychology, the mind was put back into nature. The American philosopher and psychologist, William James (who in some sense might be considered the Descartes of the twentieth century), said

---

[*] This lecture stands more or less as it was given by GME and it remains in the first person. It loses in precision what it gains in force, and we hope the reader will forgive this. It could as well have been given by George Reeke, who participated in every aspect of the work, and he is therefore a coauthor in every sense of the term.

that consciousness is not a matter of *res cogitans*. It is a process related to brain function, and we have to face the issues that follow from this conclusion.

I bring up these matters, not to discourse at length on the mind-body problem, but to make the point that it's valuable for computer scientists to recognize that physics deals with motions and not with willed actions. But minds and brains deal with volition, and also with intentions and with feelings. In modeling the brain we must somehow take this into account.

I used to believe that the world could be described by equations that said things like $F = ma$, or $S = 1/2gt^2$. Considering the brain as part of the world, I no longer believe that. I would like to make a plea for another point of view.

Let me try to give you a feeling for what has to be incorporated in addition to such equations, by telling you a story that relates to the physical structure of the world but also reflects the problems we face when we consider the brain.

It is the story of a young man who had the suspicion that his girl friend was carrying on with someone else. On a very hot summer night he came home early from work, and he searched through the closets and under the beds, screaming and yelling. They had a wonderful fracas, but he didn't find anybody. At the end of all this, he found himself at the back window of this cold water flat. In his rage, he looked out of the window and saw a chap on the fire escape below, wiping his brow and loosening his tie. He flew into an even greater rage and grabbed a huge refrigerator, smashed it through the window, aimed it, and dropped it on this fellow's head. At this point, he dropped dead.

The scene switches to Heaven and St. Peter is admitting three souls. He tells them, "You have met the requirements for admission, but for the sake of the bureaucracy, you have to say how you died."

The first fellow said, "Well, I thought there was some hanky-panky going on, so I came home early and I couldn't find this guy. But finally I found him on the fire escape. I must have had an adrenalin fit. I lifted a 500-pound refrigerator and dropped it on his head and then I guess I had a heart attack."

The second fellow said, "I don't know what happened. It was a hot day and I came home from work a little early. I can't afford an air conditioner, so I stepped out on the fire escape to cool off and this refrigerator fell on my head."

And the third fellow said, "I don't know. I was just sitting in this refrigerator minding my own business!"

I believe that this story poses what the philosophers call the problem of intentionality, and it sets our theme. This is one example of the problem one faces in considering brain function, and we will consider others. In discussing them, I will present some rather complicated biological facts without making any pretense of describing them in detail, but only at the level necessary to give the flavor of a set of ideas. Those ideas bear upon my initial remarks, and I am going to make a somewhat radical and bold set of statements to embed them in your memory.

First, I do not believe the brain is a computer. In other words, I do not believe Turing-machine functionalism aptly describes either the evolution or the performance of the brain. It may describe some aspects of the collusion of brains with culture to yield brilliant inventions like the computer, but it does not describe what brains do.

Second, the cortical mantle of the brain is one of the most intricate structures that we know of. If we unfolded the human cerebral cortex, it would be perhaps the size of a very large table napkin, and the same thickness. It would have approximately ten billion neurons—we don't really know the number—and a million billion connections. If you counted one connection per second it would take you 32 million years. No two such cortical structures are identical in terms of their cellular connectivity. Figure 1 gives some feeling for the density of cells in the brain and the way they are arranged in a series of layers. In fact, the density is so great that if all the cells were stained you would just see a pitch black mass.

How is this brain made? It's very important to understand that, because it's germane to the question of computing and the brain. I can't go through all of neuroembryology, but suffice it to say that a sheet of cells, for example in a chicken embryo, enlarges, receives signals from other cells, and finally develops into something called a *neural plate*. This plate then folds into a tube which closes. At a certain point, every neuron in that structure, or rather every cell that's going to become a neuron, is a gypsy. Each cell moves either up and down between layers or from one place in the brain to another. The processes that drive this extraordinary mechanism to yield the intricate wiring of the brain are cell-movement and cell-death, both of which have a certain stochastic element, and cell-division. These processes are controlled by cell-adhesion and by signals from collectives of cells that go back and forth, turning on different kinds of genes and inducing the target-cells to differentiate.

This is a most intricate process. If you look at it very carefully, it becomes clear that even identical twins will never end up with the same neural architecture at the finest ramifications because of the stochastic nature of the forces driving network-formation. Having said that, I believe we are left with a series of rather extraordinary challenges which collectively define a crisis. (I should add that I think a crisis is the best place to be in science, because it means that there is a really exciting problem to solve.)

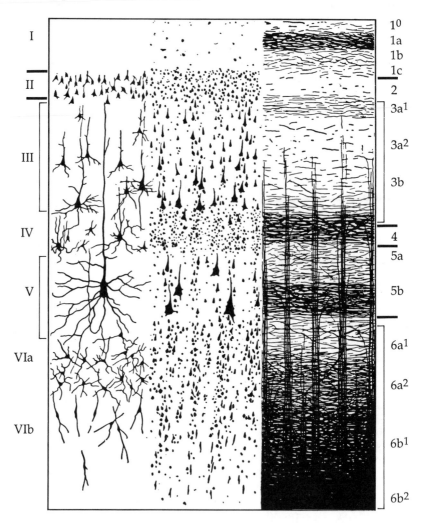

Figure 1. An illustration of a small segment of human cerebral cortex made by Brodmann showing the arrangement of cells in multiple layers using three different staining techniques (reproduced with permission from Ranson and Clark, 1959).

To begin with, precise, prespecified point-to-point wiring is excluded by the nature of the developmental process. Second, uniquely specific connections cannot exist. It just isn't conceivable that the green wire goes to the red node and the red node connects with the violet wire, et cetera, as in an engineering diagram.

Thirdly, as Professor Merzenich covers in more detail in his paper, the arbors which come out of these cells are extraordinary in their degree of overlap, which is vast compared to their size. They cover very large amounts of neuronal space, and a particular cell has no way to tell which of the particular 10,000 synapses that happen to connect onto its dendrites comes from which particular source. Certainly not in the sense that you would demand if you were to develop a computer architecture.

Figure 2 illustrates the structural crisis with a few examples. The first panel is a diagram taken from work by Goodman and Pearson showing the contralateral descending motion detector neuron of the common locust. It's a neuron that regulates the so-called *extensor tibia response* that occurs when the locust launches itself from a surface and begins flying. The diagrams make use of techniques for staining individual neurons. Four examples of the same neuron are stained here, from four different locusts. There are enormous structural diversities, yet each of these locusts will have roughly the same kind of behavior.

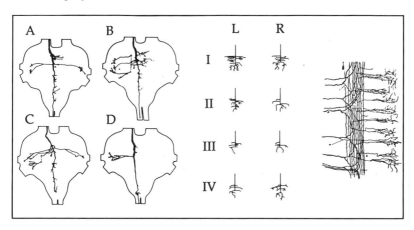

Figure 2. The structural crisis: drawings of (a) descending lateral motion detector neurons from the common locust (reproduced with permission from Pearson and Goodman, 1979), (b) identified neurons from the visual system of *Daphnia magna*, from clonally identical individuals (reproduced with permission from Macagno, Lopresti, and Levinthal, 1973), (c) neurons from the rabbit cerebellum (reproduced from Ramón y Cajal, 1904/1952).

Perhaps an even more dramatic example is shown in the second panel. This is taken from work by Macagno and coworkers at Columbia, who have studied *Daphnia magna*, the water flea. These animals are parthenogenetic females, and therefore each of them is a member of a genetically identical clone. Four specimens are shown in the figure. Stained neurons from the left and right sides of the visual system are shown for each insect. Notice the enormous divergence in these structures, even though they are from genetically identical individuals.

Finally, the third panel gives us a look at a higher organism. It is the work of the great anatomist, Ramón y Cajal, and shows some of the repeating structures found in the cerebellum of the rabbit. If you look from repeat to repeat, no two are alike.

These anatomical diagrams pose a massive problem. One can't get away from it by talking about noise and invoking error-correcting codes. Indeed, it has a little bit of the flavor, as you shall see, of what happened when Darwin looked around and said, "But wait a minute, that spotted animal has stripes," and people said, "That is a sport. It's a mutant. Ignore that. Tigers are tigers."

So, I hope these examples gives you a sense of the structural crisis. Now let's turn to some of the functional crises.

If you actually put electrodes in certain portions of the brain, you would find that the majority of the synaptic connections that exist anatomically are not expressed functionally at any one time. Furthermore, as Dr. Merzenich has shown in a brilliant piece of work, there are major temporal fluctuations in the maps of the brain. (I am going to come to why there are maps a little later). The variability of these maps depends very much upon the available input, and upon what events occur peripherally in the system. How these maps change is one of the ingredients of the functional crisis.

Another element of this crisis has to do with what I think is the fundamental operation in rich nervous systems—what I shall call *perceptual categorization*. Perceptual categorization precedes learning—it is what a baby can do without anybody teaching it. For example, a baby learns within several weeks of birth that syllable-lengths in its mother's and father's voices are different, even though it doesn't know what English is. This kind of recognition is carried out with an extensive capacity for generalization, and it is seen not only in humans but also in animals that don't have the use of language at all.

To round out my list, there is the problem that your brain has multiple sensory maps, and yet you have a unitary perception of the world in spite of the fact that your perceptual processes are, in fact, based on this enormous number of different interactive maps. This bears on the issue of perception in a fundamental way.

Let me take up perception, then, and offer you, first of all, the statement that it is not necessarily veridical in the sense that a physicist would insist on for his measurements. This is illustrated by the Wundt-Hering illusion in Figure 3. Most viewers agree that the two lines at the top are parallel, and I think most of you would say that the middle panel shows lines that are bowed in while the bottom panel shows lines that are bowed out.

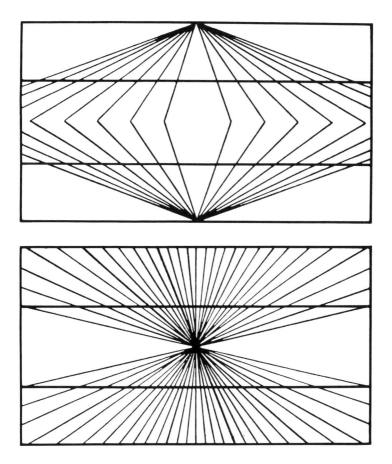

Figure 3. The Wundt-Hering illusion (reproduced with permission from Edelman, 1987).

Wundt and Hering were great physiological psychologists (or psychophysicists if you will), and they were describing what people actually perceive. You mustn't think that this illusion is an error—it is a percept that may indeed reflect some of the profound adaptive properties of the visual system. To repeat my point, perception is not necessarily veridical, but that doesn't mean that when it isn't it is "wrong". Please notice that this is an incorrigible illusion. Even if you know what to suspect, you can't help but see it. What you would do as a scientist is to measure orthogonal distances with some error bound, and show me that the distances are alike. You would be willing to act upon the results, which are that the lines are parallel. But the bowing is very real.

Another fascinating property of perceptual categorization is its relation to generalization. A really extraordinary thing is the capacity of animals to generalize on a very small set of samples. Professor Cerella at Harvard presented pictures of oak leaves to pigeons in an operant-conditioning experiment. He conditioned the pigeons with a reward on *Quercus alba*, the white oak, and then, within a small number of trials, the pigeons recognized that all oak leaves are in the same class, and rejected all other kinds of leaves, such as maple leaves.

This result does not depend in some obvious way on the fact that pigeons evolved with leaves and therefore might have some special innate capacity for recognizing patterns in leaves because of selection for wiring in their brains. That would not be very interesting. To demonstrate this point, Professor Hernnstein at Harvard took a thousand colored slides of trees in various contexts and mixed eighty of them at random in a projector with slides of objects that were not trees, but that resembled trees. He conditioned the pigeons, and quite promptly they were able to recognize all kinds of scenes of trees and to reject the pseudo-trees. That boggles the mind.

But still, pigeons evolved in trees. You could easily say that natural selection could take care of recognition like this, although you'd have to ignore the statistics of the trial runs. To control for this possibility, Professor Hernnstein repeated these experiments using pictures of fish of different sizes and scales (pun intended). The pigeons gave high scores on "recognizing" these pictures of fish. Pigeons do not eat fish. They do not live with fish—at least as far as I know, but perhaps in New York. They do not evolve with fish. So how do they recognize them?

For those of you who like puzzles, Figure 4 shows a way of categorizing that I think may be at the heart of these remarkable capabilities to generalize perceptual responses in the absence of language. The figure shows some groups of objects. Those groups on the left of the line are, and those on the right are not, members of a particular so-called polymorphous set, a set which doesn't have a list of either necessary or sufficient conditions for membership. This figure was given to a group of Cambridge students by Dennis, Hampton, and Lea some years back with the task to state the rule for set membership. After being allowed a maximum of ten minutes for cogitation, only two out of six subjects got any answers at all, and theirs involved tortuous and incorrect logic.

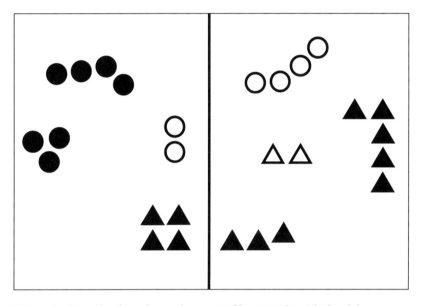

Figure 4. Example of a polymorphous set. Objects in the right-hand frame are members of the set; objects in the left-hand frame are not members of the set (reproduced with permission from Dennis, Hampton, and Lea, 1973).

I won't put you through this agony. Pigeons do it perhaps better than you do. In the example shown here, at least two of the following must be true of a group in order for it to be a member of the set: *is a group of dark objects, is a group of round objects, is a symmetric group of objects.* My suspicion is that disjoint samplings of various characteristics of the world are involved in these kinds of perceptual acts and generalizations.

Having stated that I don't believe Turing-machine functionalism is the answer to how the brain works, I would like to submit that the evidence I have given you will at least suggest why I have taken this position.

The question is: What are the alternatives? One is not trying to deny the extraordinary power of Turing-machines, but rather to indicate that there may be other kinds of approaches. To take a central and challenging example, animals evolved. Do you think

evolution is a Turing-machine?   If so, please tell me what the
effective procedure is.   Selection occurs *after* variation - it is an *ex
post facto* event.   This observation leads us to consider what are
some of the properties of selectionism in contrast to those of
functionalism.   The man who had this most remarkable idea of
selection was Charles Darwin.   Natural selection is absolutely the
most important and the most ideologically extraordinary idea in
biology, and it is important to understand the gist of it.

What Darwin really did was to consider the consequences of
selection against preexisting diversity.   A point of significance for
understanding of the nervous system is that selection of this kind
brings about structure.   An ecological example may help make this
clear.   In Panama, there are perhaps ten times as many species of
birds as in Puerto Rico, which is an island ecosystem; the jungles,
however, are very similar.   If you stratify the trees into five
layers and count the species in each layer, the picture you would
get in Panama would be that birds of a kind would fall together
in the layers.   Of course, there would be some overlap in the
layers, and there would be a few generalist birds that would fly
around in all the layers.   But if you looked in Puerto Rico where
there is relatively little competition, the canopy would have
relatively little structure.   Thus, out of competition in a system
with variance, you can get structure.

A second example is given by the immune system.   When it was
first understood that the body could recognize a vast set of
different foreign chemical structures, the remarkable fact emerged
that it could distinguish even very similar organic chemicals like
dinitrophenyl and picryl from one another.   If you made a
molecule that never existed before in the history of the world,
injected it into the blood, and then looked a few weeks later, you
would find antibodies that positively bind that molecule.   To
explain this result, Linus Pauling proposed the *instructive* theory
of antibody formation.

This instructive theory is a Turing-type theory.   Pauling said
that all antibodies are initially equivalent in their potential
ability to bind different antigens.   One of these antibodies
acquires the ability to recognize a particular antigen by folding up
in space around that antigen.   In this way the antigen *instructs* the
antibody to take on its particular steric pattern in three-
dimensional space.   The process is similar to the way a cookie
cutter forms a cookie.   When the antigen is removed, the antibody
is there waiting for that antigen to come along again.

A beautiful idea, but it's wrong.

The right idea was proposed by Macfarlane Burnet and it's a
selectionist idea.   It said that the immune system doesn't know
anything about what it's going to encounter, just as a newborn baby
doesn't know what its genes mean, except perhaps after it has

gone to Harvard. Macfarlane Burnet's theory was that every single cell that is going to make antibodies in fact makes only one kind. There is a mechanism for diversifying the antibodies made by the different cells. This generator of diversity operates in somatic time, after you're born. So as an individual you end up with a huge repertoire of different antibodies. In fact, you may have millions of different shapes waiting, each on an individual cell. When a foreign molecule comes in, whatever its name, it binds to a particular subset of those antibody shapes more or less well. There is a mechanism to bring about differential amplification of those cells bearing antigens that happen to bind above a particular threshold. You make more of those cells, changing the population, so that there are, for example, more antidinitrophenyl binders when you have been exposed to dinitrophenyl.

In general, in no two individuals are there the same antidinitrophenyl binders, but nonetheless the scheme works marvelously well. When we did the structure of the antibody molecule, we found that these molecules have a set of variable regions and a set of constant regions. Perhaps a hundred thousand of these molecules of a given shape sit floating in the cell membrane with the variable part sticking out, ready to bind any antigen that comes along and happens to fit it.

Every cell of a certain type makes the same constant regions, but every cell does a little jiggle in the DNA for antibodies to make different variable regions. Since they're not matched up to the antigens ahead of time, you end up making a lot of antibodies that may turn out to be nonsense. That is the price you pay for being selectionist, for being able to match many new antigens that come along that you've never been exposed to before.

Having given you some examples, I can perhaps attempt to confront our crises and propose a neural counterpart of these selective systems (Figure 5).

Consider that perhaps when the nervous system is wired up, it isn't hard-wired, but rather that repertoires of circuits are created by epigenetic processes in which the driving forces of development create an immense variation (Figure 5, top). In the view I shall take, such variation isn't noise at all, it provides the grounds upon which selection will occur.

Now, suppose that after most of the nervous system is built, synapses in various combinations are selected by strengthening them or weakening them (Figure 5, middle). Instead of increasing the numbers of cells in these circuits by growth or by cell division, you simply change their possibilities of influencing the responses of other cells by synaptic change.

And finally, suppose that in order to match the spatio-temporal continuity of the world, which doesn't have any labels and is not a computer tape, the nervous system evolves in such a way that it organizes into certain kinds of maps. These maps are connected in a special way that allows their properties to be linked (Figure 5, bottom).

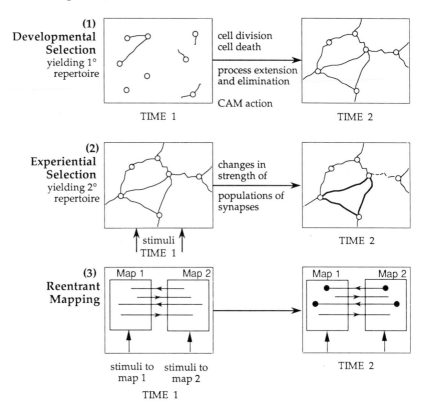

Figure 5. Schematic diagram illustrating principles of the theory of neuronal group selection. (Top) Formation of neuronal structures and connectivity during embryonic development - epigenetic events involving selection determine the finest details of the architecture of the nervous system. The result is a primary repertoire of neuronal groups. (Middle) Interaction with the environment results in neuronal group selection through differential modification of synaptic strengths, enhancing the probability of behavioral responses that have adaptive value for the individual organism. The result is a secondary repertoire of neuronal groups. (Bottom) Reentrant signalling between maps correlates responses arising from different sensory modalities, permitting categorizations based on disjunctive sampling of an unlabeled world (reproduced with permission from Edelman, 1989).

Let me go very quickly through some consequences of these ideas, which form the basis of what I call *the theory of neuronal group selection*. First of all, it must be obvious that in such variant repertoires of nerve cells it won't do to have just a few recognizers, just as it won't do to have just five antibodies - with such an immune system you'd soon be dead. You have to have hundreds of thousands and millions of them. In fact, there's a relationship between the degree of specificity you need for effective recognition and the number of recognizing elements you need in a selective system (Figure 6). If, for instance, you assume that you have a preexisting repertoire in which each element has an equal *a priori* probability, p, of recognizing any signal that might come in, then you can compute the probability, r, that *at least one* member of the repertoire will respond to any such arbitrary signal. For a repertoire of N elements, this comes out to be

$$r = 1 - (1-p)^N.$$

This equation gives the familiar sigmoidal curve shown in Figure 6 when r is plotted as a function of N.

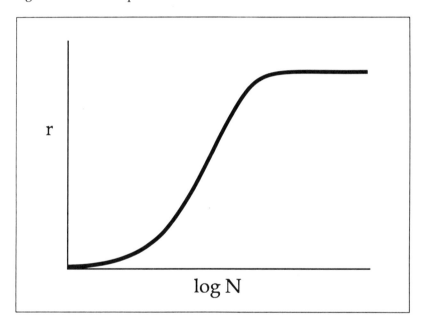

Figure 6. Probability, r, that at least one group in a repertoire will respond to any given stimulus as a function of repertoire size, N. Assuming that any member of the repertoire is equally likely to respond to the stimulus with some probability, p, it may be shown that $r = 1-(1-p)^N$ (reproduced with permission from Reeke and Edelman, 1984).

For a fixed value of p, you can't expect recognition below a certain number N, because the chance of recognizing anything is too low. Above some large value of N, it won't help you to make more recognizers, because you already recognize everything well enough, and there is no perfection in such systems. The crossover point between these two extremes, the point where r is $1/2$, occurs when N is roughly equal to $1/p$.

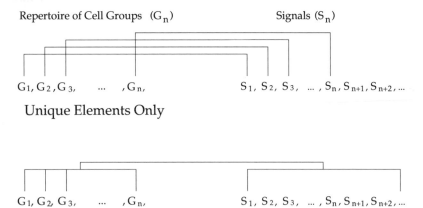

Figure 7. Schematic illustration showing failure of a selective system in the extreme cases of (a) total specificity (for a repertoire of N groups, one can always find an N+1'th stimulus for which there is no match), and (b) total degeneracy (the same response occurs for all possible stimuli) (reproduced with permission from Edelman, 1978).

Furthermore, it's important to understand that if you demand an exact match between signals and recognizers, it won't help to have even a very large number of unique elements, because you can always construct a signal that isn't in the set of recognizers, and that could be the one that kills you (Figure 7, top panel). So the smart thing to do is to make the repertoire degenerate (each recognizer is able to respond to more than one signal). However, if the system is completely degenerate (Figure 7, bottom panel), every element will recognize every signal and you won't have any specificity to the responses. That won't do, either. So you must stay at some intermediate point between complete specificity and full range. That is exactly how the immune system works, and that is exactly how I would propose the nervous system must work as a selective system.

This idea has several consequences. First, it suggests that you don't have a hard-wired nervous system, and you don't have a set of molecules to specify which cell is wired to which other cell, as you might, for example, in writing a computer program to design the wiring on a chip. Second, it says that you should get variant maps. I'll have a lot more to say about that in a moment. Third, it is consistent with the idea that perhaps some form of reentrant signaling between maps to solve the polymorphous set problem is one way in which you can make sense out of an unlabeled world.

If everything isn't prespecified, what is the mechanism for getting pattern with diversity? To answer that question, I need to tell you a little bit about some of the molecular developmental biology of the nervous system.

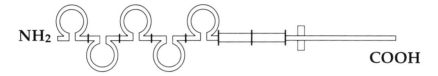

Figure 8. Structure of N-CAM, the neural cell adhesion molecule. The molecule exists in several variants that express different numbers of coding regions (exons) of the N-CAM gene. All variants have the five immunoglobulin-like regions denoted by the loops at the left. The position at which the molecule passes through the cell membrane is indicated by the shaded vertical area just right of center. Interactions between neural cells mediated by N-CAM are an important determinant of primary repertoire formation in the nervous system.

Figure 8 is a diagram of a molecule we discovered in our laboratory called N-CAM. It's one of the major glues of your brain, indeed of many parts of your body. It is one of the key molecules responsible for linking cells together in these extraordinary neural circuits. But it doesn't work by an addressing code - it's not as if I numbered the cells and then numbered their places like seats in an auditorium. The pattern arises instead as a result of a rather more dynamic picture of gluing and ungluing as a function of place, similar over some local area, but with great variation. It has been a source of some aesthetic satisfaction that when we did the structure of the gene for this molecule, it turned out to be homologous to the genes for antibodies, upon which we worked so long. In fact, the entire system of immunity derives from a precursor of this molecule, a long time ago. Relatives of this molecule, are for example, present in fruit flies, which don't have immune systems.

The main point is that, as a cell moves into a particular locale, a signal comes and changes various CAMs from one type to another in a very dynamic loop. That changes the binding, the movement, and then the next signaling event, and eventually creates the structure of the nervous system (and, indeed, of the whole embryo). What this means is that no two individuals can be alike. It also means, I believe, that it's unlikely that the variation in the structure of the nervous system is just noise. Instead, I would propose that it is an origin of diversity in a selective system.

Selection in Somatosensory Cortex

This explains something about anatomical diversity and selection and to some extent relieves our structural crisis. What about synaptic selection? To understand how this might work, I'd like to discuss an experiment that Michael Merzenich performed, which is described in more detail in his chapter in this volume. He mapped the so-called *somatosensory* portion of a monkey's cerebral cortex by looking for those neurons, say in area 3B (see Figure 9), in which he could find a response with an electrode when he touched one of the monkey's fingers. This procedure gave a very definite map. Merzenich found that no two monkey's maps were alike.

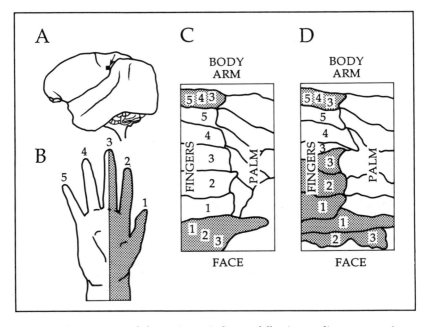

Figure 9. Progression of change in cortical maps following median nerve section. (a) Overall view of monkey cerebral cortex showing location of somatosensory areas 1 and 3b (arrow). (b) Monkey hand showing numbering of the digits used in (c) and (d). Stippled area is served by the median nerve. (c) Typical map of neuronal responses in somatosensory cortex. Cross-hatched areas respond to touch on dorsal surface of hand; unshaded areas to glabrous surface. (d) Map taken from same animal as in (c) after median nerve section. The cortical areas that originally responded to glabrous portions of digits 1, 2, and 3 now respond to dorsal surfaces; map borders in nearby areas are rearranged (based on Merzenich *et al.*, 1983).

Then he performed a series of truly inspired experiments in which he cut one of the three nerves that serves the sense of touch in the monkey's hand. For example, figure 9D shows what happened when the median nerve was cut. This nerve is normally connected to the glabrous or smooth portion of those fingers that are stippled in the figure. Merzenich found an extraordinary rearrangement of the map immediately; then, over time, the maps adjusted further, leaving the cortical regions that previously responded to the median nerve now responding to the other two nerves serving the hand. These results are very difficult to explain except in terms of some kind of dynamic multilevel readjustment occurring across the entire map.

We have tried to model these variable maps in terms of the neuronal group selection theory by simulating a hand in a computer with four fingers and a palm, and mapping it roughly as we know it maps in monkeys. Input was brought into each region of the map from both the dorsum and the glabrous surface, in a very wide spread of overlapping arbors. The dynamics of the network followed the principles that I discussed earlier.

In this model, we used a synaptic modification rule that is different from the so-called *Hebb rule* that is frequently used in these sorts of models. According to the Hebb rule, a connection becomes strengthened when the pre- and post-synaptic cells are both active simultaneously. However, this rule does not give an adequate explanation of the data. Instead, we used what is called a *hetero-synaptic rule*. In the model, as in the nervous system, the so-called *pre-synaptic* neurons generate a chemical signal, a neurotransmitter, that binds to the post-synaptic receptor and sets off a new wave of electrical activity there. A key part of the model is that the transmitter also acts as a signal to alter another chemical at the post-synaptic membrane, a so-called *second messenger*. Coincident (so-called *hetero-synaptic*) activity elsewhere on the dendritic arbor of the same post-synaptic cell makes a difference as to whether that second messenger leads to modification of the strength of the synapse or not. The hetero-synaptic rule gets its name because other synapses are involved in determining whether or not there is a change at this given synapse. When such a rule is in effect, a most remarkable set of behaviors resembling Merzenich's data was observed in the model. We felt, from a consideration of the evidence, that the unit of selection in a nervous system is a *group* of neurons, not a single neuron, and we wanted to see how these groups could arise from the working of the hetero-synaptic rule and how they would change with changing input.

Figure 10 shows some data from a simulation in which there were about 1,500 neurons, about 50,000 input connections from the hand, and another 70,000 connections from one cell to another within the network, for a total of 120,000 connections. That is a very large number for a computer simulation, although it represents only a small fraction of those found in the actual nervous system. The connections were all initially set up with random strengths, chosen from a normal distribution. These starting conditions are shown in the first picture of Figure 10 where the different connection strengths are represented by the brightness of the different lines. You can see that the connections primarily have a medium level of strength.

INITIAL FORMATON

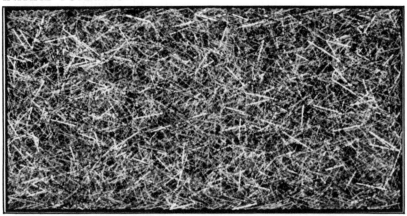

GROUP FORMATION

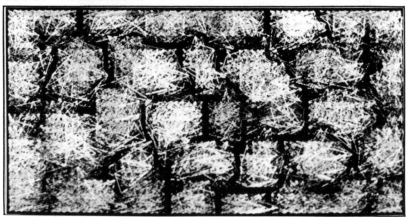

Figure 10. Group formation in simulation of monkey somatosensory cortex. (a) Connection strengths in simulated cortex before any stimulation. Different connection strengths are represented by lines of different brightness. Strengths are taken from a Gaussian distribution. (b) Connection strengths in same map after repeated random stimulation of simulated hand. Connection strengths have changed, giving rise to groups (collectives of cells with strong interactions) separated by "moats" of weaker interaction strengths (reproduced with permission from Pearson, Finkel, and Edelman, 1987).

We then tapped at random on the simulated hand while letting all the cells respond according to the rules we had put in.

The tapping gave rise to synaptic impulses, first in the connections from hand to cortex, then in the internal connections from one part of the network to another. Those impulses released transmitter, bringing the hetero-synaptic rule into play. After tapping several times on each part of the hand, we got the second picture shown in Figure 10.

It should be stressed that no connections are made or broken in the model. Nonetheless the uniform distribution of connection *strengths* does change drastically. Cells begin to interact cooperatively with each other as they receive correlated stimulation from nearby locations on the skin; this encourages them to strengthen their synapses to nearby cells to form a neuronal group, a bunch of cells more tightly connected to each other. At the same time, connections to cells outside the group are weakened, leaving a moat of weak connections around the group. All of this keeps changing in a dynamic fashion as the input is altered.

Our computer program allowed us to construct a so-called receptive field map, which shows what region of the hand each cell responds best to. Each cell received roughly an equal number of input connections from the dorsum and the glabrous surface. At the beginning of the experiment, all the cells in a group had rather large, diffuse receptive fields and there was a response to stimulation on either side of the hand. After we tapped, a choice was made—cells in a group become either dorsal or glabrous responders. The fields are much smaller, but the response is stronger when the stimulation is in the right place. Of course, underneath it all, the neuroanatomy is still there that will permit other possibilities, depending on the input and the neural structure.

When we did the whole map of the hand, we got something that looked very much like Merzenich's results. When we did an experiment he pioneered, which is to have a monkey tap a lot with one finger, the area allocated to the glabrous portion of the finger extended into other areas, capturing neurons, as it were, by this dynamic interaction. When we cut a nerve (comparable to the median nerve), immediately the dorsal areas, which are the darker areas in each map, took over and enlarged (Figure 11). When we tapped some more after making the cut, we got effects that were more or less similar to those that I already showed you in the monkey.

Why is this important? The point of the results with modeling the somatosensory cortex as a selective system is that the nervous system seems to be working as a multi-layered structure, a little bit like the birds in Panama. There is a kind of *neuroecology*. The behavior of the different neurons depends on what signals are coming in, what kind of competitions exist locally, and on a very extraordinary set of diversification rules and synaptic rules. Selection upon variance is at the very heart of such systems.

Receptive Field Maps

NORMAL MAP   HAND

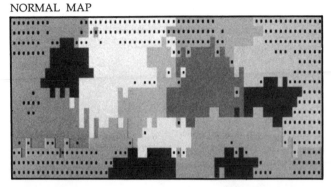

AFTER NERVE TRANSECTION   HAND

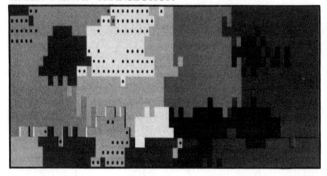

Figure 11. Receptive field maps obtained with the simulated cortex of Figure 10. Different shades of gray indicate regions responding to different portions of the simulated hand, as shown on the key at right in each panel. Small black dots indicate cells that respond equally well to dorsal or glabrous stimulation. (a) Normal map obtained after initial random stimulation. (b) Reorganized map obtained after simulated median nerve section. Large black areas give no response (reference given in Figure 10 legend).

Can we make use of this neuroecology to help us understand perception? What I have said so far is that the evidence doesn't seem compatible with the idea that the brain is a functionalist system. The evidence is, indeed, more compatible with selectionism than with functionalism. Can we use these ideas to get at the problem of perceptual categorization? Can we construct an automaton that carries out perceptual categorization?

In fact, we have been working on that goal, and we have come up with some tentative conclusions that may be of some interest.

Darwin II, an automaton for perceptual categorization

A key element of the automata we have simulated is the use of maps of the kind I have just discussed. Suppose the brain has maps with particular properties that are built in by evolution, and these maps quite independently sample some particular portion of space. For example, let's take a map which responds to lines oriented at certain angles and another one that integrates over exploratory motions involving touch. Let's assume that the maps map to each other (see Figure 12), and that the way they are mapped has a particular geometric distribution. Suppose that the mapped fibers going back and forth are uniformly distributed over each map, but that their arbor branches, which overlap, have a normal distribution locally. Let us assume also that there is a synaptic rule operating such that events in these two maps that happen to be correlated lead to strengthening of synapses in the reentrant connections between them.

These principles have in fact been embodied in an automaton called *Darwin II*. The two sets of maps have been named after Darwin and Wallace, two of the pioneers of the theory of natural selection. Darwin, the part of the system on the left (Figure 12), consisted of two networks. The first of these had particular characteristics that we built in, much as evolution might have done in a real nervous system. These characteristics enabled its neuronal groups to respond to local features of objects, such as a part of the horizontal bar in the letter A. These groups were connected at random to groups in a higher-order network (R-of-R, see figure 12), and these connections could change strengths depending on what was presented.

Wallace, the part of the system on the right (Figure 12), dealt with certain aspects of complete objects. It would trace around an object, and give responses that were more or less independent of the size and direction of the various lines, but instead depended on the relations between them. This tracing was done in Darwin II by artificial means, because Darwin II did not have an arm to trace with, but as we shall see shortly, there was nothing about it that could not be done by a creature with an arm and a simple nervous system. Indeed, we have implemented just such a system in our more recent automata. The results of the tracing were expressed in Darwin II by the activation of a set of neural groups (G_1 through G_{27} in figure 12) that were in turn fed into a higher order network that we called 'R_M' for *recognizer-of-motion*. R_M thus responded to arbitrary combinations of the feature relations found by the trace, just as R-of-R responded to arbitrary combinations of the purely local features found by the R network.

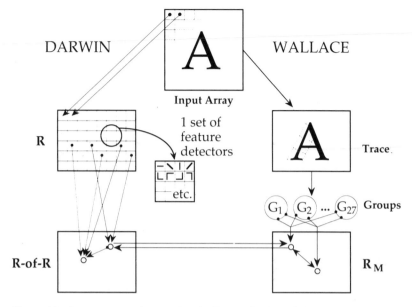

Figure 12. Arrangement of repertoires in Darwin II. Stimuli are presented on an input array (top). The "Darwin" section (left) responds to local features of the stimuli, such as oriented line segments or bends (R network, middle left). A higher-level network (R-of-R, lower left) responds to arbitrary combinations of these local features. The "Wallace" section (right) responds to correlations of features that are frequently characteristic of stimulus category. A trace mechanism (upper right) excites a set of neural groups (G_1, G_2, ... G_{27}, middle right) according to the presence of complete contours and their relationships (junctions of various kinds). A higher-level network (R_M, lower right) responds to arbitrary combinations of these featural correlations. Reentrant connectivity between R-of-R and R_M (horizontal lines at bottom) forms a "classification couple", permitting the system as a whole to categorize based on both individual (Darwin) and class (Wallace) characteristics of stimuli. Systems containing classification couples are capable of generalization and the formation of associations between related stimuli without need for an external "teacher" (reference given in Figure 6 legend).

The R-of-R and R_M repertoires of the Darwin and Wallace networks were connected together randomly by reentrant connections in both directions. The function of Darwin was to generate individual responses to particular portions of an input signal, but not to recognize an object as a whole; on the other hand, Wallace was supposed to recognize an object, but not to be sensitive to its fine features. Together, the two systems produced a kind of associative memory because the synaptic strengths of their reentrant connections could change.

When we tested Darwin II, we found what you would expect from this description. Figure 13 shows the responses in Darwin and Wallace to the presentation of a tall, narrow A, a fat A with a low bar (labelled A'), and then an X. If you compare the two

Darwin   Wallace
R   R-of-R   R$_M$

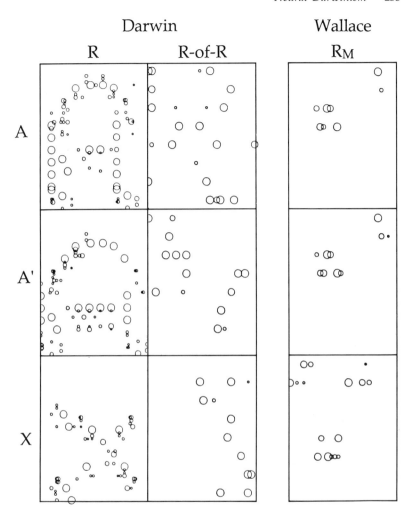

Figure 13. Responses of Darwin II when presented with two A's and an X. Panels at left show responses in the feature-detecting (R) and the abstracting (R-of-R) layers of the "Darwin" network; panels at right show responses in the abstracting (R$_M$) layer of the "Wallace" network. Note that the responses to the two A's are similar in R$_M$ but unlike in R-of-R. Sizes of circles represent strength of group firing (reference given in Figure 6 legend).

A's, you will see that you can recognize their shapes in the low-order part of the Darwin side, but in the R-of-R representation there is really no pattern that looks alike to the eye. By statistical tests, however, there is some correlation between these patterns. In Wallace, on the other hand, the patterns are also abstract and therefore not recognizable, but you can readily see that there is a relationship between the responses to the two A's. In fact, these patterns are also reasonably invariant to rotation.

When the Darwin and Wallace patterns are allowed to interact through the reentrant connections, it is possible to get an association built up between patterns that are different in Darwin but similar in Wallace. However, this does not happen between patterns that are generically different, for example, the responses to the A versus the X that are shown in Figure 13.

It is important to understand that there was no programming involved at the overall system level in getting these responses. We programmed the simulation of the individual groups, of course, but then we just let it run without any teacher to give "correct" answers to the system, and the properties of the network emerged from the properties of the individual units.

Darwin III, an automaton with global reentry

Darwin II performed reasonably well, but it had a terrible problem. It was an angel, not a beast. You had to look at it using a God's eye view to see what it was doing. We have now constructed something more like a real beast. That beast is called Darwin III. It is actually a sessile creature with an eye and a four-jointed arm that is simulated in a very large computer. It sits in a world of objects of any shape which move by it randomly.

What it does, using the principles of selection and several kinds of reentrant mappings, is to make a number of responses to things. It has three senses. It has *vision*, it has *touch* at the end of its finger, and it has *kinesthesia*. In its nervous system, it has neurons and synapses arranged in repertoires with reentrant connections between them. The synapses can change strength according to their activity and the build-up of modulating substances; they work much like a simplified version of the synapses we already saw in the model of somatosensory cortex.

Darwin III has about 46 repertoires, so it is quite a complicated beast—it is about at the level of a simple insect in its complexity. It has about 6,000 neurons, and about 150,000 synapses. Our present versions have gotten even more complex, and some of them have several million synapses. Simulating a system that large on any computer is a rather vicious problem, but it's a natural for parallel processing, which is discussed in other chapters of this volume.

Darwin III is really a very dynamic creature, and it is unfortunate that the movie used in the oral presentation cannot be reproduced in this book. Instead, still figures will be used to show the most important aspects of its construction and performance. What the simulation allows us to do is what William James always hoped we could do. We can look at a creature, with its external phenotype (its arm and its head), its internal phenotype (its nervous system), and the world, all simultaneously in time chunks, one after the other. We still can't do that in neurobiology and the fact that we can't often leads to what James, in his *The Principles of Psychology*, called the *psychologist's fallacy*, which is the imputation of the goals, beliefs, or point-of-view of the observer to the mental object or psychological system being studied.

In constructing Darwin III, we found very early on that the machine wouldn't work unless we put in *values*, *i.e.*, a set of simple, evolutionarily constructed innate goals for the organism, such as, for example, *seeing is better than not seeing*. Value is signaled by sets of specialized cells and synaptic connections that respond to the consequences of behavior (such as, in this example, moving the eye so that the amount of light falling on the central part of the retina increases). By the way, these value-sensitive cells don't tell the organism *how* to do anything, they just evaluate after something is done whether the net effect of the action was of value for that organism or not.

In order to do machine behaviorism, we also built some higher values into Darwin III. These are tendencies to perform certain behaviors. One of them was this: when the simulated creature decides *on its own* that something is an object, and that object is categorized perceptually and found to be bumpy and striped, then it will tend to exercise a reflex and swat with its hand. This allows us to observe the consequences of a categorization event without looking into the nervous system. That means we can switch off our displays of the nervous system and just be machine behaviorists. Alternatively, we could tantalize the machine neurophysiologist, switch off the animal's actual behavior, and just show the nervous system along with the stimuli.

Figure 14 is an overall schematic diagram of Darwin III showing that it has four neural subsystems. Its world is shown at the upper left. Its visual fields are marked by two squares - an outer one showing the boundary of peripheral vision, and a smaller inner one showing central, or foveal vision. Its arm, which has four joints, is shown reaching up from the bottom center. The four sets of neural repertoires are shown around the bottom and at the right. It has an oculomotor system that moves its eye, a reach system that moves the arm by pairs of agonist and antagonist muscles, a tactile system, and a higher-order nervous system for doing categorization.

I am going to present one example of the operation of each system, beginning each time with a creature born naive into the world. Keep in mind that no programming of neural responses is going on here. Random-number generators are driving the neural activity, and also, independently, from a different seed, the world.

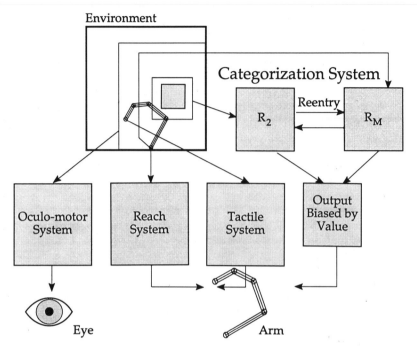

Figure 14. Schematic showing the four principal functional subsystems of Darwin III. For explanation, see text (reproduced with permission from Reeke, Sporns, and Edelman, 1989).

Figure 15 shows the setup of the oculomotor system in more detail. The visual fields (shown as squares) project onto a model retina (VR) and from there onto a higher order repertoire (SC) that has some of the properties of an optic tectum. (At any time I mention a particular brain region in connection with Darwin III, I intend to suggest a functional analogy only, and not that a detailed, "anatomically correct" model of that region has been constructed). Finally, there are more connections from there to a set of motor neurons (OM) that move the eye in various directions. The strengths of these connections are averaged for us by the computer and shown in the cross-shaped part of the diagram at the top right. The four segments show connections hooked to cells that are going to move the eye in the four directions up (U), down (D), left (L), or right (R). A value-dependent hetero-synaptic rule operates to alter those connections according to what happens when the creature encounters an object in an unknown world.

One such object is shown by the heavy square in the visual field in Figure 15. When that object registers on the retina, neurons fire there and then in the colliculus-like region, and finally the eye motor cells fire. When the creature is first born into the world, it moves its eye around pretty much at random at the same time the object is moving around at random. At this point we cannot predict what the eye is going to do, because its motions are not correlated with the motions of the object.

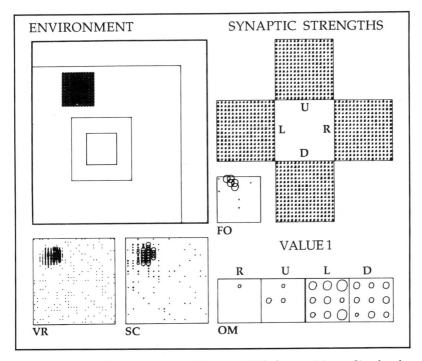

Figure 15. Oculomotor system of Darwin III before training. Simulated environment with visual fields and heavy square stimulus object is at upper left and the retinal (VR), superior colliculus-like (SC), and oculomotor (OM) repertoires are across the bottom. Cross-shaped diagram at upper right maps average connection-strengths (represented by sizes of small squares) for connections onto motor neurons that will move the eye up (U), right (R), down (D), or left (L), respectively. Positions in each map correspond to locations of source cells in the overall visual field. At this initial stage, connection-strengths are random.

As the object jerks and jumps around, and the eye sometimes moves towards it, sometimes away from it, particular neuronal groups become favored over others. Their synaptic strengths are gradually enhanced, until after about two thousand trials the movements are no longer so random - the eye still doesn't do very well, but it is beginning to track the moving object. After another two thousand trials, the distribution shown in Figure 16 is found, and the eye tracks quite well. Each instance of Darwin III ends up with a different synaptic population. It's remarkable how insensitive the creature's global behavior is to the particular scales or other conditions that the connections are set up with.

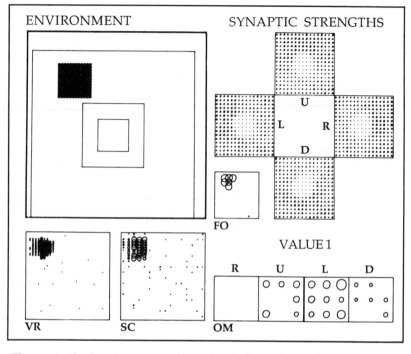

Figure 16. Oculomotor system of Darwin III after training. Conventions are same as for Figure 15. Connections between visual system and oculomotor neurons are no longer random, but have organized in such a way as to generate leftward motion of the eye when the object is at left of the visual field, and so on (reference given in Figure 14 legend).

Unlike a machine vision device, Darwin III has a kind of primitive protoattention. It arises because the visual cells can sustain firing for only a limited amount of time (this phenomenon is called *depression*), and there is also lateral inhibition. So if two objects are put in at the same time, they will compete and one will win out because of the lateral inhibition - after a while the cells it stimulates will stop responding and then the other object will take over. Of course, you can't predict just when the switch will occur.

Another part of Darwin III has to do with how a creature with an arm comes to move that arm around until it can touch objects that come into its field of view. That is a considerably more complicated problem, even when the eye has been shown the world for a bit. Figure 17 shows some parts of the nervous system of Darwin III that are involved in this task.

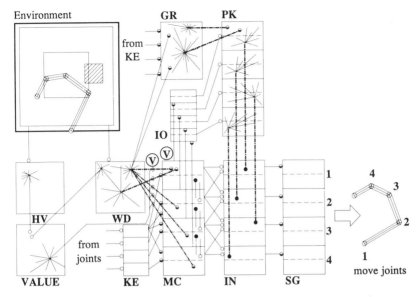

Figure 17. Arrangement of the nervous system of Darwin III for reaching. The various neuronal repertoires are described in the text (reproduced with permission from Reeke *et al.*, 1989).

Value in this case is registered when the arm finds itself near the object, which will be more or less in the center of the visual field when the eye is tracking it. Any synapses in the arm-motor system that have been active just before this happens have a higher chance of being amplified. When the arm actually comes in contact with an object, its sense of touch fires off; this will be important when we get to the next stage, which is tracing the object.

The nervous regions controlling the arm include an area that resembles a brain region called the cerebellum (top center in Figure 17). In the model, this is an inhibitory area that modulates the flow of traffic going from a motor-cortex-like area to an area that is something like the spinal cord, the pathway by which neural signals finally get to the arm muscles (lower right in Figure 17). The cerebellum has the job of filtering out gestures of the arm that are inappropriate for reaching, that is, gestures that move the arm away from the object rather than towards it. As a result, the arm eventually gets better and better at reaching. In effect, the number of degrees of freedom with which it can move becomes less, as in Bernstein's theory of synergies (Whiting 1984).

While it is still quite clumsy, the improvement in reaching that you can get with this simple scheme is quite remarkable. Figure 18 shows some trajectories of arm motion before and after the arm has been trained to reach out for objects. Initially (left panel), you observe motions randomly selected from a set that is constrained by the phenotype of Darwin III. Later on (right panel), a particular cluster of those actions is selected out. Thus, neuronal group selection solves a profound problem of kinematics related to the coupled motions of joints, a problem which has proven very difficult for robotics researchers to deal with.

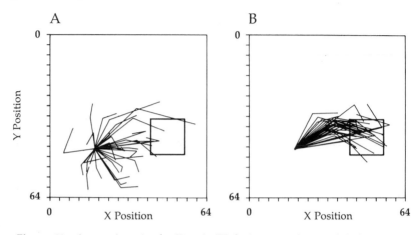

Figure 18. Arm trajectories for Darwin III during a reaching task before (left) and after (right) training. Note that successful trajectories are selected from a repertoire of arm motions that occur spontaneously in the absence of training (reproduced with permission from Reeke and Edelman, 1988b).

To simplify the next stage of the simulation, we built a reflex into the model that causes the arm, when it touches an object, to straighten out in much the way a praying mantis would take up a posture to grab a prey. Once the reflex is activated, a different set of arm-control repertoires comes into play, and the automaton begins to explore the object it has touched. It does this by jittering around the object using agonist-antagonist pairs of muscles. The cortical circuits that control these muscles are biased by a value-scheme that favors pressure on the touch sensors, at least up to a certain maximum. As a result, the arm will hunt around until it finds an edge of the object. (The pressure is higher at the edges than it is inside an object, because the area of contact is less at an edge. Of course, this pressure is also higher than when contact with the object is lost entirely). Once the edge is found, the arm moves around it, maintaining roughly uniform pressure. Sometimes the arm changes direction and falls off or goes into the center, but mostly it just moves around the edge. The result is an entirely neural implementation of the trace that was done artificially by the Wallace part of Darwin II.

While all this jittering is going on, the shoulder joint is sending a characteristic set of kinesthetic signals to a map in the creature's brain.   At this point, the creature is independently and disjointly sampling the stimulus-object with a visual detector and a set of movements of the eye, and at the same time with a kinesthetic detector and a set of movements of the arm.   The higher-order maps in these two sensory systems are connected to each other by reentry in such a fashion that when selected neuronal populations in the two maps happen to be activated at nearly the same time, the reentrant connections between them are strengthened.   This strengthening acts to coordinate the two maps, giving the basis for categorization.

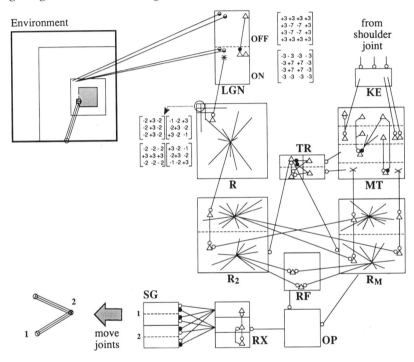

Figure 19. Arrangement of the nervous system of Darwin III for categorization. The various neuronal repertoires are described in the text (reference given in Figure 17 legend).

Figure 19 summarizes all these arrangements.   The environment is at the top left as usual, with the straightened arm visible at the bottom center.   To the right of the environment is the visual system, with a primary map whose output is sampled by a higher-order map.   At the far upper right is the touch system, with a primary kinesthetic map feeding similarly to a higher-order map.   The two higher-order maps are connected to each other by a dense set of reentrant connections, and selective rules for synaptic modification operate on both channels.   This combination

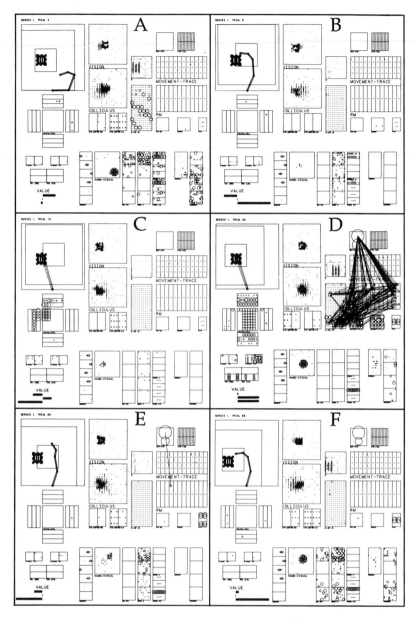

Figure 20. Sequence of diagrams taken from a movie of Darwin III, showing a categorization and rejection reflex sequence. (a) Eye fixates on target object. (b) Arm assumes straightened posture and traces around boundary of target. (c) Reentry between visual and kinesthetic sensory systems signals that the automaton has arrived at a categorization and is triggering a rejection response. (c) The arm swats the noxious object away.

of two maps with reentry forms a classification couple just like the one in Darwin II. The classification couple connects in turn to motor repertoires that are involved in moving the arm. The behavior we get when an object is categorized (say as striped and bumpy) is our second built-in reflex—a rapid, forceful motion of the arm that tends to swat away the object as if it were a biting insect. This reflex is actuated by a simple neuronal oscillator in the "spinal cord" that overrides everything else and makes the arm twitch. This motion is the equivalent for Darwin III of a rejection response.

Figure 20 shows how the whole automaton works when a stimulus comes along that meets the criteria for rejection—being both stripy and bumpy. This is a typical sequence, at least after the creature has had some experience, but keep in mind that it never plays out exactly the same way twice. First you see the arm approaching the object just after it has been visually fixated; then you see the arm in its straightened posture as it feels around the edge of the object. In the third frame, this examination has been going on for some time, and we have caught the burst of reentrant activity that signals that the automaton has decided on a category. The last frame shows the swatting response as the arm gets rid of the stimulus. Of course, there is a lot of undercurrent of activity going on in between these frames that you can't see, but the most important elements of the response are there.

This behavioral sequence demonstrates that we have a very primitive selective recognition automaton, one that is based on the idea of selection in maps. Of course, we have short-circuited the embryology and acted like evolution in building up the phenotypic structures of this creature, but once that has been done, we step back from the simulation and just let the whole thing run. We can't influence anything. We just look and see what happens.

We have done various control-experiments to identify the critical features of this complicated system. For example, we can cut out one of the value networks, the one that says *light is better than no light* and that gives a small selective advantage to any neuron that was active just before light is detected. When that is done, the eye never is able to track moving lighted objects.

Another thing we can do is to cut off the nervous system view and just score the behavior the way a psychologist does with his pigeons. As I mentioned before, this ability to look at any combination of organism, nervous activity, behavior, and stimulus gives us a remarkable opportunity to get away from William James' psychologist's fallacy, one form of which is the idea that you can assume the system you are studying has the same point of view that you do. Certainly Darwin III does not.

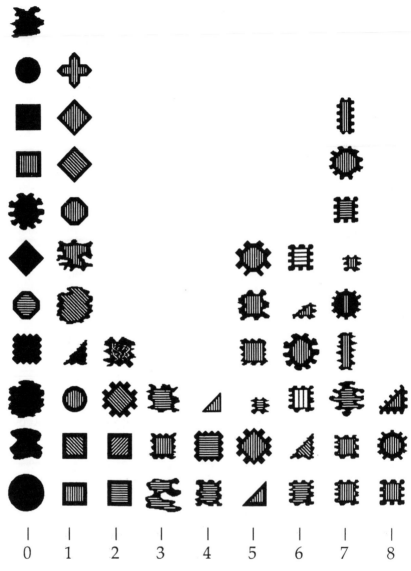

Figure 21. Frequency of rejection responses by Darwin III for 55 objects exhibiting various degrees of striped interior and rough boundaries. Abscissa: number of rejection responses in 8 trials with each object. Objects that have smoother edges and interior tend to be rejected less often (left) than those with rough edges and striped interior (right) (reference given in Figure 17 legend).

Finally, I will present just one example of the kind of behavioral data we can collect on Darwin III. This experiment was carried out by Olaf Sporns, who is a great machine behaviorist. It gives you some sense of the individuality of these simulated creatures. Out of an infinite set of possible objects of the appropriate general size, he picked the 55 objects shown in Figure 21 for testing. They have been arranged in columns according to the number of times each object was rejected in eight trials. This number is shown along the abscissa. The objects at the left were rejected zero times out of eight, then one, two, and so on. Finally, the ones on the right were rejected eight out of eight times.

This diagram shows the data for one particular exemplar of the creature Darwin III. When several other exemplars were tested, they behaved grossly the same way, but no two are *exactly* alike in how they classify those 55 objects. This is because there are internal variables which are characteristic of that creature's history, its growth, and the selections it has undergone.

Conclusions

Let me draw some conclusions. First, these kinds of dependencies, which are certainly seen in humans, suggest very strongly that we are not Turing-machines. The extensive variance found in the nervous system suggests the same thing. If you look at this variance, it's just enormous at every level, from the molecular level all the way on up. The variance in brains is not noise. You'd never get away with building a computer with that degree of variance. You would have to come up with incredible error-correcting codes to compensate for the errors. This conclusion should not disappoint those people who are individualists. I believe there is considerable value in individuality.

A second reason the brain is not a Turing-machine is very interesting. It comes from the fact that the world cannot be a piece of tape. If, in fact, the world *were* a piece of tape, Charles Darwin would have had to have been wrong. We wouldn't see the diversity in that jungle of birds. We'd just see creatures that had found out sooner or later how to read that tape, and they'd all be the same.

This notion of informational certainty and the world as a piece of tape reminds me of the guy who buys a cello, goes to the country, and plays the same note with a dreamy look on his face for two weeks. Finally his wife says, "Look, when I go to a concert in New York, they move their fingers all over the place." He says, "Those damn fools are looking for the note. I've found it."

The world is not a piece of tape. In fact, it's infinitely partitionable, and our problem both as neuroscientists and as computer scientists is to try to figure out how we and other animals partition it without depending on mathematics and language, both of which are themselves dependent on prior partitioning. In other words, we don't want to fall into the trap of saying, as the mouse did to his buddy, "You know, I've got my psychologist trained. Every time I run the maze, he gives me a piece of cheese."

If you name the world as Adam did and you call each neuron the such and such neuron you will find exactly what you put in. But, in fact, all the evidence is that biology and neurons do not work that way. I believe the correct view is the one first proposed by Darwin. I believe the challenge to us is to try to understand the brain from a genuinely biological stance—that of development and evolution. While not denying that there are ideas we can export and import back from field to field, I believe that the correct road to that understanding is to examine the consequences of the assumption that the brain is a selective system.

Finally, if it ever does come to pass that we can devise perception-machines that are not Turing-machines, but rather are probabilistic machines based on selection, I think their capacity to deal with novelty and categorization when coupled with true Turing-machines would be so great that it would mark a new epoch. It would be one of the most exciting things that has ever happened in the history of human efforts to understand how we can classify things in our richly structured world.

DISCUSSION
Question: Can you say something about the machine and the language that was used for the simulation?
Answer: The automaton I presented was simulated on IBM 3090s at the Cornell National Supercomputer Facility. Assembler language was used for the critical parts that consume most of the computer time, and FORTRAN was used for the rest—the graphics, statistics, and so forth. The whole thing amounts to about half a megabyte of executable code. The most important feature is that George Reeke has devised a language in which you can sit down at a console and dial up a nervous system. This is done with a package called CNS (Cortical Network Simulator), which enables someone who is not a programmer to sit down and write a specification for a simulation of any kind of nervous system he wants to construct.
Question: What is a trial?
Answer: Within any one particular experiment, what we call a trial is what happens from the time a new stimulus is presented until the automaton completes its response to that stimulus, either because it makes a behavioral response, or because it fails to do so and a timer runs out.

But let me speak more broadly of the general scheme for running an experiment. The idea is that each experiment should begin with a newborn creature, that is to say, a creature that has been set up in the computer but has never had any exposure to sensory signals. In practice, we can also start with a creature that has had some previous experience, because we can record the state of its nervous system on disk at any time and then start over from there. Either way, we then expose the creature to a world in which we specify the kind of objects that are going to come along and the general rules for how they are going to move. The details are determined by the program using a random-number generator, so we don't know any more than the creature does exactly which object is going to be picked out next or exactly which way it will move.

The experiment is to ask, in terms of either machine behaviorism or of some specific question about the nervous system, whether there is a significant change as compared to a control. For a machine behaviorist, an experiment would involve the obliteration of all knowledge of the nervous system. He wouldn't even want to know the ecological background: whether the creature preferred objects that were striped and bumpy, or whatever. Then he could come in and do with Darwin III what he does with an animal: he would notice, operantly, that when an object of a certain type does this, the machine does that, and he would score it. Unlike the behaviorist, however, we can also do the same thing with complete knowledge of what the nervous system is doing. That is what I have shown you.

Question: I suppose there's a saturation, a limit to the learning of this machine?

Answer: This is a deep question. Unlike the situation with so-called 'neural nets', where you can partition everything in advance and do information-theoretic analyses, in selective systems, it doesn't go that way.

The lady says "How do I know what I think until I see what I say?". There's a certain stochastic element, and the reason is a very deep one and a very important one which I would like to leave with you.

Let me go back to the immune system to explain that. The immune system can recognize molecules that have never existed before in the history of the world. I can go into an organic chemical lab and make any compound I want, as Dr. Landsteiner, my predecessor at the Rockefeller University who also found blood groups, did. By doing this, he showed that antigen-antibody reactions were a branch of organic chemistry. You could make some extraordinarily complex ring structure that never existed before, and you could immunize a rabbit with it. Bang. The blood serum of that rabbit picks out a hundred molecules of just that thing, out of nowhere or out of a complex mixture. You would say, "Well, that's miraculous", until you look at how it works.

This actually involves a problem of thresholding. To measure it, we have a method of selecting cells out of the spleen (an organ of the immune system) on the basis of what they will bind to. When I did this experiment on a mouse that had not previously been exposed to the antigen I was testing, I found that whatever I picked off the organic chemical shelf, one per cent of the spleen cells bound to it. But that means after a hundred trials, forget it, you've used up all the cells. But then I looked at the *function* of those cells and it became clear what happens to get specificity. If you look at the *strength* of binding, which is roughly an indicator of the triggering threshold, there is a curve that falls off and the cells with weak binding strengths never trigger. Now immunize the mouse with compound A. What I saw is something like a delta function at the extreme end of the binding strength distribution, a population with high affinity that is one thousandth of the binding population but one that triggers and gets amplified to the Nth degree. All the other ones, which bind more weakly, do not trigger. They're going to be used for some *other* antigen, because there's no degree of perfection in their binding. So the system acts like a high pass filter with an enormous gain. It works well but not perfectly. Perfection is a doctrine of the dead in biological systems.

In some sense, one cannot determine the saturation, because of the unknown matches that can be made. Given this and the *ex post facto* nature of selection, you can only determine failure and success but cannot get a strict measure of information.

Selected Readings[*]

Anderson, J.A., and Rosenfeld, E., (editors) *Neurocomputing: Foundations of Research.* MIT Press, 1988.

Dennis, I., Hampton, J.A., and Lea S.E.G.   *Nature* 243, 101-2, 1973.

Edelman, G.M. Antibody Structure and Molecular Immunology. *Science* 180, 830-840, 1973.

---

[*]   Because it is a record of a lecture, this chapter does not contain the usual scholarly citations, which are given fully in other publications from our group. However, for the benefit of the interested reader, we provide here a short bibliography of our own work as well as of other books and papers giving more extensive discussions of some of the philosophical and scientific points raised here.

Edelman, G.M. Group Selection and Phasic Reentrant Signaling: A Theory of Higher Brain Function. *The Mindful Brain: Cortical Organization and the Group-Selective Theory of Higher Brain Function,* by G.M. Edelman and V.B. Mountcastle, pp. 51-100. MIT Press, 1978.

Edelman, G.M. *Neural Darwinism: The Theory of Neuronal Group Selection.* Basic Books, 1987.

Edelman, G.M. *Topobiology: An Introduction to Molecular Embryology.* Basic Books, 1988.

Edelman, G.M. *The Remembered Present: A Biological Theory of Consciousness.* Basic Books, 1989.

Edelman, G.M. and Reeke, G.N. Selective networks capable of representative transformations, limited generalizations, and associative memory. *Proceedings of the Natlonal Academy of Science of the USA* 79, 2091-2093, 1982.

Grossberg, S., (editor). *Neural Networks and Natural Intelligence.* MIT Press, 1988.

Hebb, D.O. *The Organization of Behavior: A Neuropsychological Theory.* Wiley, 1949.

James, W. *The Principles of Psychology.* Holt, 1890. Reprint, Dover, 1950.

Macagno, E.R., Lopresti, V., and Levinthal, C. Structure and development of neuronal connections in isogenic organisms: variations and similarities in the optic system of *Daphnia magna. Proceedings of the Natlonal Academy of Science of the USA* 70, 57-61, 1973.

Merzenich, M.M., Kaas, J.H., Wall, J.T., Nelson, R.J., Sur, M., and Felleman, D.J. Topographic reorganization of somatosensory cortical areas 3b and 1 in adult monkeys following restricted deafferentation. *Neuroscience* 8, 33-55, 1983.

Pearson, J.C., Finkel, L.H., and Edelman, G.M. Plasticity in the organization of adult cerebral cortical maps: a computer simulation based on neuronal group selection. *J. Neurosci.* 7, 4209-4223, 1987.

Pearson, K.G. and Goodman, C.S. Correlation of variability in structure with variability in synaptic connections of an identified interneuron in locusts. *J. Comp. Neurol.* 184, 141-65, 1979.

Pylyshyn, Z.W. *Computation and Cognition: Toward a Foundation of Cognitive Science.* MIT Press, 1984.

Ramón y Cajal, S. *Histologie du système nerveux de l'homme et des vertébrés.* Translated by L.Azoulay. Maloine, Paris, 1904. Reprinted by Instituto Ramón y Cajal, Madrid, 1952.

Ranson, S.W. and Clark, S.L. *The Anatomy of the Nervous System—Its Development and Function,* 10th edition. W. B. Saunders, Philadelphia, 1959.

Reeke, G.N. and Edelman, G.M. Selective networks and recognition automata. *Ann. N.Y. Acad. Sci.* 426, 181-201, 1984..

Reeke, G.N. and Edelman, G.M. Real Brains and Artificial Intelligence. *Daedalus (Proc. Am. Acad. Arts and Sciences)* 117, 143-173, 1988. (See also the other papers in this issue of Daedalus.)

Reeke, G.N. and Edelman, G.M. Recognition automata based on Neural Darwinism. *Forefronts* 3, 12, 3-6. Cornell University, Center for Theory and Simulation in Science and Engineering, Ithaca, New York, 1988.

Reeke, G.N., Sporns, O., and Edelman, G.M. Synthetic neural modelling: comparisons of population and connectionist approaches. *Connectionism in Perspective,* (edited by R. Pfeifer, Z. Schreter, F. Fogelman-Soulié, and L. Steels), 113-139. Elsevier, 1989.

Reeke, G.N., Finkel, L.H., Sporns, O., and Edelman, G.M. Synthetic neural modeling: a new approach to the analysis of brain complexity. *Signal and Sense: Local and Global Order in Perceptual Maps* (edited by G.M. Edelman, W.E. Gall, and W.M. Cowan) Wiley, 1989.

Rumelhart, D.E., McClelland, J.L., and the PDP Research Group, (editors). *Parallel Distributed Processing: Explorations in the Microstructure of Cognition* (2 volumes). MIT Press, 1986.

Turing, A.M. On computable numbers, with an application to the entscheidungsproblem. *Proc. London Math. Soc.* 42, 230-265, 1937.

Whitehead, A.N. *Science and the Modern World.* The Free Press, New York, 1925.

Whiting, H.T.H. (editor). *Human Motor Actions: Bernstein Reassessed.* North Holland, 1984.

IV

PARALLELISM IN
ARTIFICIAL INTELLIGENCE

Chapter 10

MEMORY-BASED REASONING

DAVID L. WALTZ

Introduction

Memory-based reasoning (MBR) systems (Stanfill and Waltz 1986, Stanfill and Waltz 1988, Wolpert 1989) are made possible by the availability of parallel machines. The memory-based reasoning approach is applicable to practical problems, but also has relevance to the problem of understanding cognition, and particularly to problems that traditional Artificial Intelligence (AI) methods have not been able to solve.

MBR makes use of a database which consists of a set of *items*, each with a corresponding *classification*. For example, each item in a database of medical information might consist of a number of characteristics: age, name, height, weight, and so on, and its classifications might be diseases or treatments.

An MBR system decides how to classify each new item by comparing it with all the items previously seen, seeking a set of items are 'close' to the new one. Some particular algorithms that can be used to do this are described below. Once such a set of items is found, the new case can be classified by assigning to it the same classification as that of the 'nearest' item (the *precedent* for the decision), or by computing a classification for it based on those of a set of nearby items.

There are several interesting properties of this model:

(1) An MBR system behaves like an expert system. However, unlike an expert system, which generally requires interviewing experts to find out what rules they use to classify items, no such 'knowledge entry' is needed. All an MBR system needs is a database of prior decisions.

(2) MBR systems can provide a measure of certainty, which has traditionally been difficult to estimate in expert

systems. An MBR system can recognize when it cannot classify an item; if no item in the database is sufficiently 'close' to the new one to serve as a precedent, the system will identify those which are closest, but say that none of them are really close enough.

(3) MBR systems degrade gracefully if noise is added, as will be shown below. This pleasant property has not traditionally been associated with AI systems, although it has been a feature of neural networks.

(4) MBR systems are able to provide explanations: namely, the decision to classify a new item is explained by citing the precedent or set of precedents. This is a nice kind of explanation, easy to express and understand.

(5) MBR systems can change instantaneously in response to additions to or deletions from the set of precedents. AI systems that depend on learning require time-consuming retraining to cope with changes.

(6) Finally, MBR systems have the desirable property that, the larger the database, the better are the classifications: since the chances are then greater that one of the items in the database will be quite close to the item to be classified, and it is therefore more likely that the resulting classification will be 'correct'.

Since it was the Connection Machine which originally inspired the idea of MBR systems, and because MBR systems represent a natural, highly efficient application for the Connection Machine, we first summarize the Connection Machine architecture. We then describe how MBR systems actually work, and contrast them with other systems which have been used for similar tasks. Some test results are then described, followed by two MBR applications for document retrieval and visual object recognition, to illustrate the breadth of the idea. We next discuss the relevance of MBR to cognitive science, and in particular propose that MBR modules can be used to generate associative memory modules, which are an important building block for constructing cognitive architectures. Finally, we try to draw some messages or morals from all of this.

Connection Machine architecture

There are basically two ways to construct a parallel machine. The most common way is to take the *instructions* and divide them up among several ordinary processors. This solution introduces problems of *communication* and *synchronization*. For example, each processor needs to know when the values of the variables it uses are valid. Processors must communicate with each other in order to discover this. This method is appropriately named *control parallelism*, since each processor has an independent flow of control. One problem with control parallelism is that of *load-balancing*: different processors have different amounts of work to do, so that some processors are busy while others are idle. Another problem is that it may be difficult to find the parts of a program which can be executed in parallel in this way. And, most seriously, one cannot in general scale up the performance by adding more processors, since control-parallel solutions are compiled with respect to a specific number of processors.

A second way to exploit parallelism is to divide the *data* among processors. Imagine we have many processors, enough so we can assign each data element to its own processor. We can execute the program in a serial machine that sends its instructions to all the processors, which then operate on the distributed data simultaneously. Thus each of the many processors executes the entire program on its local portion of the data. This idea is called *data parallelism*. The Connection Machine is based on it.

In a data-parallel system, a processor sometimes needs to use data that it does not have locally. This means that a data-parallel machine must be able to communicate data between its processors. In the Connection Machine this data communication is handled by a hardware *router*.

The Connection Machine (CM-2 1988, Hillis 1985) has up to 65,536 processors, each of which has its own 32 kilobytes of memory, for a total memory size of up to 2 gigabytes for a full machine. This will increase by a factor of four when 4 megabyte DRAMS become available in 1990. By virtue of built-in software it is possible to program the Connection Machine as if it had many more 'virtual' processors than the 'actual' 65,536 processors it in reality has. The system software in effect divides up the memory of each actual processor into many smaller virtual memories, which are operated on serially by the processor. Thus a programmer can have the illusion that there are very many more virtual processors in the machine than there are actual processors; if the memory of each virtual processor is made just big enough to store one 32 bit number, the whole 'virtual' Connection Machine will appear to have *500 million* processors!

The machine physically consists of 4,096 processor chips; each chip contains 16 processors and routing hardware, and is connected to external memory. Each processor is an extremely simple device which takes three one-bit inputs, two bits from memory, one bit from a set of registers or flags, and generates two output bits, one to a flag and one to its memory. If the processor is adding, it takes two bits to be added, plus a carry bit, and generates one output bit to memory and a carry bit to a register. There is also a hardware floating-point option. With this option, 2048 floating-point chips are fitted, one for every 32 bit-serial processors. The programmer interacts with the Connection Machine at a higher level than this, however, when programming the system. All high-level instructions are in fact little programs built from fine-grain instructions, but the details are invisible to the programmer.

There is also a *communication   network* over which any processor can receive information from any other processor or send information to any other processor. This communication is supported physically by a twelve-dimensional hypercube network. The important feature is that each processor can get information from anywhere else and send it to anywhere else. There is elaborate hardware within the routing system that supports *message fan-out*, whereby one processor can send a message to many different processors, as well as *message fan-in*, whereby messages from many processors are combined en route to a single processor, to avoid creating a bottleneck at the receiving processor when more than one message arrives there at the same time. The communication network of the Connection Machine can be dynamically reconfigured. Thus the processors can be interconnected in a regular grid pattern, where every processor talks to its nearest neighbors north, south, east, and west; but they can also be interconnected in an arbitrary pattern, moreover one which can change as the computation develops, in a manner which the programmer specifies as part of the program.

Basic description of memory-based reasoning systems

Each MBR system is built on an underlying database, which I will assume for ease of illustration is a simple relational database, although, as I will show later, this assumption is not essential. One database we have used in our tests (Stanfill and Waltz 1986, Stanfill and Waltz 1988) is the set of words and their pronunciations used in the NETtalk experiment of Sejnowski and Rosenberg (1986). The NETtalk task is to use this database of letter-context pronunciations to infer the pronunciation of words that are not already in the system.

Suppose we want the system to pronounce the new word *translation*. The system views this input word as eleven 'windows', each centered on one of the eleven letter occurrences *t-r-a-n-s-l-a-t-i-o-n*. The system looks at each window in turn and tries to figure out how to pronounce its central letter occurrence. For example, in order to decide the pronunciation of an occurrence of the letter *s* when it is preceded by *t-r-a-n-*, and followed by *l-a-t-i-* the MBR system would first search its database for items that are similar to the item

   t-r-a-n- s̲ *-l-a-t-i-*

in order to find out which item or set of items is most similar to this one. The pronunciation of the most similar item would then be adopted as the pronunciation of this unknown items. The 'correct' pronunciation of the *s* in this context is taken to be Z (although some English speakers would pronounce it as S).

For example the search of the database might produce the seven entries:

t-r-a-n-	*s̲*	*-i-t-i-o-*	pronounced	Z
t-r-a-n-	*s̲*	*-p-o-r-t-*	pronounced	Z
t-r-a-n-	*s̲*	*-p-o-s-e*	pronounced	Z
a-n-	*s̲*	*-w-e-r*	pronounced	S
m-e-n-	*s̲*	*-w-e-a-r*	pronounced	Z
m-e-n-	*s̲*	*-u-r-a-t*	pronounced	S
e-n-	*s̲*	*-l-a-v-e*	pronounced	S

ordered from most similar to least similar. In each of these entries there are several attributes, one for each letter occurrence. For example, in the first entry we have the attribute that *t* occurs four places to the left of the central *s* and that the pronunciation of the central *s* is Z, and so on.

The difficulty here is to decide which attributes of each retrieved entry need to match the letters in the test pattern, or alternatively to decide how relatively important various inexact matches are. In this particular example it is the letters before the *s* that are important. But we can invent other cases where a following letter, for instance, a final *e*, will affect the way a preceding vowel is pronounced—*e.g.* whether it is long or short. So we cannot say in advance which of these positions adjacent to the letter-occurrence is the most important one; it depends on the individual case.

The upshot of this is that in order to do memory-based reasoning, we have to go through the entire database and assign a *score* for each attribute of each entry, representing how close it is to the sample case. We originally accomplished this by executing a variety of statistical operations: essentially, for each letter in a particular position, the system had to decide how often that letter's occurring in that position is associated with the particular pronunciation of the central letter, and how often it is associated with some other pronunciation of the central letter. Alternatively, one could select sets of weightings at random, and use the ones that test best on a training set (Wolpert 1989); or one could select those database entries that lie on classification boundaries, omit those entries that are surrounded by entries with identical classifications, and then use nearest-neighbor techniques (Kibler and Aha 1987).

Once we have obtained an 'importance weight' for each attribute of each entry, we then add up all the different importance weights of a given entry to arrive at a total score for that entry. We can then use their total scores to decide which entries are most similar to the test pattern. While this represents the basic idea, there are many possible variations.

There are also many possible complications; for example, certain attributes can be extremely important in one case, but in a very similar case quite unimportant. In a medical database, for instance, we would assume that in general the sex of a patient matters very little in diagnosing the patient's problem. The symptoms of the common cold do not vary much between males and females. In certain special cases, however, the sex of the patient would be most relevant. Certain symptoms in a woman, for example, might point towards a diagnosis of pregnancy, whereas the identical symptoms in a man would not. Nor would the diagnosis of pregnancy be indicated for women more than, say, sixty years old.

How can the system deal with that? Ordinarily we would want the sex of the patient to have a small importance, but in a few cases to have an extremely large importance, in selecting the correct diagnosis. Our MBR system can automatically determine this for us.

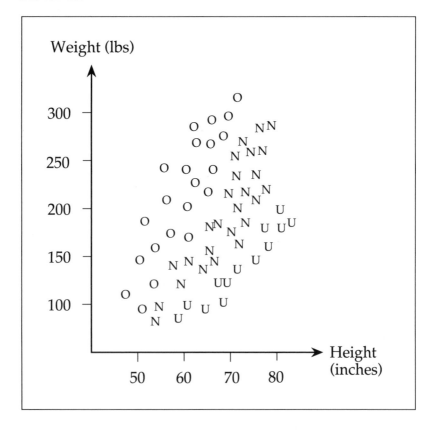

To give a concrete example, consider the very simple 'toy' medical database containing the entries as the preceding graph, in which there are two variables (Height and Weight) and three diagnoses (Normal, Overweight, and Underweight). (We have in fact been working with the Framingham Heart Study Database, which has 40 variables).

How can we actually solve a problem of this sort? There are many ways.

Traditionally AI has tried to solve problems like this by forming a set of rules. One method was devised by Ross Quinlan, in his system called ID3 (Quinlan 1986). ID3 builds rules that can then be used to drive an expert system. ID3 decides which attribute, *e.g.* W or H, and what value of that attribute, offers the best way to divide the database, so as to maximize the information in the two newly created subsets of data.

In this case, the best way to make the division is probably a horizontal cut at about 190 pounds, because all the U cases are below 190 pounds, and none of them are above. Having made that cut (numbered 1), we can then recursively divide up the two resulting subsets in the same manner.

The upper set is divided (by cut 2a) at height 67 inches, which separates out all the Ns in that set from almost all the Os in that set; the lower set is similarly divided (by cut 2b) at about height 62 inches. If one repeats this process, eventually the plane is divided into a set of rectangular regions, each of which has only one uniform classification within it, as follows:

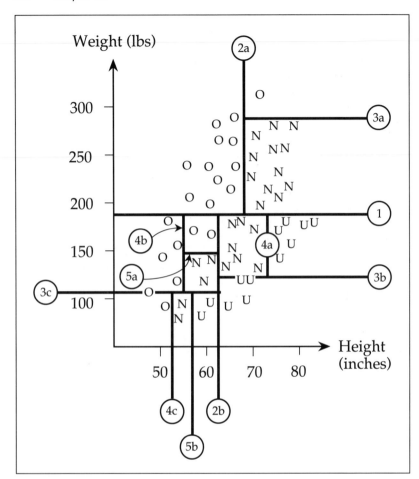

This partitioning can then be used to draw up the following decision tree:

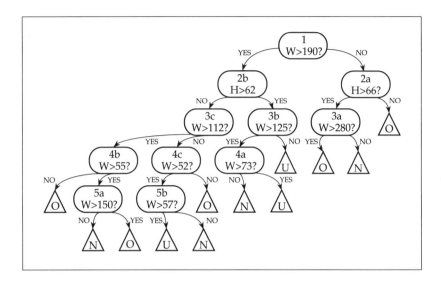

Each of the triangles at the leaves of the decision tree is a classification. The reader can verify the correspondence between the decision tree and the regions of the divided plane.

For building expert systems, knowledge engineers have used either this type of *rule-induction* method or, more commonly, they have used interview methods, where, for example, a physician attempts to express his/her knowledge about how to diagnose patients with different symptoms.

Another possibility is to perform a statistical analysis in order to find curves that divide the regions reasonably well:

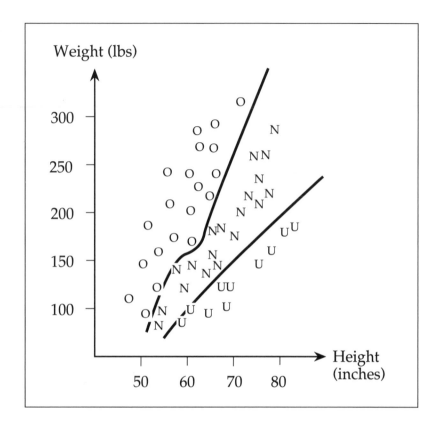

One of the important discoveries of neural network researchers is that one can achieve a similar division with multi-layered networks which have been trained with the samples; such systems can learn to approximate the divisions:

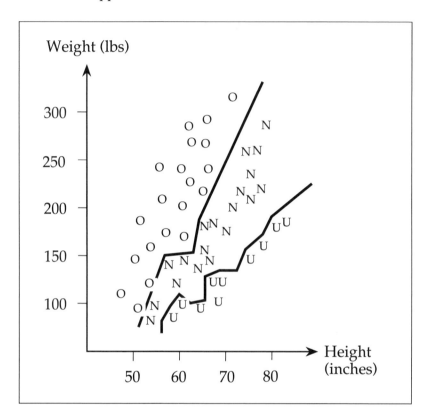

Memory-based reasoning

Let us compare these methods with memory-based reasoning techniques. MBR is a nearest-neighbor technique; one can imagine it to be doing roughly the following thing:

(1) find the n cases nearest to the current case to be classified; and

(2) use a weighted majority vote procedure to select one classification, or list one or more near cases with associated likelihoods.

Thus if we have a case surrounded by neighbors that all share the same classification, it is easy to see that memory-based reasoning does the right thing. In cases where the nearest neighbors represent two or more different classifications, the important thing is to form a weighted decision. To do this, the system must judge how important it is to match the different attributes of the case to be classified.

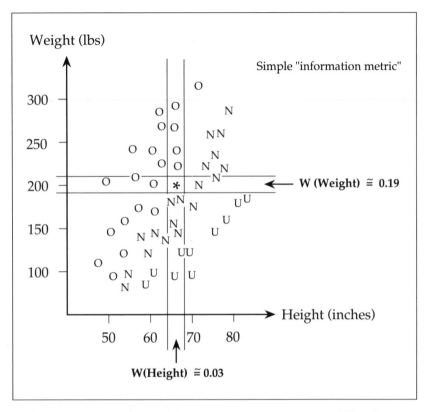

Let us suppose that we have a new case, represented by the star in the figure above. How shall we classify it: as an O, an N, or a U? We would like to judge whether height or weight is important, and if so, how relatively important each is. In this case, if one looks at all the cases that are close in height, one can see that weight says little about whether the person is overweight or not. There are four overweights, four normals, and two underweights that are close to the new case, so this really does not give much information, since the distribution of classifications for people with similar height is very nearly identical to the overall distribution of cases. On the other hand, if you look at cases with similar weights, there are three overweight and two normal patients. This actually gives a lot more information, since this distribution is very different from the overall distribution.

We can use a simple kind of information measure to judge the importance of each attribute, and to produce a numerical weight to represent the importance of each. We count up the number of examples of each classification for patients similar in each dimension. We introduce the expression for W_i; the weight of the ith attribute:

$$W_i = \Sigma \mid C_{ji} \mid^2 / (\Sigma \mid C_{ji} \mid)^2 - \Sigma \mid C_j \mid^2 / (\Sigma \mid C_j \mid)^2$$

where $\mid C_{ji} \mid$ is the number of cases with classification j that are identical (or close) in the ith attribute to the case to be classified, and $\mid C_j \mid$ is the number of cases with classification j.

Thus as shown in the figure, of those patients nearly equal in height to the new one, four are overweight, four are normal, and two underweight. Square each of those numbers, and take their total (16+16+4 = 36), then divide by their sum (10) squared (= 100) to get 0.36. Finally, subtract a similar term that covers the entire set of cases (0.33), to get 0.03, or W_{Height}. This small number tells us that Height is a relatively unimportant dimension on which to match. We repeat this calculation for Weight. Of the cases with similar weight, two are normal, three are overweight, and none are underweight: this gives us $W_{Weight} = 0.19$, which tells us that matching on weight is substantially more important than matching on height, for estimating closeness of resemblance among cases.

This approach would, for example, let us take a database in which one of the classifications is pregnancy, and, without having to identify and input the fact as a rule, discover that men do not become pregnant. One could take the view that this is basically a statistical method, and that there is nothing much new here. I would not strongly oppose this view. The main new contribution is the idea that a program can do dynamic on-line statistics. When you want to answer a question, you could actually set up the equivalent of a large-scale statistical experiment on the data, and complete it in a matter of a few seconds: that is the essence of what I have shown so far. However, when one wants to reason using databases that are semantic networks, or other less-structured collections of data, then MBR techniques start to look less like statistics, and more like AI.

Test cases for MBR

One of the tests that we have carried out is a comparison of the neural net approach with an MBR program. We used the NETtalk training sample as its database. The NETtalk task is very much like the pronunciation task discussed earlier. The task was solved by a neural network with about three hundred units and sixteen thousand interconnections, arranged in three layers. The input units look at a seven-letter window. There is a set of thirty output units; groups of three output units correspond to each output phoneme. The system was trained to generate pronunciations by repeatedly presenting it with a training set of a thousand words (about four thousand seven-letter windows), and using the neural net method called *back propagation*. This method basically computes an error vector across the output units (the difference between the actual and desired outputs) and then uses those errors to adjust the weights connecting units in each layer, until the error is no longer decreasing.

Let us compare NETtalk with our memory-based reasoning system MBRtalk. (We are not trying to pick on neural nets, but are really looking for ways of comparing MBR with other learning systems). Memory-based reasoning offers an alternative for neural-net-like tasks, using a radically different internal mechanism but without sacrificing any of the advantages enjoyed by neural nets.

The most interesting point of comparison is generalization, *i.e.*, the ability to judge the correct pronunciation for novel words not in the training sample. Seventy-eight per cent of the guesses NETtalk made were correct on a letter-by-letter basis. With a seven-hundred-word database MBRtalk achieved exactly the same accuracy. With sixteen thousand words, MBRtalk produced somewhat better behavior: 91 per cent. The sixteen-thousand-word experiment has not been done on NETtalk, and it would be relatively difficult to do it, requiring a much larger network and a training session at least sixteen times as long. More recent work by Wolpert (1989) has achieved 93-per-cent accuracy for the thousand-word NETtalk task.

NETtalk generates about 85 per cent correct guesses (on a letter-by-letter basis—not per word) on the training sample after ten passes through the corpus, *i.e.* after training the system ten times on each example. After about 50 passes, NETtalk produces 95-per-cent guesses. MBRtalk is a hundred per cent correct from the beginning on the training sample, because those samples are exact matches.

NETtalk used a thousand-word dictionary, and it would need a much larger network for a larger dictionary. It would also need to be retrained from scratch. MBRtalk was able to move quickly between seven-hundred- and sixteen-thousand-word dictionaries. In general, updating is costly for neural nets, and very cheap for MBR.

It took about a hundred hours to train the original NETtalk system on a VAX 780. Using a recently devised algorithm (Singer 90, Farber 1989) the same task requires less than five seconds on a CM-2. It takes no training-time to do ordinary MBR, though about a hour is needed to generalize the database for MBRtalk (on a CM-1). By generalize, I mean that we take each item in the database, compare it to all the others, and assign extra weight on the matching fields of the nearest correct database neighbor. Thus, generalization finds and marks the important characteristics for deciding how a given letter should be pronounced within the context of a particular word. After generalization, the performance of MBRtalk improves quite substantially, to about 93 per cent correct on novel words using the sixteen-thousand-word database.

Neural nets exhibit graceful degradation (Stanfill 1987; Stanfill and Waltz 1988); when there is a lot of noise in the inputs, or if some of the units in the neural net are changed or removed, the system's performance falls off gradually. This is in sharp contrast to expert systems or computer programs in general, where small changes can lead to dramatic degradations in performance.

Memory-based reasoning also degrades gracefully in the presence of noise, or after damage to its database. We experimentally introduced noise into the MBRtalk database by putting random letters in place of existing letters until more than 90 per cent of the letters were replaced. The system performance fell off only by about 10%. When we added noise also to the output fields, performance fell off somewhat faster, but still slower than linearly. Generalization made the MBRtalk even more resistant to noise.

MBR applications areas

We are currently doing further experiments using the Framingham Heart Study Database, a study of five thousand people for twenty years, with ten physical examinations per person during that period. This database has been used to establish most of the modern results relating high blood-pressure, obesity, smoking, stroke, and heart disease. We have been trying to replicate published studies, and have also recently shown that we can make substantially more accurate predictions than those in the literature about the time-course of blood-pressure, whether patients are treated for the condition or not.

We are working on the protein-structure prediction problem (Zhang, McKenna *et al.* 1989). Here we have applied both neural nets and memory-based reasoning, and have found that MBR performs somewhat better in this task, but that the two methods have somewhat different domains of accuracy. We are hoping that we can combine their advantages to build a system more accurate than either taken alone.

We are also interested in the possibility of building natural-language-understanding systems using memory-based reasoning. The idea here is to build up a large database of text which has been pre-processed. This could involve, for example, parsing the text, assigning parts of speech, and assigning the correct dictionary definitions to words in the text. We can then take a new text which we would like to process, compare it to this entire body of already-processed text, looking for similar passages, and then use these passages to judge how the new text should be processed. We have done some preliminary tests of these ideas, which look quite promising. In essence an MBR system would perform operations quite like those explored by Ken Church at Bell Labs, using a very different methodology (probabilistic transition-networks) (Church 1988).

Recently, Chris Atkeson at MIT has been using an MBR variant to control a robot arm (Atkeson 1987).

We believe that there are many more applications amenable to this kind of technique, such as: evaluating loan-applications, insurance underwriting, hardware or software troubleshooting, and even weather forecasting.

Document retrieval

I will now turn to the first real application of MBR ideas, a document retrieval system called DocuQuest now available as a commercial service through Dow-Jones (Stanfill and Kahle 1986, Waltz 1987, Stanfill, Thau and Waltz 1989, Weyer 1989). The system has been in continuous operation since January 1989. About 40,000 people had accounts as of June 1989. In this system, each of the database elements is a document: a piece of text such as a newspaper article.

The prime goal of the system is ease of use. The system operates by a method called *relevance feedback* (Salton 1970). The basic idea is to select one or more of the articles that you like, and tell the system to find further articles which are similar. The user can make these selections from a menu, or can simply point to them using a mouse. The system then uses *all* the words in the user-selected documents, and finds those documents in the database that have the greatest overlap of words, weighted by scores that are high for rare words and low or zero for common words. The system is fast, completing 99.95 per cent of its searches in less than one second.

The internal operation of the system can be understood through the following analogy. Suppose that I give a different document to each of sixty-four thousand people in a football stadium, along with a pocket calculator. All the terms that were being sought would be read out over the public-address system, along with a score-value for each term. Every person in the stadium would scan his or her document to see if it contained the term, and if it did, would add the appropriate score on the calculator. At the end of this process, each person would have a total score for his or her document. Then the people would have somehow to assemble themselves into an order from those with the highest score to those with the lowest, or at least must locate the highest scores. This is hard to do in a stadium, but (fortunately) easy to do on a Connection Machine.

This application also illustrates the usefulness of MBR for *clustering*. In a very large collection of articles from many newspapers there will inevitably be many stories that are nearly identical, and we probably do not want to show a user who is interested in some topic every identical story on that topic. Instead, we would like to group similar articles together, choose one of them to stand for all the others, and then show the user only that one article, announcing the fact that there are a number of other stories that are almost the same. So clustering is an important issue, and will become more important as more and more text is put on line. It is very easy to do clustering in a MBR system by taking an item and computing rapidly how similar each other item is to it.

The document retrieval application has another nice feature, namely the ability to support *browsing*, or moving freely around the database somewhat as in a hypertext system. If you happen serendipitously to encounter, during a search related to one topic, another topic you are also interested in, you can suspend the current search and go off in the new direction. This is in sharp contrast to traditional methods of search, which require a user to start from scratch in formulating each new search query.

Object recognition

Moving to a quite different application: we have also used a variant of MBR for computer vision (Tucker *et al.* 1988). This demonstration system consists of a simple video camera pointing at a scene consisting of small objects on a table. We have made this into a two-dimensional problem by assuming that the objects are always the same distance away from the camera. The system learns new objects as they are presented to it by the experimenter, and can then later recognize them, even when they are partially occluded by other objects.

For example, in learning to recognize a plastic refrigerator magnet shaped like the number 5 the system first finds edges in parallel, and then finds lines and corners, using a piecewise linear decomposition for edges which are curved. It then saves this set of vertices, angles and edges as its model of what the object looks like. We repeat these operations for a number of other kinds of object.

Having thus built a database of object models, we can then present the system with a scene that contains several of these objects, possibly overlapping each other. The system then finds all the vertices and edges in the entire scene, in much the same way as it did for the each separate object. It then broadcasts the features in the scene to all the models. Each model tries to imagine how it might be rotated and translated so that it could account for each feature in the multi-object scene.

So, any given object that has several features will give rise to many "explanations" (model-name, rotation, and translation) that overlay each other. For some objects almost all the models will lie on top of one another, and there will be no other objects that can explain the vertices except one. Other objects may seem to the system to be quite ambiguous. Thousands of hypotheses are generated about how the total-scene features might be explained. The system then clusters the explanations (simply by sorting them), and it uses explanations with many aligned "votes" to identify and name each object in the scene. The time required to do this is relatively independent of the number of object-models. For up to about 150 models, recognition takes about ten seconds on an 8K CM-1.

Cognitive modeling with MBR

What does this have to do with cognitive science? As described so far, almost nothing. In part, this is because cognitive science has mainly concentrated on modeling task-performance and timing, not on cognitive architecture—we have not had much information on which to base models of cognitive or brain architectures. As is evident in much of the research described in Part III of this book, our knowledge about the structure and function of the brain is growing at a very rapid pace. I maintain that MBR is a leading candidate for implementing associative memory modules, which are highly general building blocks that can, among other things, be useful in modeling cognitive modules. I believe that methods derived from memory-based-reasoning can provide a basis for artificial intelligence that is superior to its current foundations.

The dominant paradigm in artificial intelligence for its entire history has been *heuristic search*. Heuristic search uses trial-and-error to generate and explore all possible solution paths in the hope that one of them ends up at a goal. Heuristics are used to order the search, so as to try the most promising paths first. The difficulty with this method, which is the basis of expert systems and much else in AI, is that it cannot operate fast enough. Really large heuristic search systems will suffer from a combinatorial explosion, and therefore in any case cannot be the mechanism used by the brain.

This clearly follows from the *hundred-step rule* originally formulated by Jerry Feldman (1988): many perceptual tasks and sensory motor decision tasks require *on the order of a hundred milliseconds* for their performance. We know that each neuron introduces roughly a one-millisecond delay from the time that inputs arrive at its dendrites until the time that it actually fires. This means that the longest path from the initial sensing neuron(s) to the last motor effector neuron(s) cannot consist of more than a hundred steps. Thus the brain can be doing little, if any, trial-and-error searching and backtracking; far fewer than 100 hypotheses could be considered in this time. Heuristic search therefore cannot explain how we operate, at least for such rapid responses. Trial-and-error is certainly a possible explanation for many tasks that take seconds or longer, *e.g.* solving mathematical problems.

Another key assumption in traditional AI is the *physical symbol-system hypothesis*, which contends that the most important thing about the brain is that it somehow implements a universal logic machine, and that the actual physical details by which it does so are irrelevant. *Any* machine that is able to generate Turing-universal abilities would then in principle be capable of exhibiting intelligence. It seems clear, however, that the brain is not just implementing a universal logic-machine, and that the physical details of the brain's operations really do matter. That indeed is one of the underlying themes of this book.

There is also a kind of *extreme neural network* position according to which, once it is shown to be possible to take a few thousand neural net nodes and generate, or learn, a solution to a problem, one should conclude that the only thing that needs to be done to build a whole brain is to construct a very much larger network, and then teach it using an appropriate set of training samples. Unfortunately, that is not like the brain either. The brain seems to depend on extensive innate wiring (*e.g.* for vision). Another problem is that learning procedures are unlikely to scale well as networks become very large. In particular, some neural net learning procedures are NP-complete problems, so that learning may not be possible in a reasonably short time. Also, systems may get stuck in local minima, that is, they may come to have weights that can't be improved by small perturbations in any direction, even though they still do not yet solve the overall problem satisfactorily (Rivest and Blum 1988, Judd 1987).

To summarize my view: *an artificial intelligence based only on logic will not work.* By the same token, a neural-net-based artificial intelligence system that starts with random initial weights and a large homogeneous network will not work either.

So what is the solution—what is a reasonable approach? One possible answer is to use information about the way the brain operates at a rather crude structural level, and to build an analog of that structure, without necessarily incorporating low-level details. We need not use analog neurons! If we include a module that divides the perceptual world up in a reasonable way, we may be able to use learning methods that are relatively tractable and understandable.

One such method is *parameter adjustment*. If you have a structured initial system, you can probably adjust its parameters (possibly with hill-climbing methods) so that it comes to perform somewhat better. A second method is to use *rote-remembrance of groups of features that co-occur*. Such memories are proto-schemas of events, and the rote-remembered experiences can be used to construct memory-based reasoning and generalization systems. A third method is *generalization* of events and proto-schemas, given that certain kinds of events have occurred over and over again. Compositions and modifications of schemas can be used to form new schemas. I believe this is the right general approach

What kinds of components would we want to use to build such a system? I would like to argue that associative memory models are potentially a nice kind of universal building block—analogous to the use of NOR-gates or NAND-gates as universal elements for constructing any kind of computing device. Associative memories may not be universal—I am not sure we can build a vision system or motor system out of them—but they can serve as the basis for many kinds of components.

Craig Stanfill at Thinking Machines Corporation has done an experiment that uses memory-based reasoning systems as elements of a somewhat more complicated architecture (Stanfill 1988). The system he built is called Johnny, and it learns to read. Johnny simulates a four-year old child who has not yet learned to read, that is, not yet learned how to look at pages of text and correctly say words of the text aloud. We imagine that the child has watched Sesame Street, and has formed a notion of the simple rules for associating letters with their possible sounds, and for combining these sounds into words. Thus, the child knows that C sounds like K or S or Ch (in combination with H). We also assume that the child knows many words (and their meanings) by the *sound* of the words.

Johnny consists of three memory-based reasoning systems, one for generating possible pronunciations from rules, a second that contains known pronunciations and matches these to hypothetical pronunciations, and a third that stores word-pronunciation pairs, and is very similar to MBRtalk.

When we put in a new word like *cat*, Johnny generates, through its simple rules, a set of plausible pronunciations, and compares these with ones that it knows; if it can find a best match, it then generates a new entry for the MBRtalk-like module, stating that "cat" is pronounced "k@t".

The main method Johnny uses is unsupervised learning: it adds each new word-pronunciation pair assuming that it is correct. There is a separate path direct from inputs to the MBRtalk module, so that if Johnny ever sees "cat" again, the memory-based reasoning module can judge that it knows how to pronounce "cat" already, so it will not again go through the whole effort of generating pronunciations from rules. This is because the direct MBRtalk path will succeed first and suppress the more complex processing. For an unknown word it will however use the complex method. Each time it encounters a new word, it generates a word-pronunciation pair, and adds it to the MBRtalk dictionary.

After seeing a thousand words, and starting with an empty MBRtalk component, Johnny performs with about a three per cent error rate. If you remove some of the pronunciation rules, *e.g.* all the rules that apply to consonant clusters such as *th, ch, sh*, and *ng*, the systems starts off with fairly bad performance. But eventually learning reduces the error to about the same level as the system which started with all the rules. If you add some supervision to the experiment, *i.e.* if you tell Johnny whether or not it has the right answer, it eventually gets close to a zero error-rate.

This general architectural idea of multiple modules can be useful in many ways. One of the problems in AI for which it has been traditionally criticized is that it has dealt largely with toy problems that do not scale up. An associative memory module might become a general tool for turning a large full-scale problem back into a toy problem. Basically, a system could judge which domain you were working on through the use of associative memory, and use this information to propose only the operators and subgoals that are essential for solving that case. We have at any given moment perhaps thousands of actions that we might take, and such a system could help decide which two or three are actually the best ones to consider, if there is no exactly-matched action appropriate to that situation.

Thus, using associative memory which can be built out of memory-based reasoning modules, as well as out of many other technologies, may be very useful as a way of interfacing with traditional AI knowledge. I believe that ultimately the correct way to model intelligence is as a *society of mind* (Minsky 1986), a model very similar to what was called a *pandemonium* model in the 1950s (Selfridge 1959). Essentially, a system should have many interconnected *demons*, each of which knows only one little thing and accordingly is responsive to only one situation.

Conclusion

Finally, let me offer some broader morals.

First, models in AI and psychology are heavily dependent on available and imaginable hardware. Until we had the possibility of building neural nets or Connection Machines, models of the types I have been discussing (and their implications) were not taken very seriously. We should not, however, become too smug and believe that we have now thought of all possible basic paradigms: when next year's hardware comes along, we may suddenly find some other newer ideas about how it might be used to model the brain and the mind.

Memory-based reasoning is a natural method for Connection Machines and other parallel machines, and I think it is likely to prove an important idea. There is a strong technological momentum towards building data-parallel systems of this sort:

• *Memory size is increasing and its costs are coming down.* These systems are highly regular, and therefore it is possible to put more and more components on chips and wafers, including full MBR systems, which are mostly memory.

• *Memory, especially associative memory, is very important*, and likely to become more so, both as a building block for cognitive models, and also for practical applications that can make AI real.

• *Programs using the data-parallel approach are simple to write.*

For any given problem there are usually many solutions. For example, to build associative memories we have looked at MBR, genetic algorithms, neural nets and several other methods. Each method has different economics and different ranges of applicability. It may be that better silicon devices, or gallium arsenide devices, or optical devices, will support yet different kinds of solutions. They may or may not favor brain-like technology. We just don't know at present. I doubt that neurons will be built out of silicon, because the branching factors will have to be too large. In the brain each neuron has an average of ten thousand connections to other neurons, and you cannot very well get that kind of fan-out electrically, at least in our current technology.

We are by no means yet at the end of AI's story. Many problems remain to be solved or to have their solutions refined. Even so, I believe that parallel hardware provides a good basis not only for most problems in artificial intelligence but also for cognitive modelling. I believe we are just on the threshold of a very exciting and important explosion in theoretical and applied cognitive science.

Suggested further reading

Atkeson, C. Roles of knowledge in motor learning. *Massachusetts Institute of Technology Technical Report 942, 1986.*
> Shows how MBR-like systems can learn to control a robot arm or hopper with better accuracy than traditional control systems.

Blum, A., and Rivest, R. Training a 3-node neural network is NP-complete. *Proceedings of Neural Information-Processing Systems, 1988.*
> The conditions for the proof are fairly restrictive, but this result sounds a general warning that neural networks may not scale well.

Church, K.W. A stochastic parts program and noun phrase parser for unrestricted text. *Proceedings of the Second Conference on Applied Natural Language Processing,* Austin, Texas, 1988.
> Impressive performance in a system built on statistics or word frequency within local contexts.

CM-2 Technical Summary. *Thinking Machines Corporation,* 1989.
> Clear, comprehensive overview of the Connection Machine's architecture and programming models.

Farber, Rob. *Personal communication,* 1989.
> The original idea for the world's current (1990) fastest implementation of artificial neural networks.

Feldman, J.A., and Ballard, D.H. Connectionist models and their properties. *Cognitive Science* 6, 205-254, 1982. (Reprinted in Waltz and Feldman 1988).
> One of the original articles that sparked the renaissance of research into connectionist (artificial neural) systems. Good treatment of alternative models, their strengths and weaknesses.

Hillis, W.D. *The Connection Machine.* MIT Press, 1985.
> Hillis' thesis; a manifesto for massively parallel processing. While the actual Connection Machine sold today differs somewhat from this description, the basic intuitions and reasons for the current excitement about massive parallelism are here.

Judd, S.J. Complexity of connectionist learning with various node functions. *Technical Report 87-60,* Department of Computer and Information Sciences, University of Massachusetts, Amherst. 1987.
> More reasons to believe that artificial neural nets will not overcome NP-completeness.

Kibler, D., Aha, D., and Albert, M. Instance-based prediction of real-valued attributes. *Computational Intelligence*, May 1989.

> An alternative formulation of memory-based reasoning for classification. Database instances are retained only if their near neighbors' classifications differ, yielding equal classification performance from a smaller set of instances.

Minsky, M.L. *Society of Mind*. Simon and Schuster, 1985.

> An eloquent, accessible argument that our minds are composed of a large collection of specialized cooperative autonomous agents, and that our minds are not, as AI has long supposed, merely 'inference engines'. Packed with ideas and observations, organized into one-page 'chapters'.

Quinlan, J.R. Induction of decision trees. *Machine Intelligence* 1, 81-106, 1986.

> Describes the widely-used ID3 learning method, which builds decision trees that are optimal from an information-theoretic viewpoint.

Salton, G. *The SMART Retrieval System—Experiment in Automatic Document Classification*. Prentice-Hall, 1971.

> Classic summary of the heyday of information science in the 1960s. Little that has happened since has found its way into fielded applications.

Sejnowski, T.J. and Rosenberg, C.R. NETtalk: A Parallel Network that Learns to Read Aloud. *The Johns Hopkins University Electrical Engineering and Computer Science Technical Report JHU/EECS-86*, 1986.

> The most famous artificial neural net system, its data base has been widely used to test and compare different learning models. Caught public imagination by feeding its output to a speech synthesizer, yielding baby-like babbling for the partially trained system, and shading gradually into intelligible child-like speech as the system learned.

Selfridge, O. *Pandemonium*: a paradigm for learning. *Mechanization of Thought Processes*, Volume 1, 511-531. London: H.M. Stationery Office, 1959.

> The original source of the idea of 'demons' in programming.

Singer, A. Implementations of artificial neural networks on the Connection Machine. *Parallel Computing*, June 1990.

> A comparison of several methods for implementing back-propagation networks on a Connection Machine, together with comparative timings. Gives insight into efficient algorithms for massively parallel machines.

Stanfill, C. Memory-based reasoning applied to English pronunciation. *Proceedings of the Sixth National Conference on Artificial Intelligence (AAAI-87)*, Seattle, Washington, July 13-17, 1987.

> Fairly detailed account of the experiment comparing MBR with back-propagation networks. Also demonstrated the robustness of MBR when noise is added to its database.

Stanfill, C. Learning to read: a memory-based model. *Technical Report RL88-2*, Thinking Machines Corporation, 1988.

> Shows how MBR models can perform a variety of functions (*e.g.* implementation of rules; pattern completion; reasoning from precedents) that can be interconnected to build an interesting system that carries out unsupervised learning.

Stanfill, C., and Kahle, B. Parallel free text search on the Connection Machine system. *Communications of the ACM*, 29, 12, 1229-1239, 1986.

> Describes the massively parallel implementation of a very fast document retrieval system that uses 'relevance feedback' to perform searches with high precision and recall (*i.e.* most articles are retrieved are on the topic of interest (precision) and most interesting articles can be found (recall)). This research led to the development of SEEKER, a system that went into commercial use in January 1989 as 'DowQuest' (Dow-Jones News/Retrieval).

Stanfill, C., Thau, R., and Waltz, D.L. A parallel indexed algorithm for information retrieval. *Proceedings of the 12th International Conference on Research and Development in Information Retrieval (SIGIR-89)*, June 26-28, 1989.

> Describes how a system can be built to search a terabyte-sized database in under five seconds, using currently available hardware

Stanfill, C. and Waltz, D.L. Toward memory-based reasoning. *Communications of the ACM* 29, 12, 1213-1228, 1986.

> The original article on MBR. Describes algorithm for nearness matches in some detail, along with results from testing on the NETtalk database.

Stanfill, C. and Waltz, D.L. The memory-based reasoning paradigm. *Proceedings of the Case-Based Reasoning Workshop*, Clearwater Beach, Florida, May 1988.

> Discussion of the MBR paradigm, its advantages, limitations and consequences.

Tucker, L., Feynman, C., and Fritzsche, D. Object recognition using the Connection Machine. *IEEE Computer*, January 1987, 85 - 97, 1988.

> Description of a massively parallel system that learns (from a single trial) to recognize objects in a scene, even when they overlap. Uses machine vision methods along with a novel, clever encoding of object models. Helps illustrate the scope and generality of MBR-like methods.

Waltz, D.L. Applications of the Connection Machine. *IEEE Computer*, January 1987, 85-97, 1986.

> A summary of several applications, including MBR, and text retrieval (using MBR-like methods). Includes some examples of code (in *LISP).

Waltz, D.L. The prospects for truly intelligent machines. *Daedalus* 117, 1, 191-212, Winter 1988.

> An essay on the possibility of replacing the rule-based version of cognition with an MBR/Society of Mind-inspired model, and on the obstacles to be overcome in order to build machines that are unarguably intelligent.

Waltz, D.L., and Feldman, J.A. *Connectionist Models and Their Implications*, Ablex, 1988.

Weyer, S. Questing for the Dao: DowQuest and intelligent text retrieval. *Online* 13, 5, 39 -48, 1989.

> A perceptive and interesting review of the DowQuest document retrieval system.

Wolpert, D. *Generalization theory, surface-fitting, and network structures.* Ph.D. thesis, Physics Department, University of California, Santa Barbara, 1989.

> Describes an alternative MBR-like system in which weightings are picked by generating several sets of random weights, evaluating their performance on test data, and keeping the bast set. Wolpert's system dramatically outperformed the artificial neural network-based version of NETtalk.

Zhang, X., McKenna, M., Mesirov, J.P., and Waltz, D.L. An efficient implementation of the back-propagation algorithm on the CM-2. *Proceedings of Neural Information-Processing Systems Conference*, Boulder, Colorado, November 1989.

> Describes a fast artificial neural net implementation, not as fast as that of Farber or Singer (above) in general, but potentially better for some problems.

Chapter 11

NATURAL AND ARTIFICIAL REASONING

J. ALAN ROBINSON

Natural and artificial intelligence: Turing's test

Since the first appearance in 1950 of Alan Turing's influential essay *Computing Machinery and Intelligence* (Turing 1950) there have been many attempts to program computers to behave intelligently in various ways, and much has been written about how it might be done, or why it cannot be done.

Most people who address the matter find themselves nagged by two questions:

- what does *behave intelligently* really mean?

- if we could build an artificial brain would it be conscious?

Turing's essay evaded these questions by a clever trick. He simply asked, in effect: is it possible to design a machine (or what amounts to the same thing, to program a computer) to simulate human behavior and abilities well enough to deceive us into believing that it is a fellow human in disguise?

To spell out what that computer program would have to be able to do is to unfold, as Turing surely intended, the entire grand agenda of artificial intelligence (AI) research: fluent use of natural language, knowledge and skill acquisition, problem-solving ability, and so on. Although we are a very long way yet from being able to write a program like that, nobody has shown that it can never be done. The unconvincing impossibility-arguments of philosophers like Dreyfus (1972) and Searle (1980) suffer from the methodological difficulty of trying to reach empirical conclusions by *a priori* reasoning.

The fact is, we must wait and see. If such a program ever comes along, we ought to be able to say whether it behaves intelligently or not. It would be harder to decide whether it is conscious or not—but no harder than it already is to decide whether other humans, or animals, are conscious.

Meanwhile AI researchers will keep working towards the goal. There are two broad kinds of approach: the *natural* and the *artificial*.

The natural approach is to find out how humans and animals do things and then design machines to do them in that same way. In its purest form unfortunately this approach is going to have to await very much more progress in the behavioral and brain sciences than seems likely to happen any time soon.

The artificial approach is easier (though still difficult). It consists of taking what humans do and trying to design machines to do these things by any means at all, not necessarily in the same way that humans do them (which may well still remain unknown even if the machine works).

Nature has had plenty of time to evolve very good solutions to problems which appear to be very hard. Our brains really do work rather well. AI has the exasperating mission of trying to solve many of these same problems in the knowledge that they are solvable (since nature has already solved them) but without as yet being able to figure out how to do it at all, let alone how nature did it.

Artificial and natural chess programs

Humans play chess, some of them supremely well, but just how they do it is not as yet well understood and may never be. This is why there has not yet appeared a strong *and* natural chess-playing computer program. Today's successful chess-playing programs are all artificial, and derive their power mainly from the great speed and storage capacity of today's machines. They follow the simple basic minimax method explained in any good elementary AI textbook (*e.g.*, Winston 1984).

The natural approach to computer chess, championed notably by Hans Berliner (who is himself both a former world correspondence chess champion and a professional computer scientist) may or may not reach this level (Berliner 1981). We shall see. The motive for trying to write such a program is not, in the end, to win chess matches but to understand how humans are able to.

Heuristic methods in theorem-proving and in general

Humans reason deductively, some of them supremely well. This includes discovering proofs for theorems, and following and understanding proofs found by others. If we look closely at natural ways of proving theorems, we find that humans use intuition, backward and forward chaining, pattern-matching, guessing, trial-and-error, means-end analysis and all manner of other 'heuristic' methods. Testimony by prominent mathematicians who have reflected on their own mental processes in finding proofs strongly suggests that much remains hidden, below the level of conscious awareness. But however a human theorem-prover does it, we find that often the same theorem could have been proved artificially by a systematic logical analysis, by a mere mechanical process of executing a certain algorithm. So in this problem domain of theorem-proving there have been opportunities to compare 'pure' natural with 'pure' artificial programs.

Perhaps the best known early heuristic theorem-proving program is Newell and Simon's LT (Logic Theorist) (Newell and Simon 1956). In designing this program they made explicit a number of the tricks and tactics humans seem to use when searching for proofs of logical formulas in the *Principia Mathematica* system of Russell and Whitehead. LT was set up to use these same heuristics.

Soon afterwards (starting in 1957, and described in Newell and Simon 1963) the same researchers generalized the heuristic goal-seeking scheme of LT so that essentially the same problem-solving plan could be applied to subject-matter other than formal proof-finding. Their GPS program (**G**eneral **P**roblem **S**olver) was intended to be a direct, although somewhat stylized, imitation of the way humans tackle goal-seeking problems of any kind. In retrospect one can see how this early work eventually blossomed into today's 'expert system' programs, in which the main idea is to represent some restricted area of human knowledge or expertise as a corpus of heuristic rules which can be captured in a computer program (see, *e.g.*, Webber and Nilsson 1981).

LT was not a very good theorem prover. However, this does not mean that it was not a reasonable simulator of a certain kind of human problem-solving behavior (the not-too-successful kind, perhaps). It did prove some theorems, but only a few, and only easy ones, and only very inefficiently. By comparison, an artificial theorem-prover written soon afterwards (Wang 1960) proved these and many much harder theorems of *Principia Mathematica* very quickly and efficiently.

Of course Wang's systematic artificial algorithm can in principle also be carried out, although slowly, by a human (as of course can any algorithm written for a serial computer). For that matter, humans could also play chess artificially by using the minimax algorithm. But they don't. What is fascinating about ordinary—let alone unusually brilliant—natural human performance is how a human can manage to do such sophisticated things so rapidly and so well despite being built from such slow components and having such a small short-term memory.

Parallel methods in theorem-proving

The advent of parallel computers has only served to sharpen the distinction between natural and artificial reasoning. Computers are no longer merely bigger and faster one-thing-at-a-time performers—and thus different only in degree from ourselves—but now they can reason artificially in a quite alien many-steps-at-a-time fashion.

At the level of fundamental neural events, the brain is of course itself a massively parallel system. Yet at the higher level of explicit ratiocination, humans seem to be irredeemably serial devices, limited to one stream of consciousness. Complex natural real-time problem-solving behavior may indeed involve paying attention to many concurrent processes (consider, for example, conducting an orchestral performance or piloting a helicopter in a storm) but this quasi-parallel control always turns out to be done by skillful fast switching of a single flow of conscious attention. Humans can only simulate parallel algorithms, never actually execute them in a truly concurrent manner. They do it by timesharing, just as serial computers do.

Some surprising new phenomena emerge when we consider the use of parallel computers in artificial ways to do formal reasoning. A simple example of this is the process of *proof-checking*.

Parallel proof-checking

Suppose we are given an alleged proof of some sentence P and challenged to determine whether it really is a proof of P. How do we go about this? To simplify matters, we assume that we can recognize an axiom when we see one and that we can readily tell whether or not a given sentence follows from given others by a sound inference rule. This means that it is clear what counts as a proof of P: it has to be a tree structure each of whose nodes is labelled by a sentence, so that the following is true at each node of the tree:

either   the node is the root of the tree, and is labelled by P;

or   the node is a leaf of the tree, and is labelled by an axiom;

or   the label of the node follows by one of the sound inference rules from the labels of the sons of the node.

A human being, or a *serial* computer, could straightforwardly verify that a tree is a proof of P (or discover that it was not one) by 'walking the tree' in some order, and checking the truth of the above proposition node by node along the way. *One node at a time.*

But with a *team* of humans (or a *parallel* computer) available, one could examine every node in the tree *at the same time*, by allocating one human (or processor) to each node. There is nothing whatever in the notion of a correct proof which says that you have to visit the nodes one at a time or in any particular order. The notion of a correct proof is really a parallel notion, not a serial one.

Checking a proof thus turns out to be an example of what Geoffrey Fox elsewhere in this book calls an *embarrassingly parallel* computation: it can be done by partitioning the data (here, the alleged proof) into parts on which subcomputations can be done simultaneously, by independent agents, without any communication taking place between them.

This simple analysis also suggests that, as long as the number of nodes in the proof tree does not exceed the number of processors available, parallel proof-checking can be done *in constant time* no matter how large the proof is. Actually this is true only when there is some fixed bound on how long it takes to verify a single inference. We shall soon see that for machine-oriented, artificial inference rules, such fixed bounds no longer need exist.

We conclude that the apparent serial character of proof-checking is *only* apparent. The natural proof-checking as done by you and me is serial only because of the (logically) contingent fact that we can consciously do only one reasoning step at one time.

But then, just what is a *single* reasoning step? Here again, our usual ideas are heavily influenced by our own human information-processing limitations. The logical inference patterns which are traditionally studied turn out, on closer inspection, to be a tiny subset of a much larger variety of possible inference patterns. Machines not being limited in the same ways as humans, it is possible to organize machine reasoning systems whose individual reasoning steps are very large indeed by human standards.

Natural single steps are limited in size; artificial ones can be arbitrarily large

The amount of information a human can process in a single mental or perceptual act is admittedly a contingent matter. One can certainly imagine—and simulate on a computer—a more powerful reasoning agent capable of taking in (or putting out) much more inferential complexity in a single step than a human can.

In reality individual humans vary considerably in this respect among themselves, either innately or because of practice and experience, or both. A chess master typically can accurately recall a board position from a game after having looked at it for only a very short time. Is this done by a very rapid serial scan, or by a parallel, vision-like act involving a rich high-level set of 'expert pixels'? Tests show that a nonsensical configuration of chess pieces is memorized no more easily by an expert than by a beginner (de Groot 1965).

Traditional systems of logic are *human-oriented*. Their axioms and inference rules are abstracted from actual human reasoning patterns, and are designed to be used comfortably by humans in formal deductions. Both axioms and rules of inference are therefore kept simple enough so that the single-step-capacity limits of human information-processing are not exceeded. The proofs sanctioned by these natural systems of formal reasoning are trees whose nodes satisfy 'small' locally-verifiable conditions of correctness.

When we design *machine-oriented* logics we need not limit ourselves in this way. The result is that we now have examples of logics in which proof-checking is artificial even though it is serial: the single inference steps are typically much too large to be handled as such by a human, who is forced to treat them as composite transactions, as multistep proofs with the interior steps hidden away.

A good example of this is what happens in proofs built according to the so-called *resolution* inference principle (Robinson 1965). Humans usually find 'large' resolution inferences difficult even to grasp, let alone to generate. The patterns involved are rather more complex than those which enter into the more traditional, human-oriented inference patterns. For example, the following is a single 'hyper-resolution' inference. In human terms it consists of several steps; in machine terms it is a single primitive step:

for all x,y,z,u,v,w: **if** [P x y u] **and** [P y z v] **and** [P x v w]
                   then [P u z w];
for all r,s: [P [G r s] r s];
for all a,b: [P a [H a b] b].

∴ **for all** a, s: [P s [H a a] s]

All resolution inferences, except the very simplest ones, require subordinate pattern-matching computations in which a set of symbolic equations has to be solved in order to construct most general common instances of different expression-patterns. These subordinate *unification* computations can in principle be arbitrarily complex and are hard for humans even when they are small-scale.

For example the above inference requires the simultaneous solution of the three symbolic equations

$$[\,P\,x\,y\,u\,]\ =\ [\,P\,[\,G\,r\,s\,]\,r\,s\,]$$
$$[\,P\,y\,z\,v\,]\ =\ [\,P\,a\,[\,H\,a\,b\,]\,b\,]$$
$$[\,P\,x\,v\,w\,]\ =\ [\,P\,[\,G\,r\,s\,]\,r\,s\,]$$

in the sense that we must find the most general way in which the variables x, y, z, u, v, w, r, s, a and b can be replaced by expression patterns so that each equation becomes an identity.   It turns out that a general solution is (as can be verified by substitution into the three equations):

$$x = [\,G\,a\,s\,], \qquad y = a, \qquad u = s, \qquad r = a,$$

$$z = [\,H\,a\,a\,], \qquad v = a, \qquad b = a, \qquad w = s.$$

If these substitutions are made in the three premisses of the inference, the premisses become the following instances of themselves:

for all a, s: **if** $[\,P\,[G\,a\,s\,]\,a\,s\,]$

                    and $[\,P\,a\,[\,H\,a\,a\,]\,a\,]$

                    and $[\,P\,[G\,a\,s\,]\,a\,s\,]$

                    then $[\,P\,s\,[\,H\,a\,a\,]\,s\,]$;

for all a,s: $[\,P\,[G\,a\,s\,]\,a\,s\,]$;

for all a: $[\,P\,a\,[\,H\,a\,a\,]\,a\,]$.

From these the conclusion

for all a, s: $[\,P\,s\,[\,H\,a\,a\,]\,s\,]$

follows immediately.   The overall inference is thus based on several smaller subinferences, one of which is the construction of the general symbolic solution of the three equations by the unification process.

Let us next review the idea of unification and get a feel for the way this type of artificial symbolic reasoning is done.

Unification of expression patterns. Most general common instances

Unification is a pattern-computation process involving expressions as data. For illustration purposes we will borrow from the programming language LISP and take expressions to be: atoms and lists of expressions. We will write atoms as strings of uppercase letters, and write lists by enclosing their members in a pair of square brackets. Thus

BIG

BEN

[BIG [[[BEN]] [BEN] BEN] [ ] END]

are three expressions. The first two are atoms, and the third is a list with four components. Note that a list can in particular be the empty list [ ] or a singleton list like [A] or [[[[ ]]]].

The third expression above

[BIG [[[BEN]] [BEN] BEN] [ ] END]   (1)

is an instance of the pattern

[BIG [[[BEN]] [x] x] [ ] y]   (2)

in the sense that we get (1) from (2) if we substitute 'BEN' for 'x' and 'END' for 'y' in (2). But there are many other patterns of which (1) is an instance. For example, it is also an instance of

[z w [ ] END].   (3)

(1) comes from (3) if '[[[BEN]] [BEN] BEN]' is put for 'w' and 'BIG' is put for 'z'. This means that (1) is a *common instance* of (2) and (3). There are many (in fact infinitely many) other expressions which are common instances of (2) and (3) Here are two more:

[BIG [[[BEN]] [DOG] DOG] [ ] END]   (4)

[BIG [[[BEN]] [[A B]] [A B]] [ ] END]   (5)

The instances (4) and (5) correspond to two solutions of the *equation*

[BIG [[[BEN]] [x] x] [ ] y] = [z w [ ] END] (6)

namely, the solution:

$$x = DOG, \quad y = END, \qquad z = BIG,$$

$$w = [[[BEN]] [DOG] DOG]$$

and the solution:

$$x = [A \ B], \ y = END, \qquad z = BIG,$$

$$w = [[[BEN]] [[A B]] [A B]].$$

These are *particular* solutions of (6). There is also a *general* solution of (6), namely:

$$y = END, z = BIG, w = [[[BEN]] [x] \ x]$$

which corresponds to the 'most general common instance'

[BIG [[[BEN]] [x] x] [ ] END]   (7)

of (2) and (3) which, although not itself an expression, is a expression-pattern of which *every* common instance of (2) and (3) is an instance.

Every equation like (6) is either unsolvable (meaning that there are no common instances of the two expression-patterns which it equates) or else has a general solution which corresponds to the most general common instance of the two expression-patterns.

Moreover there are systematic ways to determine whether or not an equation of this kind is solvable, and to construct a general solution in the positive case. These are known as *unification* algorithms. There is interest in computer solutions of expression-pattern equations because the process of finding most general common instances of expression-patterns (the unification process) plays a crucial role not just in resolution methods but in most modern methods for automatically proving theorems.

Differences between expression patterns

It is useful in computing with expression patterns to define the *difference* $\Delta(A, B)$ between two expression patterns A and B.
$\Delta(A, B)$ is the set $\{ \{ A, B \} \}$, except in the two cases:

$$\Delta(A, A) \quad\quad\quad = \{ \};$$
$$\Delta([A_1 \ldots A_n], [B_1 \ldots B_n]) = \Delta(A_1, B_1) \cup \ldots \cup \Delta(A_n, B_n).$$

Thus the difference between two expression patterns is a collection of *unordered* pairs, and it is empty exactly when the patterns are identical.

An *ordered* pair <W V> consisting of an expression-pattern W and a variable V is called a *reduction* of the difference $\Delta(A, B)$ if {W, V} is in $\Delta(A, B)$ and V does not occur in W. The reason for the name is that if we substitute W for V everywhere in A and B, then A and B will be 'less different' than they were.

For example, the difference between (2) and (3) above is

$\{ \{ \text{ BIG, z } \}, \{ [[[\text{BEN}]] [x] x], w \}, \{ \text{ END, y } \} \}$,

so it has the three different reductions:

$< \text{BIG } z >, < [[[\text{BEN}]] [x] x] \ w >, < \text{END } y >.$

If we apply, say, the reduction $< \text{END } y >$ to both (2) and (3) they then become respectively

$[\text{BIG } [[[\text{BEN}]] [x] x] [ ] \text{END}]$ (2')

$[z \ w \ [ ] \text{END}]$ (3')

and their difference is is reduced to

$\{ \{ \text{ BIG, z } \}, \{ [[[\text{BEN}]] [x] x], w \} \}.$

Unification: natural but slow

The following iterative process of *successive difference reduction* can be applied to any equation between expression-patterns A and B:

while $\Delta(A, B)$ has a reduction <W V>

do   substitute W for V throughout A and B.

The repetition will eventually come to an end, since each successive reduction yields a new A, B in which there is one fewer variable than in the previous A, B, and the number of variables is of course finite.

If on termination A and B have each become the same expression-pattern C, then C is a most general common instance of the original A and B. A general solution of the original equation can then be immediately written down by comparing C with the original A and B. On the other hand if at termination the A and B are still distinct, then the original problem has no solution.

It is easy (though tedious) for a human to solve unification problems by the successive difference reduction process. In this sense it is a natural process. On the other hand this is a highly inefficient way to do unification. For example, to solve the equation

$$[[F x x] [F x_1 x_1] \ldots [F x_{n-1} x_{n-1}]] = [x_1 x_2 \ldots x_n] \quad (8)$$

by the method of successive difference reduction requires the eventual transformation of both sides into the expression pattern

$$C(n) \quad = \quad [D(1) \ldots D(n)]$$

which is their most general common instance, where:

$$D(0) \quad = \quad x$$

$$D(n+1) \quad = \quad [F D(n) D(n)].$$

For example, C(4) is the expression-pattern

$$[[F x x]$$
$$[F [F x x] [F x x]]$$
$$[F [F [F x x] [F x x]] [F [F x x] [F x x]]]$$
$$[F [F [F [F x x] [F x x]] [F [F x x] [F x x]]]$$
$$[F [F [F x x] [F x x]] [F [F x x] [F x x]]]]]]$$

which contains 26 'F's and 30 'x's.

In general the expression-pattern C(n) contains $2(2^n - 1) - n$ 'F's and $2(2^n - 1)$ 'x's. Thus the time and the space required by the successive difference reduction method to solve equation (8) both grow exponentially with n. Fortunately one can do unification much better than this. Even on a serial computer, it is possible to solve a unification problem of size n in time and space approximately proportional to n, and there are ways to parallelize the process which speed it up even further.

Unification: fast but artificial

The faster unification techniques use distributed representations of expression-patterns which can exploit indirect addressing and the sharing of subexpressions. The computations called for are quite artificial—inhuman even when done serially, and in parallel versions wholly alien and impossible for the human mind to follow.

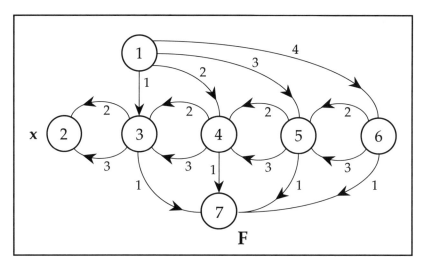

Figure 1.

Graph representation of expression-patterns

In a typical distributed representation scheme, expression-patterns are economically represented as nodes of a directed labelled acyclic graph. For example, C(4) is represented by the root node (node number 1) of the 7-node graph shown in Figure 1.

Each node in Figure 1 represents an expression-pattern.

node   expression-pattern represented

1   C(4)
2   x   = D(0)
3   [F x x]   = D(1)
4   [F [F x x] [F x x]]   = D(2)
5   [F [F [F x x] [F x x]] [F [F x x] [F x x]]] = D(3)
6   D(4)
7   F

In general, expression-patterns are represented by nodes in directed acyclic graphs like the one shown in Figure 1. These graphs are constructed according to the following plan:

A non-leaf node represents a list $[A_1 \ldots A_n]$ by having exactly n out-arcs, numbered respectively 1 to n, whose destinations represent the respective components $A_1 \ldots A_n$.

A leaf node represents the atom or variable by which it is labelled.

Fast unification: an example

Let us look again at how we might solve equation (8). Consider the case n = 4, which is equation (8'). We represent the two equated expressions in equation (8') as nodes in a graph. They are the roots (nodes 1 and 2) of the first graph shown in Figure 2. We solve the equation by a series of steps we shall call *equatings*.

As the first step, we equate the two roots. This represents the requirement that the equation

$$[[F x x] [F x_1 x_1] [F x_2 x_2] [F x_3 x_3] = [x_1 x_2 x_3 x_4] \quad (8')$$

must be true.

To do this, we simply *merge* node 1 with node 2. One can imagine doing this on a computer screen: we just pull the nodes next to each other, dragging their out-arcs along with them, and 'fuse' them into a single node. The result is the second graph shown in Figure 2. The new fused node is now the origin of arcs which formerly originated in node 1 and also of arcs which formerly originated in node 2.

The general rule for proceeding is the following: if a graph contains nodes α, β and γ such that $\alpha[i]\beta$ and $\alpha[i]\gamma$ then the two nodes β and γ must be equated.[*] Thus as long as there is a node in which two distinct arcs originate which have the same label, the graph is not in final form. In the second graph of Figure 2 there are four such nodes. The rule says that we must equate:

nodes 3 and 7	(because {1,2} [1] 3 and {1,2} [1] 7),
nodes 4 and 8,	(because {1,2} [2] 4 and {1,2} [2] 8),
nodes 5 and 9,	(because {1,2} [3] 5 and {1,2} [3] 9),
nodes 6 and 10	(because {1,2} [4] 6 and {1,2} [4] 10).

These equatings can be done in parallel.

---

[*] The notation $\alpha[i]\beta$ means that there is an arc labelled by i whose origin is α and whose destination is β.

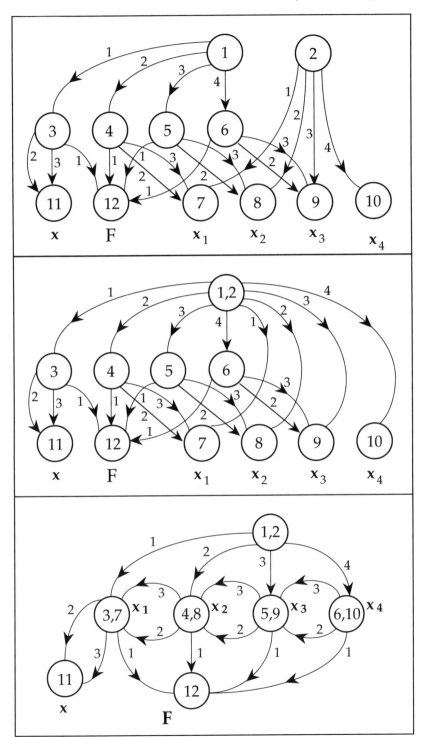

Figure 2

The result of doing all of them is the third graph in Figure 2. Note that when a leaf node is equated to another node, it contributes its label (atom or variable) as a label of the merged node. The third graph is now final; no more equatings are required.

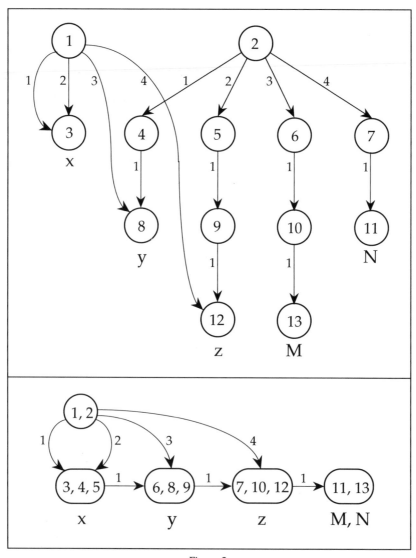

Figure 3

One can see that the root {1, 2} of the third graph in Figure 2 represents C(4). This final graph is in fact isomorphic to the graph in Figure 1 if we ignore the labelings of the non-leaf nodes These labelings actually represent the solution:

$$x_i = D(i), i = 1, ..., 4.$$

The 'node-equating' unification algorithm also detects unsolvability. For example, the equation

$$[x x y z] = [[y] [[z]] [[M]] [N]]$$

is not solvable. Initial and final graphs for this problem are shown in Figure 3. The reader should now be able to carry out the successive equatings to get from the initial to the final graph.

In the final graph, the node {11,13} is labelled by two distinct atoms—an impossibility. The original problem is therefore unsolvable.

This is the first of three 'local' properties of a graph which indicate unsolvability. The second is the equating of two nodes of different degrees (which therefore represent lists of distinct lengths) and the third is a non-leaf node labelled by an atom. These conditions can be recognized immediately by local inspection of each node.

However, there is a fourth property of the final graph which is not locally recognizable in this sense: this is the presence of *cycles*. For example, the equation

$$[x [F x]] = [[G y] y]$$

is represented by equating nodes 1 and 2 in the left graph of Figure 4. This then requires the equating of node 3 with node 5, and node 4 with node 6, producing the final graph on the right in Figure 4.

The cycle between node {3,5} and node {4,6} represents an impossible syntactic structure in finite expressions. The root node {1, 2} of the final graph indeed represents the 'expression':

$$[[G [F [G ...]]] [F [G [F ...]]]]$$

which is in fact a correct solution of the equation in the domain of *infinite* expressions. It is the presence or absence of such cycles in the completed graph which determines whether the solution represented is infinite or finite. The analysis needed to detect a cycle or to prove acyclicity can be performed in time proportional to the size of the collapsed graph.

The best known serial methods of completing a unification graph need, in the worst case, an amount of time and space which is either strictly linear or almost linear in the size of the graph. The problem of parallelizing the unification process has been investigated.[1]

---

*   For example by Dwork, C., Kanellakis, P.C., and Mitchell, J.C., The sequential nature of unification, *The Journal of Logic Programming* 1,

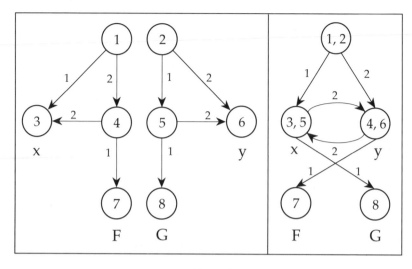

Figure 4

The node-merging unification algorithm can easily be extended to the case of simultaneously unifying more than two expression-patterns; one simply starts off by merging all of their nodes into one node. Indeed one can in general start off with several merged nodes, each representing a set of expression-patterns to be collapsed to a singleton.

In summary: unification can be done very rapidly by the process of equating pairs of nodes in the graph representing the problem. Portions of this process can be carried out in parallel, but even the serial version of the process is acceptably fast and is the one in use today within most resolution theorem-provers, and all implementations of Prolog.

Unification is part of a resolution inference

As was said, one of the main uses for the unification process has been as an auxiliary device in making resolution inferences.

A basic resolution inference obtains a conclusion from two premises. All three sentences are so-called *clauses*—universal

35-50, 1984, and by Vitter, J.S., and Simons, R.A.,, New classes for parallel complexity, *IEEE Transactions on Computers*, C-35, 403-418, 1986. Vitter and Simons showed that the running time in an idealized shared memory parallel computer with P processors is approximately $E/P + V \log P$, where E and V are respectively the number of arcs and the number of vertices in the expression graph.

generalizations whose bodies have a special **if...then** form in which both the **if** part and the **then** part are unordered sets of atomic sentences. A sentence of the form

$$\text{if } \{A_1, ..., A_m\} \text{ then } \{B_1, ..., B_n\}$$

is taken to mean that there is at least one A_i which is false or at least one B_j which is true. Either or both of m and n can be 0; if both are 0 this means that the sentence is false and it is called the *empty* clause.

The overall resolution inference looks like:

for all $\{x_1, ..., x_{m_1}\}$ **if** $\{A_1, ..., A_{m_2}\}$ **then** $\{B_1, ..., B_{m_3}\}$;

for all $\{y_1, ..., y_{n_1}\}$ **if** $\{C_1, ..., C_{n_2}\}$ **then** $\{D_1, ..., D_{n_3}\}$

∴ **for all** $\{z_1, ..., z_{k_1}\}$ **if** $\{P_1, ..., P_{k_2}\}$ **then** $\{Q_1, ..., Q_{k_3}\}$

where the A's, B's, C's, D's, P's and Q's are atomic sentences and the x's, y's, and z's are variables. The conclusion is constructed from the two premises with the help of the unification process, as follows.

First, we construct the expression graph in which all the atomic sentences are represented as nodes, and equate one or more of the B's with one or more of the C's. These are the *key nodes* for the inference. This graph is then completed; that is, the nodes are all transformed into various instances of themselves and in particular the key nodes are all transformed into their most general common instance.

The conclusion is then formed from the completed graph by taking the P's to be the A's and C's which are not key nodes, and the Q's to be the D's and B's which are not key nodes; the z's are then just the variables (if any) which occur in the P's and the Q's.

Other forms of resolution are defined by placing various restrictions on the form of the premises and conclusion. Still others (such as the hyper-resolution of which we earlier saw an example) consist in effect of two or more simultaneous basic resolutions.

Logic programming

One of the more interesting uses of a restricted form of resolution underlies the idea of *logic programming* (Kowalski 1979). Since the early 1970s this idea has been mainly associated with the Prolog programming language (Colmerauer 1985), which is essentially a controllable resolution theorem prover based on a restricted form of resolution in which the clauses must have a singleton set or the empty set as their **then** part (and thus be so-called *Horn clauses*). Logic programmers call such clauses *assertions* if their **then** part is a singleton, and *goal clauses* if their **then** part is empty. An assertion is *unconditional* or *conditional* depending on whether its **if** part is empty or not. A Prolog computation step is just a resolution inference with a goal clause as one premiss, one or more assertions as the other premisses, and a goal clause as conclusion.

A Prolog deduction is a chain of Prolog inferences whose assertion premisses all come from a fixed set of assertions called the *knowledge base.* The goal clause serving as premiss of the initial inference is a given *initial goal clause.* Each subsequent inference uses as its goal clause premiss the one which is the conclusion of the previous inference. Such a deduction is *complete* if the conclusion of its final inference is the empty clause (both its **if** part and its **then** part are empty).

The interesting twist is that Prolog deductions are completed merely in order to harvest, as output, the corresponding cumulative unification solutions; indeed, Prolog users think of the initial goal clause G as simply serving to generate all such solutions, corresponding to all the different ways in which the empty goal clause can be deduced by Prolog inferences from the knowledge base together with G.

If an inference step involves more than one assertion then the work can be done in parallel; moreover the different complete deductions for a given initial goal clause can be developed in parallel. The formidable decade-long Japanese Fifth Generation Computer Project, due to end in 1992, has as one of its goals the implementation (in a suitable mix of hardware and software) of a logic programming system in which such opportunities for parallel speed-ups are exploited as much as possible.

Reduction; normalization

Reduction is the kind of reasoning we have to do in order to evaluate a simple numerical expression step by step. For example, if we want to work out the number

$$\sqrt{(((3 + 2) \times (8 - 6))^2 \div \sqrt{(11 + 5)})}$$

we have perform as many 'reduction steps' as are needed to get rid of all the operations:

$$\sqrt{(((\mathbf{3 + 2}) \times (8 - 6))^2 \div \sqrt{(11 + 5)})}$$
$$\sqrt{((5 \times (\mathbf{8 - 6}))^2 \div \sqrt{(11 + 5)})}$$
$$\sqrt{((\mathbf{5 \times 2})^2 \div \sqrt{(11 + 5)})}$$
$$\sqrt{(\mathbf{10}^2 \div \sqrt{(11 + 5)})}$$
$$\sqrt{(100 \div \sqrt{(\mathbf{11 + 5})})}$$
$$\sqrt{(100 \div \sqrt{\mathbf{16}})}$$
$$\sqrt{(\mathbf{100 \div 4})}$$
$$\sqrt{\mathbf{25}}$$
$$5$$

and at the end we know that the expression we started with denotes the number five, which presumably we didn't know when we started.

Each of these eight reasoning steps is of the same general kind. We change the current expression into a new expression by locating an occurrence of some subexpression in it, such as '3 + 2', whose denotation is known to us, in the sense that we know what numeral has the same denotation: in this case the numeral is '5'. So we replace the occurrence of '3 + 2' by an occurrence of '5'. This change does not alter the denotation of the whole expression: whatever number it denoted before the change it still denotes after the change.

Logicians call such an immediately replaceable subexpression a *redex*. In the example above the redex selected for replacement in each expression is printed in bold face. Note that there are three redexes in the first expression. Any of the three could be chosen in order to reduce the first expression. Each choice would reduce the first expression to a different second expression. The redex '3 + 2' happened to be the leftmost of the three and so it is the first to be encountered in a left-to-right scan of the expression. Because of the freedom to choose any redex as the basis for each reduction step, the overall evaluation process can take many different paths.

Most people know how to figure out that

$$\sqrt{(((3 + 2) \times (8 - 6))^2 \div \sqrt{(11 + 5)})}$$

is 5, and could get through the steps fairly quickly and almost without conscious thought. But it would have to be done 'on paper'—there are definite limits on how large a task of this sort can be done in one's head. The one-redex-at-a-time transformations in this example are chunks of work which lie comfortably within human information-processing capacity, but the overall organization of the task is too complex to manage entirely without any external aids. Of course even a single redex can be too big to do mentally as a single chunk of work: the reasoning by which we multiply 2534152635243546 by 56784536456735456 to get 143900682702919366036218653366976 has many separate steps, and we need to keep track of the details by writing them down.

But there is no *logical* requirement to stick to one-redex-at-a-time. All the redexes in an expression can be replaced at once. For example, if we do all redexes at the same time, the same example normalizes in larger but fewer steps:

$$\sqrt{(((3 + 2) \times (8 - 6))^2 \div \sqrt{(11 + 5)})}$$

$$\sqrt{((5 \times 2)^2 \div \sqrt{16})}$$

$$\sqrt{(10^2 \div 4)}$$

$$\sqrt{(100 \div 4)}$$

$$\sqrt{25}$$

$$5.$$

Here there are three redexes in the first expression, and two in the second, but then only one each for the rest of the way, but this is enough to see how reducing an expression in parallel gets the work done in fewer but larger steps. The architecture of our brains won't let *us* do it this way, but parallel machines can exploit such logical opportunities.

The organization of natural proofs

In the (more or less) formal reasoning examples we have looked at, the inferences take place in planned and controlled patterns. In these cases the conscious mind is really being dragooned to serve only as a computing device. It is being restricted to do only what we can also make a computer do. In general, however, the mind is not at its best when it is being used merely as a computer.

The mind reasons rather differently when left free to operate in its own natural style. It is interesting, for example, to see how different are the actual natural proofs found in mathematical writings and lectures, from the artificial proofs met with in formal logical systems. When you look closely at a serious live mathematical proof you see that it is something like an informal guided tour of a richly-connected knowledge network already in place. A proposition is *revealed* as true, by showing it from various other places in the network and by drawing attention to its relationship with other true propositions. The emphasis is more on one's being brought to *see why* the proposition is true—on being provided with an *understanding*—and not so much on simply being given a guarantee *that* it is true. Of course a good proof offers both an explanation and a guarantee, but usually the guarantee is just a side-effect of the explanation. Ironically, it is the explanation aspect which often seems to get lost when the proof is formalized. Formal proofs therefore tend to be *only* guarantees.

Covering the mutilated checker board

For example an exhaustive finite search exposes the fact that there is no way to cover, with 31 tiles each the size of two adjacent squares, the 62 remaining squares of a checker board whose two diagonally opposite corner squares have been removed:

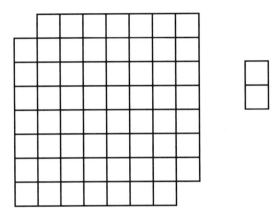

The record of such a search with its negative outcome would be a kind of formal proof guaranteeing the fact that no such covering exists, but it would give no hint as to why not, and so would not much help our understanding of the situation. The reason for the impossibility is made more apparent in the more natural proof, which points out that the two missing squares are of the same color, so that the mutilated board has more squares of the one color than of the other, and that the two adjacent squares covered by one tile have different colors:

so a board must have exactly as many squares of the one color as of the other in order to be coverable by such a tiling.

Bertrand's conjecture

A similar but more complicated example is the proof by Erdös of Bertrand's Conjecture: *for all $n > 1$, there is a prime number between n and $2n$.* To understand this elegant, powerful proof requires no more than some elementary algebra, including the idea of proof by induction, and a knowledge of the logarithmic and exponential functions. An acquaintance with the factorial function $n!$ and with the *binomial coefficients* $n!/m!(n - m)!$ is also assumed. These latter numbers form *Pascal's Triangle* when arranged down the page in rows corresponding to $n = 0, 1, ...,$ and from left to right in each row according to $m = 0, 1, ... n$. We will need to know that the sum of the numbers in the nth row of Pascal's Triangle is 2^n.

The proof exploits certain features of the 'central' binomial coefficients $(2n)!/(n!)^2$ and $(2n+1)!/n!(n-1)!$ — those which are the largest numbers in each row of Pascal's Triangle:

$$
\begin{array}{c}
1 \\
1 \ \ 1 \\
1 \ \ 2 \ \ 1 \\
1 \ \ 3 \ \ 3 \ \ 1 \\
1 \ \ 4 \ \ 6 \ \ 4 \ \ 1 \\
1 \ \ 5 \ \ \mathbf{10} \ \ \mathbf{10} \ \ 5 \ \ 1 \\
1 \ \ 6 \ \ 15 \ \ \mathbf{20} \ \ 15 \ \ 6 \ \ 1 \\
1 \ \ 7 \ \ 21 \ \ \mathbf{35} \ \ \mathbf{35} \ \ 21 \ \ 7 \ \ 1 \\
1 \ \ 8 \ \ 28 \ \ 56 \ \ \mathbf{70} \ \ 56 \ \ 28 \ \ 8 \ \ 1 \\
1 \ \ 9 \ \ 36 \ \ 84 \ \ \mathbf{126} \ \ \mathbf{126} \ \ 84 \ \ 36 \ \ 9 \ \ 1 \\
etc.
\end{array}
$$

The main idea of the proof rests on properties of the exponents in the prime-power-product representations of the numbers

$$1, 2, 6, 20, 70, ...,$$

which lie in the center of the *even*-numbered rows, that is, the numbers $(2n)!/(n!)^2$, for $n = 0, 1, ...$

To fix ideas let us consider the case $n = 50$, and look at the exponents in the representation of $100!/(50!)^2$ as the product of prime powers:

$$2^3 3^4 11^1 13^1 17^1 \ 19^1 \ 29^1 31^1 53^1 59^1 61^1 67^1 71^1 73^1 79^1 83^1 89^1 97^1.$$

Some patterns to notice are: that no prime larger than 100 is a factor; that *all* primes between 50 and 100 are factors, moreover with exponent 1; that no prime contributes more than 100 to the product; and that no prime between 33 and 50 (*i.e.*, none of the primes 37, 41, 43, and 47) is a factor.

Similar patterns occur no matter what value of n we consider. In general, in the representation of $(2n)!/(n!)^2$ as a product of powers of primes:

$$(2n)!/(n!)^2 = 2^{A(n,\,2)} \cdot 3^{A(n,\,3)} \cdot \; ... \; \cdot p^{A(n,\,p)}$$

we always have the following:

A. no prime > 2n is a factor: if p > 2n then A(n, p) = 0;

B. the exponents of the primes between n and 2n are all 1;

C. no prime contributes more than 2n: $p^{A(n,\,p)} \leq 2n$;

D. no prime in the interval $(2/3)n < p \leq n$, is a factor.

The major theme of Erdös' proof is the pursuit of the appropriate consequences of these four facts A, B, C and D, and so it is an important part of one's understanding of the proof to see why they are true. This insight can all be based on a single simple but important idea.

The basic tool for calculating the exponents of primes in prime-power-product representations of binomial coefficients is a direct application of an simple but far-reaching observation about the *factorial function*

$$n! = 1 \cdot 2 \cdot \; ... \; \cdot n.$$

Suppose that we want to represent n! as a prime-power-product:

$$n! = 2^{E(n,\,2)} \cdot 3^{E(n,\,3)} \cdot \; ... \; \cdot p^{E(n,\,p)}$$

where we denote by E(n, p) the exponent of the prime p in the prime-power-product representation of n! To do this quickly and easily we need only know that the exponents E(n, p) are given by the equation

$$E(n, p) = [n/p] + [n/p^2] + [n/p^3] + \; ... \; .$$

The 'square brackets' notation [x] denotes *the largest integer which is not larger than* x. Thus [4.23] = 4, [5.0] = 5, and so on.

The truth of the equation for E(n. p) is easily appreciated by first noting that in the set {1, 2, ..., n} there are [n/p] different numbers which are multiples of p, each of which therefore contributes 1 to the exponent E(n, p). Next one notes that $[n/p^2]$ of these numbers are not only multiples of p but also multiples of p^2—each of which therefore contributes an *additional* 1 to the exponent E(n, p). In turn, $[n/p^3]$ of these numbers are multiples not only of p and p^2 but *also* multiples of p^3—each of which contributes still *another* 1 to E(n, p). And so on, for each power of p. Of course, eventually we come to such a high power of p that there are no multiples of it in the set {1, 2, ..., n} and so the series ends.

For example, in computing the exponent of 2 in the prime-power representation of 1000! we find that the series ends after only nine terms:

$$E(1000, 2) = 500 + 250 + 125 + 63 + 31 + 15 + 7 + 3 + 1 = 995.$$

Now, to compute the exponent $A(n, p)$ of p in the prime-power representation of the number $(2n)!/(n!)^2$ we need only observe that

$$E(\,(2n)!/(n!)^2\,,\,p) = E(2n, p) - 2E(n, p)$$

to establish the fact that $A(n, p)$ is given by the equation:

$$A(n,p) = (\,[\,2n/p\,] - 2[n/p]\,) + (\,[\,2n/p^2] - 2[\,n/p^2]]\,) + \dots .$$

When $p \leq 2n$ and $p^2 > 2n$, only the *first* term in this sum, namely

$$(\,[\,2n/p\,] - 2[n/p]\,)$$

is greater than zero, and in general all the terms in the sum vanish after the $R(n, p)^{\text{th}}$ term

$$(\,[\,2n/p^{R(n,\,p)}] - 2[\,n/p^{R(n,\,p)}]\,),$$

where $p^{R(n,\,p)}$ is the highest power of p which does not exceed $2n$.

Since $[2x]$ is always equal either to $2[x]$ or to $2[x] + 1$, each term in the sum is either 0 or 1. This means that the entire sum, namely the quantity $A(n, p)$, cannot exceed $R(n, p)$, which is the same thing as saying that $p^{A(n,\,p)} \leq 2n$.

This is the reason for A and C above.

If $n < p \leq 2n$ then $[\,2n/p\,] = 1$ and $[n/p] = 0$.

That is why we have B above.

Moreover, the first term itself vanishes whenever p lies in any of the intervals

$$(2/2k + 1)n < p \leq (1/k)n$$

for $k \geq 1, \dots$, and $p^2 > 2n$.

Which accounts for D above, when $k = 1$.

How then does Erdös bring all this to bear on Bertrand's Conjecture? Roughly and intuitively speaking, what the facts A through D indicate is that that the numbers $(2n)!/(n!)^2$ could not be as big as they are if they did not have all the primes between n and $2n$ as factors. If there were no primes between n and $2n$ then (by D) the quantity $(2n)!/(n!)^2$ would be a product of no more than $2n/3$ 'small' quantities—none of them (by C) any larger than $2n$. That turns out, on further investigation, not to be possible.

How big, then, do the numbers $(2n)!/(n!)^2$ *have* to be? The following considerations soon reveal a lower bound on their size.

The quantity $(2n)!/(n!)^2$ has to be *at least* as large as $(2^{2n})/2n$

To see this, consider the following argument. We recall that $(2n)!/(n!)^2$ is the largest of the $2n+1$ numbers in the $2n^{\text{th}}$ row of Pascal's triangle (counting the top row as the zeroth) and that the numbers in the 2nth row sum up to 2^{2n}. Since each row after the zeroth begins and ends with a 1 we have, when n > 1:

$$2^{2n} = 1 + \{ \text{ a sum of 2n } -1 \text{ terms } \} + 1$$

and so if we reckon the 1 + 1 as the single term 2 we have

$$2^{2n} = 2 + \{ \text{ a sum of 2n } -1 \text{ terms } \}$$

Since the term $(2n)!/(n!)^2$ is larger than the rest of the 2n terms on the right hand side, the right hand side will become *strictly larger* if we replace each of the 2n terms by the term $(2n)!/(n!)^2$, or in other words:

$$2^{2n} < 2n \cdot (2n)!/(n!)^2$$

which is to say:

$$(2^{2n})/2n < (2n)!/(n!)^2.$$

So here we have a strict lower bound for the quantity $(2n)!/(n!)^2$ when n > 1.

But if there are no primes between n and 2n, $(2n)!/(n!)^2$ cannot in fact be that big

This takes a little more time to see. We know (by D) that *if* there were no primes between n and 2n, *then* $(2n)!/(n!)^2$ would be a product of powers of primes no larger than 2n/3 to which no prime contributes more than 2n. We can *on that assumption* calculate an *upper* bound for $(2n)!/(n!)^2$.

To do this, we must make use of an interesting fact which we will now digress to establish. It is that *the product of all primes no larger than n is less than 2^{2n}*.

We must temporarily suspend the main argument in order to show this. Note that it is only because you and I are essentially *serial* computers at the top level that we cannot just sail on and do this subordinate proof *simultaneously* with the main argument. On the other hand we don't *have* to do it at this particular moment— it is an independent item in our knowledge base, and indeed an expert would quite probably know it already.

The product of primes no larger than n is less than 2^{2n}

This proposition is obvious when n is 3 or less. For n > 3 we will prove it by induction.
Assume that n > 3 and, as *induction hypothesis*, that

for all k < n, P(k) = product of primes in the set {2, ..., k} < 2^{2k}.

Now, when n is even, the proposition is true by the induction hypothesis, because the product of all primes no larger than an *even* number n is the same as the product of all primes no larger than the *odd* number n − 1.

When n is odd, say, n = 2m + 1, we split up the product of primes no larger than n into two factors

$$P(2m + 1) = P(m + 1) \cdot R(m)$$

where

R(m) = product of primes in the set {m + 1, ..., 2m + 1}

and we observe that since P(m + 1) is strictly smaller than the quantity $2^{2(m+1)}$ (by the induction hypothesis), the strict inequality holds:

$$P(2m + 1) < 2^{2(m+1)} \cdot R(m).$$

Now if we could only replace R(m) by the quantity 2^{2m} we would have the result we are after, since

$$2^{2(m+1)} \cdot 2^{2m} = 2^{2(2m+1)}$$

But we *can* do this: R(m) is strictly smaller than 2^{2m}. We have to see why. Here is where the binomial coefficients come in again.

The primes which divide (2m+1)!/m!(m+1)! include every prime in the set {m+2, ..., 2m+1}, as well as other primes: so the strict inequality holds:

$$R(m) < (2m+1)!/m!(m+1)!$$

But 2^{2m+1} is the sum of the 2m+1 binomial coefficients in the (2m+1)st row of Pascal's Triangle. The largest number in this row, namely (2m+1)!/m!(m+1)!, occurs *twice*, and it thus contributes *less than half* of the whole sum:

$$(2m+1)!/m!(m+1)! < (1/2) \cdot 2^{2m+1} = 2^{2m}$$

and so we have the inequality

$$R(m) < 2^{2m}$$

which allows us to strengthen our inequality further to

$$P(2m + 1) < 2^{2(m+1)} \cdot 2^{2m}$$

or in other words to the desired inequality

$$P(2m + 1) < 2^{2(2m+1)}$$

which completes the inductive proof of the subordinate result.

Resumption of the main argument

So let us continue, by rearranging the product

$$(2n)!/(n!)^2 = 2^{A(n, 2)} \cdot 3^{A(n, 3)} \cdot \ldots \cdot p^{A(n, p)}$$

and splitting it into the two factors:

{product of primes p for which A(n, p) is 1} ·
{product of primes p for which A(n, p) is 2 or higher}

The first factor will be less than $2^{4n/3}$ because none of the primes for which $A(n, p)$ is 1 exceed $2n/3$.

What about the second factor?

The primes whose exponent is 2 or higher will each contribute no more than $2n$ to the whole product (by property C). How many such primes are there? There can be no more than $\sqrt{(2n)}$ of them, since the largest such p must satisfy $p^2 \leq 2n$. So the second factor is less than $(2n)^{\sqrt{(2n)}}$.

Putting these observations together, we see that

$$(2n)!/(n!)^2 < 2^{4n/3}(2n)^{\sqrt{(2n)}}.$$

This is an upper bound on $(2n)!/(n!)^2$ for any n for which there are no primes between n and 2n.

What all this has shown is that if n is a number for which there are no primes between n and 2n, then the following inequality must hold:

$$(2^{2n})/2n < 2^{4n/3}(2n)^{\sqrt{(2n)}}.$$

Now we must employ a little symbolic computation to transform this inequality into a form which is easier for the mind to deal with. First, multiplying both sides by 2n, we have:

$$2^{2n} < 2^{4n/3}(2n)^{\sqrt{(2n)}+1}$$

whence (dividing both sides by $2^{4n/3}$):

$$2^{2n/3} < (2n)^{\sqrt{(2n)}+1}$$

and therefore (taking logarithms)

$$(2/3) n (\log 2) < (\sqrt{(2n)} + 1)(\log 2n)$$

and finally (multiplying both sides by 3):

$$2n (\log 2) < 3(\sqrt{(2n)} + 1)(\log 2n)$$

a form of the inequality which makes it easier to reason about.

This inequality is false for all n > 512

The rest of the proof is an argument showing that this inequality is false for all n > 512. This will show that an n for which no primes occur between n and 2n cannot be any larger than 512. However, all those n are ruled out: for every n ≤ 512 at least one of the primes p in the set

$$\{2, 3, 5, 7, 13, 23, 43, 83, 163, 317, 631\}$$

satisfies n < p ≤ 2n. So we only need now to see why the inequality fails whenever n exceeds 512.

Assume that n > 512, and define the quantity

$$\zeta = \{\log(n/512)\}/(10 \log 2)$$

noting that $\zeta > 0$ and that

$$2n = 2^{10(1 + \zeta)}.$$

We can now express the inequality

$$2n \, (\log 2) < 3(\sqrt{(2n)} + 1) \, (\log 2n)$$

in terms of the quantity ζ, as:

$$2^{10 + 10\zeta} < 30(2^{5+5\zeta} + 1)(1 + \zeta).$$

Dividing both sides by $2^{10+5\zeta}$ then gives

$$2^{5\zeta} < 30 \cdot 2^{-5}(1 + 1/2^{5+5\zeta}) \, (1 + \zeta)$$

and since $30 \cdot 2^{-5} = 30/32 \; < 31/32 = (1 - 2^{-5})$, this in turn gives

$$2^{5\zeta} < (1 - 2^{-5})(1 + 1/2^{5+5\zeta}) \, (1 + \zeta)$$

which, since $(1 + 1/2^{5+5\zeta}) < (1 + 1/2^5) = (1 + 2^{-5})$, yields

$$2^{5\zeta} < (1 - 2^{-5})(1 + 2^{-5}) \, (1 + \zeta) = (1 - 2^{-10})(1 + \zeta)$$

hence

$$2^{5\zeta} < 1 + \zeta.$$

On the other hand, since in general we have

$$a^b = e^{a \log b}$$

we have in particular that

$$2^{5\zeta} = e^{5\zeta \log 2}$$

which, since

$$e^x = 1 + x + x^2/2! + \ldots + x^n/n! + \ldots,$$

gives

$$2^{5\zeta} = 1 + 5\zeta\log2 + (5\zeta\log2)^2 /2! + \ldots + (5\zeta\log2)^n/n! + \ldots$$

and therefore, dropping all terms on the right after the first two:

$$2^{5\zeta} > 1 + 5\zeta\log2$$

which, since $5\zeta\log2 > \zeta$, finally yields the inequality

$$2^{5\zeta} > 1 + \zeta.$$

The assumption that there is an $n > 512$ satisfying the inequality thus implies that $2^{5\zeta}$ is both greater and less than $1 + \zeta$, which is a contradiction. So this assumption must be false.

This concludes Erdös' proof. We have given it in a somewhat more detailed form than one finds in textbooks, in order to be sure that there are no 'small' doubts left in the reader's mind. The point is to make the result fit comfortably into the network of knowledge already present in the reader's mind, and so to make it 'natural' in the sense of 'obvious when one comes to think about it'.

Erdös' argument is an excellent example of what a nontrivial but natural proof is like, and how it does its work. Indeed, it is a good example of what the 'work' of a natural proof is. A natural proof is a piece of 'obviousness engineering'. It has *to create in the mind* a network of items of knowledge which will act as a conceptual framework in which the proof's conclusion appears 'obvious'. The act of reading the proof, which is the sequential process of 'installing' it in the mind, is not what matters; what matters is the state of mind which results after the proof has been installed. It is as though the linear text of the proof itself is no more than a series of 'editing' steps whose purpose is to update one's mental structure in an appropriate way. That is why the order of the 'steps' in a proof is of little or no importance. Even calling them 'steps' may be misleading; they are simply the separate stages in the importation into the mind of the different 'elements' of the proof, and we can carry them out in any convenient order. What counts is the finished, edited structure of the knowledge network.

The mental structure set up by a natural proof is often, as in the case of the mutilated checker board example, partly based upon and bolstered by perceptual imagery: good intuitive expositions (but not always, alas, those found in professional journals and books) do tend to feature plenty of diagrams and other visual aids. A knowledge network is all the stronger and more effective for including concrete examples of relevant patterns, particular cases which act as surrogates for the general cases which they typify. We do not and indeed cannot always hold these various auxiliary information structures literally in our memories: most of us need an external, so to speak *prosthetic*, information store in which to keep at least a part of our knowledge base. Mathematical thinking has always used something like slate, paper, blackboard, sandy beach or (nowadays) a computer screen, on which to draw diagrams and display many of the details: the normal human brain just cannot hold them 'in the mind'.

The late Professor Hardy's view of natural proofs (Hardy 1929) is worth noting (italics in original):

> It is a truism to any mathematician that the 'obviousness' of a conclusion need not necessarily affect the interest of a proof. I have myself always thought of a mathematician as in the first instance an *observer*, a man who gazes at a distant range of mountains and notes down his observations. His object is simply to distinguish clearly and notify to others as many different peaks as he can. There are some peaks which he can distinguish easily, while others are less clear. He sees A sharply, while of B he can obtain only transitory glimpses. At last he makes out a ridge which leads from A, and following it to its end he discovers that it culminates in B. B is now fixed in his vision, and from this point he can proceed to further discoveries. ... If he wishes someone else to see it, he *points to it,* either directly or through the chain of summits which led him to recognize it himself. When his pupil also sees it, the research, the argument, the *proof* is finished. ... We can, in the last analysis, do nothing but *point.*

I see no way at present of mechanically arriving at such natural proofs. What happens in 'mechanical theorem-proving' is that the machine at best produces a formal, artificial proof by searching through the possibilities within some suitable formal system. The natural processes of the mind, and the interactions of the proof with the mind to bring about 'understanding' and 'insight' are not taken into account. Research is not yet very far advanced towards *understanding how we understand* mathematics.[*]

To understand more about how natural proofs work, we need to know far more than we now do about the way the mind in general works. It seems likely that Minsky's seductive 'society of mind' model (Minsky 1985) is most nearly on the right track. This model is at present no more (but no less) than brilliantly imaginative speculation, consistent with all the evidence, such as it is, that we have. If he is right, the mind is like no artificial machine we have ever known, until relatively recent times. His view is that the mind is not so much a single serial-computer-like entity as a very large collection of semi-autonomous 'agents' which interact with each other both cooperatively and competitively to arrive at 'social' or 'political' decisions. The population metaphor emphasizes the looseness of the organization and the intricacy of its dynamics. Our machines have been far smaller, neater and tidier than this in the past. It may now, however, at last, be possible to begin experimenting with massively parallel machines designed deliberately to put models like Minsky's to the test.

---

[*] But a start has certainly been made. *Cf.* W.W.Bledsoe (Non resolution theorem proving, *Department of Mathematics and Computer Science, University of Texas at Austin,* 1975) Edwina Rissland (Understanding understanding mathematics, *Cognitive Science* 2, 361-383, 1978), and A. Bundy (Analysing mathematical proofs, or: reading between the lines, *Fourth International Joint Conference on Artificial Intelligence,* 1975).

Suggested further reading

Barr, A., Cohen, P.R., and Feigenbaum, E.A., (Editors). *The Handbook of Artificial Intelligence.* 3 volumes. William Kaufmann, 1981.
> Encyclopedic coverage of the entire field of AI. Extensive bibliography.

Berliner, H.J. An examination of brute force intelligence. *Proceedings of the 8th International Joint Conference on Artificial Intelligence*, 581-587, 1981.
> An analysis of why artificial chess players are as good as they are and a discussion of how much better they will become.

Colmerauer, A. Prolog in 10 figures. *Communications of the Association for Computing Machinery* 28, 1296 - 1310, 1985.
> The original creator of Prolog authoritatively presents its conceptual underpinnings in a vivid and compact essay.

de Groot, A.D. *Thought and choice in chess.* Mouton 1965.
> A study of the way chess experts think.

Dreyfus, H. *What computers can't do: a critique of artificial reason.* Harper and Row, 1973.
> Lively, not to say passionate, philosophical argument against the possibility of artificial intelligence.

Feigenbaum, E.A., and Feldman, J., (Editors). *Computers and Thought.* McGraw Hill, 1963.
> A collection of classic AI papers, with helpful commentary.

Hardy, G.H. Mathematical Proof. *Mind* 38, 1-25, 1929.
> Reflections by a great mathematician on the nature of proof.

Hardy, G.H., and Wright, E.M. *An introduction to the theory of numbers.* Fourth edition. Oxford, 1975.
> Bertrand's conjecture is Theorem 418 in this classic textbook.

Haugeland, J. (Editor). *Mind Design: Philosophy, Psychology, Artificial Intelligence.* MIT Press, 1981.
> A useful collection of papers on various aspects of AI. Includes Searle 1980.

Kowalski, R.A. *Logic for problem solving.* North Holland, 1979.
> An inspired and inspiring introduction to logic programming.

LeVeque, W.J.   *Topics in number theory*, Volume 1.   Addison-Wesley, 1956.

> Gives 'proofs which are neither the shortest nor the most elegant known, but which seem to me to be the most natural, or to lead to the deepest understanding of the phenomena under consideration' (from the Preface) .

Minsky, M.L.   *The Society of Mind.*   Simon and Schuster, 1985.

> Profound, elegant and entertaining exposition of a novel many-agent view of the nature of the human mind and its capabilities.

Newell, A., and Simon, H.A.   The logic theory machine.   *IRE Transactions on Information Theory* 2: 61-79, 1956.

> One of the earliest AI papers. Still worth reading (but should be taken with a pinch of Wang 1960).

Newell, A., and Simon, H.A.   *GPS, a program that simulates human thought.* In Feigenbaum and Feldman 1963, 279-293.

> Describes classic early work on 'difference-engines' as models of intelligent goal-seeking agents, which was started in the late 1950s.

Robinson, J.A.   A machine-oriented logic based on the resolution principle.   *Journal of the Association for Computing Machinery* 12, 23-41, 1965. (Reprinted in Siekmann and Wrightson 1983).

> Written in 1963.

Searle, J.R.   Minds, brains and programs.   In *The Behavioral and Brain Sciences* 3, 417-424, 1980. (Reprinted in Haugeland 1981).

> The original source of the famous Chinese Room criticism of the Turing test. This *a priori* proof that a machine could never understand Chinese might be thought to show that understanding cannot exist at all.

Siekmann, J., and Wrightson, G.   *Automation of Reasoning: classical papers in computational logic 1957-1970.*   2 volumes. Springer Verlag, 1983.

> Indispensible source book for first two decades of research in 'artificial' mechanical reasoning. Includes Robinson 1965 and Wang 1960.

Turing, A.M.   Computing Machinery and Intelligence.   *Mind* 59: 433-460, 1950. (Reprinted in Feigenbaum and Feldman 1963).

> The paper which first proposed the 'Turing test'. Still the best introduction to AI and its philosophical foundations.

Wang, H.   Towards mechanical mathematics.   *IBM Journal of Research and Development* 4, 2-22, 1960.   (Reprinted in Siekmann and Wrightson 1983).

> A counterblast to Newell and Simon 1956. Describes one of the earliest artificial theorem-proving programs, whose algorithmic scheme has nevertheless a markedly natural flavor.

Webber, B.L., and Nilsson, N., (Editors).   *Readings in Artificial Intelligence.* Tioga Publishing Company, 1981.

> Chapter 2 is a good collection of papers on automated deduction. Chapter 4 has interesting articles on expert systems in chemistry, chess, medical diagnosis, geology and automatic programming.

Winston, P.H.   Artificial Intelligence, second edition.   Addison Wesley, 1984.

> A popular textbook written by a well-known AI expert at MIT.

About the authors

Michael Arbib graduated from Sydney University and has a Ph.D. in mathematics from MIT. After 5 years at Stanford he moved to the University of Massachusetts where he became chairman of the Department of Computer and Information Science. In 1986 he joined the University of Southern California where he heads the Center for Neural Engineering and is Professor of Computer Science, Neurobiology, Physiology, Biomedical Engineering, Electrical Engineering, and Psychology. His current research is on the mechanisms of visuomotor coordination in animals and robots. Among his recent publications are *The Metaphorical Brain 2* and a new edition of his classic *Brains, Machines, and Mathematics*.

Per Brinch Hansen is Distinguished Professor of Computer Science at Syracuse University and an IEEE Fellow. Previously he served on the faculties of the California Institute of Technology, the University of Southern California and the University of Copenhagen. He is the author of the first textbooks on Operating Systems (1973) and Concurrent Programming (1977). He invented the first concurrent programming language, Concurrent Pascal (1975), based on his monitor concept. His most recent programming language Joyce is designed for both multiprocessors and multicomputers.

Gerald Edelman graduated from Ursinus College, and has an M.D. from the University of Pennsylvania and a Ph.D. from Rockefeller University, where he is now Vincent Astor Professor and Director of the Neurosciences Institute. His early work on the structure of antibodies led to his Nobel Prize for Physiology and Medicine in 1972. He then turned his interest to mechanisms involved in the regulation of primary cellular processes. This led him to the discovery of cell adhesion molecules, whose function is highly significant for the development and morphology of the brain.

Geoffrey Fox graduated in 1964 from Cambridge University where in 1967 he also received his Ph.D. in Theoretical Physics. After research stints at the Institute for Advanced Study in Princeton, the Lawrence Berkeley Laboratory, the Cavendish Laboratory, the Brookhaven National Laboratory, and the Argonne National Laboratory, he joined the Physics Department of the California Institute of Technology. In 1990 he moved to Syracuse University where he is Professor of Physics, Professor of Computer Science, and Director of the Northeast Parallel Architectures Center.

Patricia Goldman-Rakic is Professor of Neuroscience at the Yale School of Medicine. She is President of the Society for Neuroscience, and has been a holder of a Senior Scientist Award from the National Institute of Mental Health since 1980. Her research interests are in neurobiology and the development of cognition. She is a member of the editorial boards of numerous professional journals and a founding editor of the journal *Cerebral Cortex*. In 1990 she was elected to the National Academy of Sciences.

Ralph Gomory is a member of the President's Council of Advisors on Science and Technology and in 1989 became president of the Alfred P. Sloan Foundation. From 1959 to 1989 he held a series of research-related positions with the IBM Corporation, culminating in that of Senior Vice President for Science and Technology. Originally a research mathematician (Ph.D., Princeton, 1954) specializing in linear and integer programming, he is one of the most distinguished contemporary figures in science and technology in the United States. He is a member of the National Academy of Sciences and the National Academy of Engineering. In 1988 he was awarded the National Medal of Science by the President of the United States.

William Jenkins is an Associate Professor in the Department of Otolaryngology at the University of California at San Francisco. He graduated in psychology and biology from Florida State University in 1973, where he also received an M.S. (1975) and a Ph.D. (1980) in psychobiology. His research interests emphasize the use of interdisciplinary approaches (electrophysiological, behavioral, surgical, biomedical and neuroanatomical) in the study of the nervous system.

David May graduated from Cambridge University in 1972 in mathematics and computer science. He then moved to the University of Warwick to work on artificial intelligence and robotics, which led him into concurrent computer architecture and concurrent programming, and to the design of a series of experimental concurrent machines and programming languages. In 1979, he joined Inmos where he is responsible for the design of the occam concurrent programming language and the architecture of the transputer. His interests include concurrent computer architecture, programming languages, silicon compilation and the use of formal methods in VLSI designs.

Michael Merzenich received his Ph.D in physiology from the Johns Hopkins University in 1968. He moved to the University of California, San Francisco, in 1971, where he is now Professor of Physiology and Otolaryngology and Director of the Coleman Laboratory, an internationally renowned hearing research center. His group played a central role in the development of multichannel cochlear prostheses that have re-established hearing of speech in deaf patients. His research in auditory, somatosensory and motor systems has focused on forebrain organization and adult plasticity, and on determining neural mechanisms.

Randolph Nudo is a 1977 graduate of Pennsylvania State University in psychology, and received his Ph.D. in 1985 in psychobiology/neuroscience from Florida State University. From 1985 to 1987 he did postdoctoral research in Professor Merzenich's Physiology and Otolaryngology group at the University of California at San Francisco. In 1988 he joined the Department of Neurobiology and Anatomy at the University of Texas Medical School in Houston, as Assistant Professor. His current research is on the cortical control of movement, using modern electrophysiological, neuroanatomical and behavioral techniques.

Gregg Recanzone graduated *cum laude* in biology and psychology from the University of California at San Diego in 1984, and is at present a researcher and graduate student in Professor Merzenich's group in the Department of Physiology, Neuroscience Division, at the University of California at San Francisco.

Alan Robinson graduated in classics from Cambridge University in 1952 and received his Ph.D. in philosophy from Princeton in 1956. After 4 years as an Operations Research Engineer with the E. I. du Pont de Nemours corporation he became Professor of Philosophy and Professor of Computer Science at Rice University, and moved to Syracuse University in 1967, where he is currently University Professor. In 1963 he devised the resolution principle, an automatic deduction technique which underlies what is now called logic programming. He is currently working on a system of automatic deduction and symbolic computation which will permit a massively parallel implementation on the Connection Machine.

David Waltz is Director of Advanced Information Systems at Thinking Machines Corporation and is also Professor of Computer Sciences at Brandeis University. He has a BS in engineering, an MS in electrical engineering, and Ph.D. in artificial intelligence, all from MIT Until 1984, he was Professor of Electrical and Computer Engineering at the University of Illinois. He has been editor of *Cognitive Science* and AI editor for *Communications of the Association for Computing Machinery*. His interests include text processing and document retrieval, massively parallel memory-based reasoning, and computer vision.

Name index

Subject index

The MIT Press, with Peter Denning as general consulting editor, publishes computer science books in the following series:

ACM Doctoral Dissertation Award and Distinguished Dissertation Series

Artificial Intelligence
Patrick Winston, founding editor
Michael Brady, Daniel Bobrow, and Randall Davis, editors

Charles Babbage Institute Reprint Series for the History of Computing
Martin Campbell-Kelly, editor

Computer Systems
Herb Schwetman, editor

Explorations with Logo
E. Paul Goldenberg, editor

Foundations of Computing
Michael Garey and Albert Meyer, editors

History of Computing
I. Bernard Cohen and William Aspray, editors

Information Systems
Michael Lesk, editor

Logic Programming
Ehud Shapiro, editor; Fernando Pereira, Koichi Furukawa, Jean-Louis Lassez, and David H. D. Warren, associate editors

The MIT Press Electrical Engineering and Computer Science Series

Research Monographs in Parallel and Distributed Processing
Christopher Jesshope and David Klappholz, editors

Scientific and Engineering Computation
Janusz Kowalik, editor

Technical Communication
Ed Barrett, editor